SEEKING GOD
DAY BY DAY

A YEAR OF
MEDITATIONS

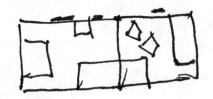

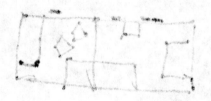

SEEKING GOD
DAY BY DAY

A YEAR OF
MEDITATIONS

FORWARD MOVEMENT
Cincinnati, Ohio

Forward Movement
www.forwardmovement.org

Foreword

In the children's game hide-and-seek, the hiding is easy. Find a good spot, settle in, and wait for someone to discover you. Seeking is the hard part. In seeking, we sometimes look in the wrong places; we may chase someone or something hard to catch. Seeking is active; it requires endurance, patience, tenacity, and desire.

By seeking God day by day, we commit to an active faith. We devote ourselves to scripture, prayer, reflection, and discernment. We move from a passive faith to one vigorously engaging the word of God.

This volume of daily meditations shares stories from the hearts of thirty-one authors. The writers differ in many ways: age, ethnicity, gender, geography, and denomination. Some are well-known writers, such as Presiding Bishop Katharine Jefferts Schori and the inspirational Bo Cox, while others are offering their stories through Forward Movement for the first time. Further, the meditations are as varied as the demographics; they are edgy, joyful, angry, gentle, struggling, loving. But what holds the stories together—and what connects all of us—is our common quest to be in a deeper relationship with God.

We invite you to incorporate these meditations into a regular spiritual practice. Read them alongside *Forward Day by Day*. Take a five-minute coffee break in the late morning to reflect upon the meditations. Use them in a small-group setting or as the foundation for your evening prayers. In all ways, our hope is that this book supports your journey as you seek—and find—God.

Richelle Thompson
Managing Editor
Forward Movement

Beginnings

This is the day the LORD has made.
Rejoice and be glad in it!

— PSALM 118:24

Ah! Give thanks for a new year!

I have never found formal New Year's resolutions terribly helpful, even though the transition of the calendar is always a time to consider the year just past. December's end offers opportunity to reflect and summarize the past twelve months, what I'm grateful for, and opportunities I see for growth. It lets me begin a new year with greater readiness to engage the new thing God is doing in me and around me.

Today is not too late to reflect on the past year. As the prayer in the New Zealand prayer book says, "what has been done has been done, what has not been done has not been done, let it be." Let it be, and dream of the new life emerging as we look to the year ahead.

The Church celebrates the Feast of the Holy Name today, remembering Jesus' naming as a week-old baby. His name means "God saves." How would you name the new thing God is doing in you? What has been birthed in you, and what do you hope will be healed/saved/ salved in you in the coming year?

I think my name this year might be *tenderized*—like pounding a tough piece of squid or abalone so that I can savor the sweetness without dislocating my jaw!

Tenderizing evokes compassion, and as the year turns, I give thanks for the times I've experienced painful encounters that became occasions of grace, and pray that I might be more open to expect the grace. —*Katharine Jefferts Schori*

Resolve to Remember

*Be present, O merciful God, and protect us through the hours of this night,
so that we who are wearied by the changes and chances of this life may rest
in your eternal changelessness; through Jesus Christ our Lord. Amen.*

— *THE BOOK OF COMMON PRAYER*, P. 133

We are one day into the New Year's resolutions—to exercise more, eat less, organize the basement—a list of changes in our lives we hope to make.

Perhaps we have an affinity for resolutions because they are changes we control. We make the decision to focus on our health instead of the heart attack that demands we do so or die. We make the decision to clean out our belongings instead of focusing on the divorce that turned our life upside down.

Life, however, is mostly filled with changes we make in response to upheavals. Life—this unpredictable, joyous, difficult event of which we are all part—is also quite unsteady. We make plans. Sometimes they work out exactly as we expected; most of the time, not so much.

When plans don't work out, and we are forced to change (oh, that word!), we may experience grief, doubt, and questions. Lots of questions.

Why? What now? How could this happen?

Often, we want life to return to what it was. Most of the time, that doesn't happen. While we are changing, shifting in life, we are invited to rest in God's eternal changelessness.

Life will bring changes. Some good, some bad, some welcome, some not. All change is uncomfortable at some level.

And we can rest in the truth that God is with us in all the changes and chances. —*Laurie Brock*

A Pilgrim's Poem

Hearing the Irish lyrical poet John O'Donohue read from *Anam Cara* was like gentle rain fetching growth from a desert floor. His mystical voice released a spirituality steeped in the rustic Gaelic tradition. Four years later, I was shocked to hear of his premature death. His prose and poetry were a glimpse of visions I could only ache to imagine.

Visiting Ireland, we made a tearful pilgrimage to O'Donohue's lonely seaside grave. Feeling a burdened grief, we realized we too stare into death's fetching. We were reminded we are mere dust.

Ireland's young poet rests in the limestone landscape of Connemara. His grave marker, a single plank of petrified oak found in a local bog, stands guard over the bard's tomb. On the day we visited, a wispy breeze fanned the sun-shocked fields of the glistening stone outcroppings.

The Irish harp was silent that day. Ravens circled, like minstrels giving announcement. Nearby cows moaned like mourners. On the hill overlooking the graveyard is an ancient church. I swore I could hear angels singing a spectral Mass.

Etched in the tombstone is O'Donohue's poem, "Beannacht." On the other side of death, nestled in the bosom of Mother Earth, the soul weaver of words offers his blessing in a sweet liturgy:

> *When the canvas frays in the curach of thought*
> *and a stain of ocean blackens beneath you,*
> *may there come across the waters a path of yellow moonlight*
> *to bring you safely home.*

As if O'Donohue's soul was floating on the clouds, our hearts leapt, filled by hope. His rhythmic dream-like words were singing solace. One day, we too will sojourn across the thin veil, passing from this life to the promise of the next.

—*Gil Stafford*

I Have No Sideways

A story is told of Ernestine Schumann-Heink, a famous German contralto of substantial girth, who had to make her way to center stage one night in San Francisco. The path through the orchestra's chairs was narrow, and she knocked over some music stands. Before the second part of the program, the stage manager suggested that perhaps she might turn sideways as she walked in. "Young man," she replied, "I haff no sideways!"

I think of Ernestine when I read God's words to the Israelites in the Old Testament, admonishing them to turn neither to the right nor to the left on their way to the Promised Land. Their path lay straight ahead. I think of her when I read of Peter's bitter tears at the realization that he had betrayed his Lord. His path had lain straight ahead, but he turned aside.

Most painfully, I think of her when I myself turn aside, from a person in need, from a task to be done, from a need to be met, from a prayer to be prayed...when I am too focused on my own plans, my own agenda, my own wants and desires to respond to the still, small voice of God, speaking quietly but clearly in my heart: "Therefore be steadfast, turning aside neither to the right nor to the left, but hold fast to the LORD your God" (Joshua 23:6, 8).

We can learn from Ernestine. We haff no sideways. Our path lies straight head, into God's beautiful dream for our lives. —*Betsy Rogers*

Taking a Load Off

Again and again in Exodus, God reminds the people to keep the sabbath holy. What's with the fetish for rest? I think it's not so much about tending to the bags under our eyes as it is about learning to trust God's providence.

You may have noticed that the way you do things shapes how you think about them. Your practice shapes your belief.

And so it is with the sabbath. Do we trust that God will give us our daily bread? Do we trust that part of that provision is having the time to do the work God has given us?

Taking a sabbath day each week, putting aside our own agendas and listening again for God's agenda, is one of the ways we live into our faith. It's a way that our practice forms our hearts. It's a way that we, with our lives, proclaim that we *do* expect God to give us enough of what we need, including time. It's a way that we learn to trust.

It's also the way we live into a lighter life. Setting aside almost seven weeks of sabbath days each year is a surefire way to pare down our schedules, to prioritize our work. It's a surefire way to become clear about what God has given us to do and what we ourselves have taken on. It's a surefire way of learning to surrender ourselves more fully into the arms of our Father, trusting him to overflow our lives with blessing. —*Kristine Blaess*

Epiphany and Transformation

The story of the Magi begins with an ominous warning that Herod was frightened by the news of a rival. It is not the part of the story we tend to focus on, distracted as we are by the marvelous scene of exotic strangers arriving with precious gifts on the occasion of a miraculous birth of a king among animals in a barn.

The warning sets up the ending. "Having been warned in a dream not to return to Herod, they left for their own country by another road" (Matthew 2:12), a little act of deception that precipitated a great atrocity. While the baby Jesus was spared, other children of Bethlehem became the victims of a murderous rage.

Baby Grace came to the early service on Christmas Eve one year. She had just returned from the children's hospital following heart surgery. A few days later her newly repaired heart just gave out. I was with her parents when a very kind nurse brought in her lifeless body, wrapped in a pink blanket, for her mother to rock one last time.

It was still Christmas. My immediate instinct was to clear the church of its decorations. The evergreens and candles had to go. The joy had to be banished. Fortunately, I thought better of it. My liturgical sense took over. The Christmas decorations stayed for the funeral.

Epiphany is the part of the story that reminds us that our deepest fears and our hopes, both death and life, live in the very same place. The coming of the Christ Child at Christmas does not mean that death is no longer part of life. It does not even mean that death takes a Christmas vacation. It does mean that both life and death are transformed.

That is why the evergreen remains green. The candle remains burning. The joy is undefeatable. The heart sings in the paradox. —*Stacy Sauls*

Making Room Again

Today is the day after the Epiphany. We're supposed to be in post-Christmas mode now.

Truth be told, many of us have been in post-Christmas mode for a while. It is hard to sustain joy for so long, especially since Christmas seems to start earlier and earlier, effectively bypassing Advent. For many of us, Christmas often is more about lists and activities and perfection and nonstop being on top of things than it is about peace and the contemplation of God with us. It is frenetic and even exhausting.

And so I welcome this time of year, when I put away my Christmas things, remembering who gave me this and appreciating that. In the name of "organization," an approved activity in our productivity-focused world, I can slow down and look, really look, at my angels and Marys and stars and the photos of friends from their Christmas cards. I can get in some stealth reflection time.

And, truth be told, I also welcome the now empty mantle and shelves, the clean and spare look of the living room when the tree is gone. It is a visual reminder that I need to make room for what God is going to be doing in my life in the months to come. I welcome the new space that is now available for Emmanuel, God with us, in my nonholiday ordinary and regular life. —*Penny Nash*

On Being and Becoming

Many New Year's resolutions already seem too ambitious. Resolving to increase the treadmill's pace in the gym seems to mirror daily life, the conveyor belt slipping behind too quickly. Such goals focus on what we're doing, but what if resolutions were about *who* we are being or becoming? Example: I could be more merciful to the person who annoys me most. I could be more merciful, forgiving myself, accepting my own limitations. What if we could become generally more forgiving, borrowing a bit of the Almighty's extravagant and tender mercy?

In 2012, I was asking God what to do next. In grief recovery, I had accepted the gift of a pilgrimage to Iona, an island among Scotland's Inner Hebrides. I wandered in the historic abbey, loved being surrounded by the sea, and reveled in pastoral scenes. I asked Highland cattle why they arranged their hair in straggly bangs over their eyes. Walking for miles, I prayed and worshiped, singing to an uncomplaining audience of sheep. But what to do for God? Not a clue.

Extended time helped me settle into awesome silence. In the abbey, a woman read from Psalm 46, "Be still, and know that I am God." A long pause, "Be still, and know that I am." A yet longer pause, "Be still, and know." A silence of rich texture. "Be still." And then, "Be."

En route home, as I still wondered what I'd be doing, an odd blend of Romans 8 and Psalm 46 blinked into my mind. "For now, be. And be convinced: neither death, nor life, nor things present, nor things to come...nothing can separate you from my love. For now, simply be." —*June Terry*

Freedom's Shadow

No one can be perfectly free 'til all are free;
no one can be perfectly moral 'til all are moral;
no one can be perfectly happy 'til all are happy.

— HERBERT SPENCER

By the time you're reading these words, I will have been out of prison for over ten years. After almost two decades in prison, it would seem that I'd had enough of that place. Why go back?

Last night I heard a man in his sixties talk about receiving his GED earlier that day in a ceremony and how proud his adult children are of him. He's doing two life sentences, so it's likely he won't ever step foot outside prison again. Yet, something inside him still wants to achieve. He often carries a folder that contains all the certificates of programs he's completed while in prison. He is proud of his growth and aware of the bittersweet reality that it came too late or, at least, at such a great cost.

Another man—a former well-known and fearfully respected drug addict and teenage death row inmate, now clean and sober and in his third decade inside—talked about how, earlier in the week, he had spoken with younger prisoners who are still using drugs. He told them about the quality of life he'd experienced in prison since quitting drugs and finding a spiritual path. His eyes lit up when he said he felt they were listening.

And, finally, I go back to the prison because I want the people who live there and who work there to know that just because you get so lost you end up in prison, it doesn't mean you can't be found. —*Bo Cox*

Doors and Other Thresholds

I have a thing for doors. I suppose it began when I saw the doors to my first cathedral—I remember climbing the wide steps leading up to doors six times my height and hearing the sounds as they opened. The doors filled me with awe and excitement. To this day, whether at cathedrals or someone's home, I get excited standing at a threshold. It is a moment of arriving, a moment of beginning.

I have come to see how I am equally enamored with the various metaphoric thresholds I encounter in my life. As a person seeking God, I have journeyed to the threshold of faith. As one in recovery, I have knocked on the door of a clean and sober life. As a father, I have come to the place where my children and I can enter into a new level of intimacy. As a husband, I have stood where I could know and be known.

Thresholds one and all...the problem is, I'm too scared to open the doors.

Rather than open the door, I stand and admire it. I celebrate reaching the threshold. I point at it for others to see. Too often, my journey ends there. Rather than enter, I'll put a fresh coat of paint on the door or polish its hardware. I'll buy a spotlight to show the door to others, but I won't open it. I'll buy another book about Jesus instead of building a personal relationship with him. I'll create another lesson plan for newcomers of twelve-step recovery instead of traveling up and down the steps myself. I'll buy my children or wife something, rather than give them myself.

At the beginning of this new year, it's a good time to stop standing at the thresholds and cross over, to stop admiring the doors and open them. There is new, and more abundant, life on the other side, but to reach it we need to open the door. —*Chip Bristol*

Of Light and Stars, and the Radiance of a Soul

There was a time when I loved the Epiphany. It is such a great story of faith and wonder—a strange star leading wise men from the east on an improbable journey to an even more improbable infant king. And then, in 1994, my mother died in the early hours of January 6 from a heart attack that came with no warning. She was only sixty-five. Epiphany became an annual time of mourning and remembrance, not celebration.

Until one Epiphany Sunday when Fr. Ray in his sermon asked us to think about who is light for us, what stars guide our journeys—and for whom we can bring light. I had been thinking of Mom, of course, and at these words I realized that while she herself was deeply troubled, by alcoholism and more, her love for us was so strong and the light she gave to all who knew her was so bright that my sisters and I are still guided by it. It was no accident, I thought, that her life-light went out on this Feast of Light—her way of telling us, perhaps, that she would never leave us, that we now must always shine on for each other.

James Joyce says an epiphany is the sudden "revelation of the whatness of a thing," the moment when "the soul of the commonest object...seems to us radiant." Mom's soul and spirit were certainly radiant. And I see them reflected in the commonest objects that fill my home this time of year—the goofy foil snowman she made when I was a child, cookies baked from recipes she perfected, ornaments she gave me, countless photos of our Christmas dinners, trees, and presents.

The Magi brought gold, frankincense, and myrrh. Mom gave us creativity, devotion to family, and unconditional love—priceless gifts, indeed. The gifts I can bring to the people I love are the promise to be light to them, in any way I can, and to count on their light to get me through my own dark times.

—*Janet Rehling Buening*

In the River with Jesus

As Jesus rose from the waters of the Jordan River, the heavens opened to him. In our baptism, we, too, plunged into a river, a river of grace from which we emerged beloved and blessed. Gregory of Nyssa once said, "The river of grace flows everywhere." At every moment, day or night, wherever we go, whatever we do, whether we are sitting or standing, walking or resting, speaking or silent, we can step again into that shining river.

The river of grace is always here, flowing through the present moment. The trick is to pay attention and stay alert. "See," says God, "the former things have come to pass, and new things I now declare; before they spring forth, I tell you of them" (Isaiah 42:9). Do we have eyes to see, ears to hear? Oh, I groan, standing impatiently in line somewhere, drumming my fingers on the counter or whipping out my cell phone, this is just another boring moment to endure.

But in fact this moment—like every moment—is not vacant, but full of possibility. In this moment the love of God is pouring into our hearts through the Holy Spirit (Romans 5:5). In this moment a voice is murmuring in our ears just as it murmured in Jesus' ears: "You are my beloved." In this moment we can step into the river of grace and recall Love's presence, listen for Love's voice. Then we can ask, "What do you invite me to do now?" And if love seems nowhere in sight, if everything seems dry as a bone, we can ask God to send forth living waters and to renew the flow. —*Margaret Bullitt-Jonas*

Come and See

Bishop Ogé Beauvoir, Suffragan Bishop of Haiti, came to visit Trinity Wall Street, the Episcopal church where I work. He told us about the challenges and opportunities people face in Haiti, about the importance of education, about the fact that Haiti is "land rich but cash poor," and about plans for sustainability and the need for training. "Come and see," he said.

It's too easy to isolate ourselves from Haiti and other places like it. It's easy to forget that we're all part of one creation, and what we do in the United States affects those in Haiti, and that the lives of people from across the world, from Africa to South America to Europe, are intricately linked with ours.

We are small beings with limited attention spans. We often cannot see past the horizons of our own shores, but we are called to see farther and better, to love larger than that.

We are blessed to live in a time when we connect with others across the world, through electronic media or by relatively easy travel. We are more connected than ever, and I think this can only increase our responsibility to those who need help. Isolating ourselves from the suffering of others is a sin. It separates us from others and from God.

Jesus came to us with his arms outstretched. He went out and spoke the good news. He listened and loved those he met; he healed the sick and advocated for the poor. We are also called out of our own villages, across the countryside, and beyond, with our eyes open and our arms outstretched. —*Jeremiah Sierra*

A God Who Hides

Truly, you are a God who hides himself,
O God of Israel, the Savior.

— ISAIAH 45:15

I found the best ever hiding place one day while playing hide-and-seek with a favorite babysitter. I had a multitude of stuffed animals, and if I burrowed under them, my petite six-year-old frame was completely concealed. If I stayed still (which had always been a talent of mine), there was no way I'd be found. Well, I wasn't found. The babysitter finally had to call the game off and feign leaving to lure me out.

Do you ever feel like God is hiding? The hiddenness of God has been a major issue in religious studies for millennia: if the Creator of the universe is real, why should this deity appear so hard to find? ("Find," in this case, often really means "prove.") I've certainly had times when God is hard to find, when I feel like a seeker in a game of hide-and-seek, except when the seeking wears on, I begin to wonder if what I am seeking is even out there. "Seek and ye shall find"—really?

I've found, though, that there is value in the seeking just as there is in the finding. God is always with us, but some seasons in our spiritual lives bring more in the way of seeking than in the way of finding, and there is beauty in these seasons, too. —*Alissa Goudswaard*

Broken Heart, Open Arms

He was my first love, and we had seriously discussed getting married. In the naïve way of newly minted adults, we had never considered the possibility that our relationship would not last.

We broke up in February, on the first snow of the year. On my way to work one morning, I realized the trees were in full bloom. It was nearly summer. An entire season had passed without my noticing.

The grief was a dull ache. I found myself praying daily, though I was not particularly religious. Then at some point, seemingly from nowhere, I began to daydream about taking communion. It didn't make sense. I was not a churchgoer. Yes, I believed in Jesus, but church? No. No to the church people. No to the sanctimonious clergy. No to the stuffy coffee hours and the dusty religion. Just no.

A few weeks later, I wandered into a church during a noonday service. I figured there was no harm in sitting quietly and listening. I was glad there were only three other people in the tiny side chapel because I didn't want to talk about "What brought me here today" or "How I found the church." I didn't want to talk at all. The priest opened his arms wide, looked over the small congregation and said, "The Lord be with you." My eyes filled with tears. Yes. Yes. This.

One day I walked into an almost empty sanctuary and knelt down to pray. And I never left. —*Yejide Peters*

Our Home Up Ahead

I am always astonished at how a new calendar year—a date on a page—can bring out such excited anticipation of newness from us. I think it must have to do with the fact that when we hang up a new calendar, we can see all those other months stretching before us. This is the time we look to the future. What's up ahead?

In *God After Darwin*, John Haught suggests that God creates not from the past, but from the future. From the future, God draws us toward a fulfillment that we call the kingdom of God. So God is not so much "up above" in heaven as "up ahead."

I like this image. I imagine God waiting to greet me when I arrive home—up ahead. After a life's journey, I trudge wearily up the front walk, and as I approach the front door, God meets me, takes me in, and welcomes me home.

Or maybe I will return home as a prodigal, starving, but repentant child, hardly daring to hope for a hot meal. But God runs out to me crying with joy. Waiting inside is not just a hot meal but a heavenly banquet—and the promise of a new start.

The Bible is full of promises of newness—a new creation, a new heaven and new earth, a God who makes "all things new." In God, every day is the dawn of a new morning, every moment like a new year when the whole cosmos turns to see the face of God in all things. God is the God of our ultimate dreams, always meeting us up ahead.
—*Joanna Leiserson*

After Twelfth Night

When I was a child, we didn't celebrate Epiphany. New Year's Day was spent undecorating the house and packing away every vestige of Christmas; I always began the year feeling bereft of festivity, picturing a stretch of gray, dutiful days until the next celebration.

Baby Jesus was all grown up, out there preaching uncomfortable words about turning the other cheek, praying for our enemies, and selling all our possessions. He was on the road to the cross and inviting us to follow. No more fun.

I was delighted to discover as a teenager that some people not only celebrate Christmas for twelve days, but also observe a long season of light after that, stretching almost into spring; to know that though we take down the tree and pack away the crèches, the star that led the Magi shines on to remind us to watch for ways to see Jesus—and *be* Jesus—as we try to carry our own crosses, with his help, through ordinary time. The joy of that still fills me, and I share it with you in this poem:

> *Now is the Feast of Taking Down the Crèche:*
> *The Holy Child (ceramic) packed away,*
> *the stable wedged against the Advent wreath.*
> *(Beneath the closet shelf are wisps of hay.)*
>
> *The Christmas wrappings went with last week's trash.*
> *Broken at once, the latest gift inventions,*
> *abandoned, too, sit sadly on the curb*
> *(along with all the New Year's good intentions).*
>
> > *Lord, who with heavenly signs the Wise Men led*
> > *to your clear starlit first Epiphany,*
> > *even now, let us see you manifest*
> > *through broken toys, discarded Christmas tree.*
>
> —Mary W. Cox

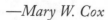

Safe Questions

Once when Jesus was praying alone, with only the disciples near him,
he asked them, "Who do the crowds say that I am?"
They answered, "John the Baptist; but others, Elijah, and still others,
that one of the ancient prophets has arisen." He said to them,
"But who do you say that I am?" Peter answered, "The Messiah of God."

— LUKE 9:18-20

Today, our church observes the Feast of the Confession of Peter, distinctive because it celebrates a story as much as a person.

Away from the crowd, with his disciples, Jesus takes a random sampling, perhaps the first recorded example of public opinion polling. He asks: *Who do people say that I am?* It's a safe enough question. Disciples weigh in with opinions. Little is at stake in their responses.

Then, with laser-like focus, Jesus asks one of the most important questions in the gospels: *Who do you say that I am?* Peter, the disciple who rarely has an unexpressed thought and speaks for the rest of the disciples (including us), offers this confession: Jesus is the Messiah, the one they've been waiting for, the one they've been seeking.

His answer is so important it merits its own feast. Peter speaks with clarity. It's a milestone in a faith journey marked by highs and lows. For example, in just the next few verses, Jesus will rebuke Peter as Satan; later, Peter will deny Jesus three times. Ultimately, Peter will declare his love for Jesus, also three times, finding restoration and forgiveness.

Peter's seeking, like ours, was marked by moments of both clarity and doubt. But he will always have that moment of confession, which made Jesus think of him as a rock. In your own journey, in your seeking, hold on to moments of clarity. Celebrate them. —*Jay Sidebotham*

A Journey in Darkness

Epiphany is a time of revelation; a time of exposure to a kind of light that has deeper meaning in darkness. The events leading up to the Epiphany, the journey of the Magi in blackness guided by the glimmer of a single star, was a journey that could only be made in the dark. The brightness of a beautiful sun-filled day would not have drawn them nearer to the place of the Holy Nativity. How paradoxical: only in darkness could they see the light of revelation, drawing them closer to the One they were seeking, the incarnation of Light in the world.

Epiphany is a time of revelation; a time of exposure to a Light that has deeper meaning in darkness. We are all children of the Light, drawn to the Light of God, even when our journey may take us through very dark valleys and places we would rather avoid. Nevertheless, like the Magi, we continue the journey until we arrive at the place of Epiphany, the place of revelation, and there, gazing into the Light, we find peace, we find comfort, and we find the blazing radiance of God right before our eyes.

Who would have thought that the shinning face of God on earth would be born in a stable among animals in Bethlehem, a city under occupation both then and now? The light of revelation will never be snuffed. Light always breaks through darkness, even when darkness and shadows abound.

Epiphany offers us an opportunity to come face-to-face with the darkness in our lives. The shining face of God is calling to us. Come and gaze, and be free of the darkness. —*Wilfredo Benitez*

Sticking with Love

At a train station, while we waited to be called to board, a young man with kind eyes asked if he could sit in the empty seat at my table. Of course I said yes.

I noticed that he was of olive complexion with a beard and had very intense eyes. He brought out a tin box filled with what looked to be small sheets of sandpaper, and in it was a nail file. I suspiciously watched him file his nails, and wondered if it could be a weapon. My heart began to beat faster as I thought there might be a terrorist among us.

He asked gently where I was going and volunteered that he was going only twenty minutes away. He was a guitar teacher. And then I noticed the guitar case by his feet. He opened it, brought out his guitar, and began to play.

Apparently, it is preferred that guitar players have rounded or sliced-to-an-angle nails, with the shorter part of the nail toward the heart. Players often use different shapes according to their level of playing or the repertoire they are playing. And that was what my table companion was calmly doing—filing his nails as he waited patiently for his train.

News reports about "just" war and drones—and noncombatants versus combatants—do strange things to the mind. He is strumming his guitar thinking only of peace and love. I am thinking of war and drones.

To quote Dr. Martin Luther King Jr. as we celebrate his birthday, "I have decided to stick with love. Hate is too great a burden to bear."
—*Westina Matthews*

Snowmageddon

The snow glistened seductively outside our living room window. The light reflected from the tiny snow crystals that had fallen the night before, each one shining like a gem embedded in an alien landscape. Only the day before had the world been various shades of gray and brown, dreary, cold, oppressive, with a side of blah. But now the world shone like the eyes of a newly engaged young couple, sparkling with newness and possibility.

There is something redemptive about snow. It blankets the earth in a clean sheen of unblemished originality. The drifts and swales of billions of ice crystals, terraforming the sleeping creation, birth something paradoxically enduring and ephemeral.

Snow also covers a multitude of sins. Those muddy tire tracks from the delivery truck that had driven up in the grass disappear. The fallen branches, the pile of leaves, and the wilted perennials transform into mere ebbs and flows of a white landscape. Which is perhaps why Isaiah wrote that, "though your sins are like scarlet, they shall be like snow" (1:18).

In our part of the country, local newscasters make pronouncements every winter about the impending Snowmageddon, Snowpocalypse, or Snowzilla when potential snowfall is forecasted. While these predictions are almost always overblown media hype, there's something deceptively true about them. It may not be the end of the world, but you can see it from here. Winter is a kind of death in which we await the rebirth of spring. The glistening new-fallen snow is a down payment on the hope that death is not the last word, that redemption is possible. —*Aaron Klinefelter*

Resting

The desert is resting. If you have lived in the desert Southwest, you have also heard it described as "not having seasons." But it does have seasons—the changes are subtle but distinct.

I often walk in the desert, and we are close friends. Sometimes she surprises me with a sign of life developing in the seeming quietness of the season (*ex profundis*—out of the depths). As I become aware of life's struggle to hold on in the harsh cold of winter, I realize how vulnerable we are physically, mentally, emotionally, and spiritually.

It is natural for our bodies to want to rest and take life a bit slower in the winter months. We are vulnerable to viruses and infections when we are not careful to rest well, eat well, and exercise. Caring for our spirit is just as important. We must be intentional to stay in relationship with creation and Creator, even when there seems to be no real evidence of life. We need to look deeply into the quiet resting earth to see those little signs of life just below the surface, waiting to burst forth at just the right time.

Look deeply within and nurture your spirit. God is present, resting inside of you and ready to burst forth at just the right moment.
—*Debbie Royals*

Delight!

My favorite Bible verse is Psalm 37:4: "Delight in the LORD, and he shall give you your heart's desire."

I am a singer, and when I sing I often remember all the blessings, promises, and miracles God has done in my life. How can I not rejoice in the God who has provided daily for me and my family? When I begin to delight in God, all at once the desires of my heart are centered on God's desires for me. I long to love more, to live more, to sing more, to be a better version of me. I long to tell others about what God has done in me. I long to share good news.

There are times when it is quite difficult to delight in anything. During a painful divorce, I thought it might be impossible. Life was so dark then. Yet, I realized later that when I was going through the most pain, I would get on my knees, with tears rolling down my cheeks, raise my arms to the sky, and sing:

Temprano yo te buscaré...early I will seek you.

Tu diestra me ha sostenido...your right hand has held me.

Suddenly the dark turned into delight.

Yes, we all can delight in God even while we dislike a situation. There have been times when anger, fear, or sorrow possess me. That is when I most need to sing. As I start singing, my heart softens and my smile returns. —*Sandra Montes*

From Heart to Heaven

My sister, Dinah, has Prader-Willi Syndrome, a rare genetic disorder that causes learning disabilities, speech problems, and more. Her inner beauty outshines her disability. She struggles to release the words of her soul that are trapped in a failed human mechanism.

At family gatherings, we pray before the meal. No one had ever bothered to ask my sister to pray until, for an unknown reason, my mother one day invited Dinah to say grace. I wondered if her earthly silence extended to heavenly communication.

Dinah bowed her head as she'd seen us do before a thousand meals. My gaze was frozen on my sister in holy expectation. I had to drink deeply into my soul every moment of this experience.

"God!" she said. It was stunning. God had been summoned. And God was there, present, at attention, and listening with attentive ears. God was bent forward, straining to hear my sister's every utterance as if she were speaking the very words God needed to hear.

There was a long silence. I could feel her communing with her soul. Then her words gushed forth like the joy of a freshly popped bottle of champagne. "I thank."

What was Dinah thankful for? She would never experience the fullness of life's ecstasy. Yet, her word was undeniable, "Thank."

"God, I thank. Mom, Dad, Gia, Cafu, Nee, Esika..." The room receded and we were transported to heaven. As objects of her prayer, we were now the thankful ones. Dinah beckoned the Divine into our midst, and I witnessed a tear roll down the face of God.

—*Gil Stafford*

A Lifelong Conversion

After Jesus meets up with Saul on the road to Damascus, Saul, now named Paul, virtually disappears into Arabia, Damascus, Syria, and Cilicia for almost two decades before he begins his public ministry. His conversion to Jesus Christ was not overnight. It clearly took many years for Paul to "get it together" following his conversion experience. Though we ultimately witness a tenacious Paul in his writings, there were many years of gestation and integration before the fullness of time when he had something to say. He waited.

Paul shows us that one dimension of conversion—from the Latin, *conversio*, "turning back"—is returning, retrieving, restoring, redeeming our previous life in a new light. God is very frugal, wasting nothing of our earlier life. What is past to us is always present to Jesus, and it's all to be used to God's glory. Sometimes we have to wait to be able to see this transformation, as Paul did.

Waiting is countercultural; waiting is un-American. And yet, for the cure of the soul, God has all the time in the world. God is not in a rush. If you are not ready or readied, don't rush. Don't cut in line. Wait. Incorporate the word "waiting" into the vocabulary of your soul. Waiting is an elixir to worrying or seething because something has not yet come to be. Our having to wait invites us into the sacrament of the present moment. A sacrament is an outward sign of an inward grace. The outward signs of our very incomplete life are not accidents, nor impediments, but rather invitations to know God's real presence in the present, all along the way.

You'll see. Just wait. —*Brother Curtis Almquist,* SSJE

Fishing for People

Follow me, and I will make you fish for people.
— MATTHEW 4:19

Jesus began his ministry just after his time in the wilderness and the arrest of John the Baptist. He was ready to be among people, to move about teaching, preaching, and healing. He trudged throughout the dusty hillsides and came to the Sea of Galilee.

This scene is the beginning of an amazing fish story. By the Sea of Galilee, Jesus found two brothers working. Their strong arms swept nets into the air and out over the water. They were fishermen. Yet the big catch Jesus is after is people, not fish.

The story takes a startling turn. *Keep fishing, but drop your nets. Follow me and fish for people. Use the heart of what you are to reach people.* His offer is outrageous. Immediately they drop their nets and follow him.

In this story, Jesus calls his first disciples. Although scripture does not portray Jesus as a fisherman, he seems to have the skills. He goes where the fish are. He knows their habits. He is observant, patient, and persistent.

His disciples are his first big catch. Fish and fishing become symbols of his ministry. As I consider my own call, it was not so swift and so sure. But the call was persistent. *Come as you are. Come "who" you are,* Jesus says. *Together we will fish for people.*

Somehow I can't help but think that Jesus has a fish story to tell about each one of us. —*Karen Montagno*

Patience and Providence

For surely I know the plans I have for you, says the LORD.
— JEREMIAH 29:11A

On January 28, seventeen years ago, I was picking out clothes, curling my hair, and heading with friends to a small, local pub—the place to hang out in a northern Indiana town. I had no idea my life would change.

On this day, the day before, I was still lonely. Many of my friends were in serious relationships. We were past the flurry of college-graduation weddings and heading into the next frenzy, from pairings made at the first or second post-college job. I was lamenting my lack of a boyfriend. Would I ever find the right person? My match? My love?

In retrospect, I can eye-roll at the drama, but at the time, I fretted deeply over the future of my love life. I wanted to marry, to have children, to spend my final days on a front-porch rocking chair, holding the hand of my beloved. I wondered about God's plan for me. I bargained: *I don't have to meet the person now, God. Just tell me I will.*

I was willing to be patient—on my terms.

I talked with a friend about my angst. Believe in yourself, he said. Believe God has great plans for you. They may—or may not—include a spouse, but if you put your faith and trust in God, then the plan will unfold as it should. I promised to try. I prayed to try.

As you might have guessed, January 28 is the anniversary of meeting my husband, of meeting the man God planned for me to love. Interestingly, we had both been going to this place on Tuesday nights for two years. And even though the pub was no bigger than a convenience store, we hadn't met before.

Even when I didn't know the plan, even when I questioned it, God knew. —*Richelle Thompson*

Whoever Heard of Sinibald?

By all accounts, the clerical career of Saint Thomas Aquinas, whom the church calendar commemorates today, got off to a bumpy start. Born to Sicilian nobility, Thomas was destined for the church. His family expected him to join the Benedictines; his Uncle Sinibald was abbot at Monte Cassino, the original Benedictine abbey. His ambitious mother Theodora hoped Thomas would land that position.

But Thomas wanted to join the Dominicans, a mendicant order with a mission among the poor. Theodora was not pleased. A bizarre tug-of-war over the young aspirant ensued. The Dominicans spirited him away to Rome and sent him on to Paris. Theodora dispatched his brothers to seize him and return him to the family castle, where she then held him prisoner for two years.

Thomas's commitment didn't waiver. In desperation, his brothers actually hired a prostitute to seduce him. Legend says Thomas drove her away with a fire iron. Finally, Theodora threw up her hands, but rather than admit defeat openly, she arranged for Thomas to escape at night through his window—thinking somehow that a secret flight was less damaging to the family's reputation.

Hardly an auspicious beginning, but Thomas went on to become one of the church's most brilliant and influential theologians. Fifty years after his death, he was a canonized saint, later a doctor of the church. His fame through the ages, which he never sought, was infinitely greater than his mother ever could have dreamed. Who, after all, has ever heard of Sinibald?

Thomas, renouncing worldly ambitions, chose a vocation among the poor, and his life bore unimaginably rich fruit. Our lives, too, can bear rich fruit, when we follow where God leads. —*Betsy Rogers*

Hoping Against Hope

I once visited a small church in my former diocese. When I got there, a group had gathered in the undercroft, maybe six or seven people. Most were women of, shall we say, mature years.

They talked about how the congregation was aging and there would be no more children and how, therefore, the church couldn't possibly grow. I expected someone to say, "Will the last person to die, please turn out the lights."

I listened and then asked one of them, the one who seemed most pessimistic and also the oldest, "Don't you know the story of Sarah?"

She thought for a minute and then chuckled. "Yes, I know the story of Sarah," she responded, "but you're not Abraham."

A few years later I visited again. This time they gave me a present. It was two framed photographs of all the children in the congregation. And there were lots of them. This little congregation is for me a place about hope. What happened is that they found their purpose, not in lasting until life ran out, but in turning outward to make a home for resettling refugees. Hope for them followed from turning their attention to others.

Abraham was an old man when God made him a promise. Sarah, too, was old and had been barren for many years. Still God made them promises, ridiculous promises, really. And in the hope of Sarah and Abraham, God's promises came to be. I would go so far as to say the hope was an absolutely necessary part of that. Without that, even God has a hard time making things happen. —*Stacy Sauls*

Potty Trained

Last week our firstborn got potty trained. My husband and I have been putting off the task, not because we love changing diapers, but because we couldn't imagine how we would potty train a child. We knew Jack understood the basics and was physically capable. The only barrier to him being potty trained was mom and dad's imaginative barrier—Michael and I couldn't potty train Jack because we couldn't *imagine* Jack being potty trained.

So last Friday, we got up in the morning and said, "Jack, guess what happened last night? You got POTTY TRAINED!" Jack screamed "NOOOO!" and cried for an hour, and then went and got a pair of underpants and put them on. Job done.

I wonder how many other things in our lives—in our families, in our work, in our congregations—we are unable to do because we just can't imagine them being done.

For example, despite extensive sailing throughout the Northern Hemisphere, no European crossed the equator until the fifteenth century, simply because no one could imagine it ever happening. Similarly, it was many years before anyone ran a four-minute mile, and when that imaginative barrier was broken, several men broke that record within a short time.

What things have we told ourselves can't be done? What limits have we placed on ourselves not because we lack skill or energy, but because we lack imagination? What calls to ministry and discipleship are we not answering because we can't imagine doing the things God calls us to do? —*Kristine Blaess*

Nameless

My great-great-great grandmother was a member of the Choctaw tribe of Native Americans. She married her husband, Sam, after he moved into Choctaw territory in Mississippi in the early nineteenth century and set up a trading post. One of her sons became a minister with and to the Choctaws. He was fluent in the language and culture.

She, was, however, not Anglo, a trait that rendered her, even up to my grandmother's generation, family best forgotten. So her name is too. I fill her in on my family tree as Name Forgotten.

Her name may be, but her legacy is not. My family may not know her name, but her descendants remain. Her presence remains. Her story has been passed down. We may not know her name, but we know her soul.

The story of our faith is often one of forgotten names of women. Many women in the Bible are simply known as "a woman," or by their role as someone's wife or mother, or by their ailments or societal shortcomings. The names we do have—Tamar, Rahab, Sarah, Ruth, Mary, Mary Magdalene, to name a few—are rare treasures.

Being nameless does not erase the worth of someone. We encounter people every day who are nameless to us. They are often known by their roles—waitress, mechanic, teacher. Or their condition—homeless, poor, prisoner.

Yet they are not nameless to God. No one is nameless to God. While we may not be able to know or remember the names of all the people we encounter daily, we can remember they all are called a beloved name by God: my dear child. —*Laurie Brock*

Walking with Brigid

God fetches the pilgrim down the burdened road of discovery if he or she is willing to walk.

I heard the fetching and went on a walking pilgrimage in Ireland, from Dublin to Kildare, visiting with the Brigidine nuns, whose motto is "Strength and Gentleness." Their stories of their patron saint were filled with serving the poor, children weaving crosses of the "Eye of God," worshiping under oak trees, of Brigid's Well, and maintaining the perpetual flame. Irish lore is often an interweaving of pagan and Christian stories.

Brigid, a contemporary of Saint Patrick, was a Druidess, tending the pre-Christian perpetual flame of goddess Brighid. Brigid converted to Christianity, cared for the poor, founded a monastery for men and women, and, legend says, was ordained bishop. Her feast day, February 1, is associated with the start of spring—probably why she is the patron of midwifery, lending to the story that she was Mary's midwife at Jesus' birth. Transformed by her grace and story, I established Saint Brigid's, an emergent and intentional community for young adults.

Years later, I walked Ireland coast-to-coast, encountering the presence of Saint Brigid continually on the journey. She was the face of other pilgrims, imprinted on the hearts of children, in doorways where the homeless slept, and on church mantels. Somewhere along the way, I introduced myself to a traveler. She responded, "Aye, Gil. Did you know Gilbride in Gaelic means "servant of Saint Brigid?" I was speechless. Indeed, God fetches us into the pilgrimage of self-discovery if we heed and will take the long walk. —*Gil Stafford*

Colors of Faith

I once believed my sister had magic powder hidden somewhere in our living room. Each time we made a fire, she would have me close my eyes; when she told me to open them I would see a blaze of colors in the flames. When she was not around, I searched the living room for her private stash of powder, but never found it. Only years later did I learn that when my eyes were closed, she put the comic pages on the fire.

I was reminded of that this morning as I sat and watched my morning fire begin. I treasure the hours before others awaken, when I have time to myself to pray and reflect. During this time I read all sorts of books and try to grow spiritually. For me, spiritual growth is as much about unlearning as it is learning.

Everything I learned about God came from my childhood. At the time, it was an understanding that was age-appropriate: God was looking down with arms crossed, watching me. I was told he loved me, that his son died for me—but there he stood watching to see how I performed. I believed God could do anything, and still do, but in too many ways God was in the image of Santa, able to care for the world and provide every sort of wonder and joy.

In recent years, I have studied and awakened to the nature of God. In no way do I believe I've figured things out, but each morning I seek to open my eyes and heart and appreciate the nature of faith. I have put away thoughts of magic powder, but the flames dance in colors all the same, and that's this morning's gift. —*Chip Bristol*

Winter Treasures

February used to be my least favorite month. It may be short, but it seems long. It's gray and cloudy and cold, and I just want it to be over.

Now that I've become a dedicated bird watcher, however, I like February a lot more. I can see things in the trees because the leaves are gone. I can see the nests from last year and how they are shaped and what they are made of, twigs and fabric and paper shards. I can see the birds themselves and watch them preening or puffing themselves up to keep warm.

What's more, where I live the bird populations actually change in winter. We have arctic birds that live here only during the winter months, while some of our spring and summer birds are gone elsewhere. I can enjoy things I don't normally get to enjoy, if I will just open my eyes to see them.

We go through all kinds of seasons in our lives, and some of them seem bleak and cold. But there are treasures to be had even then, treasures not available during other seasons. We have to have the eyes to see them, though. We have to be able to imagine that such treasures actually exist, and exist in places we didn't expect or value.

Such is life in God's time and among God's creation. It is all there for us to see and be part of, if we will, and there are pleasures in every season.

Even bleak February. —*Penny Nash*

The Mirror

'Cause every town's got a mirror, and every mirror still shows me.
— GRACE POTTER, "RAGGED COMPANY"

Thirty years ago, I used to look around at my classmates and compare myself to them. Actually, what I was comparing was what I perceived; usually a far cry from reality and who I really was. I wanted to be taller. I wanted to have those muscles. I wished I had that girlfriend. I wanted to be that popular. Almost everywhere I looked I came up short. Problem was, besides not seeing myself with clear eyes, I was comparing my insides to their outsides.

Some people are born with an accurate and natural sense of self. For others, the scenario above is a naturally occurring part of their development. Oftentimes people eventually grow out of it and develop a solid, realistic sense of self. Others, in a variety of ways, find their growth arrested.

I found alcohol and other drugs, and suddenly I felt like I fit in. As long as I was intoxicated, the world seemed a brighter place. I was smarter, better looking, cooler, tougher—whatever I needed to be. Soon, however, addiction brought a darkness into my life, and it took more and more to feel "okay." The more I used, the worse the consequences piled up and the worse my life became. It was a never-ending, destructive cycle that also prohibited me from knowing who I was.

Today, it is good to be comfortable in my own skin and to know that warts, quirks, and all, I am exactly who and where I need to be today. Most of the time, I can look in that mirror.
—*Bo Cox*

Useful Guilt

I recently read Tracy Kidder's book, *Mountains Beyond Mountains*, about Paul Farmer, the doctor and founder of Partners In Health. Farmer has devoted much of his life to helping people in Haiti. It is both an inspiring and a troubling book. Inspiring because of the difference Farmer, a single person, has made. Troubling because it challenges my relative complacency. How can I, having health care and all the food I need (and then some), live comfortably when so many others do not have enough to eat and die from treatable diseases?

We're less keen on guilt nowadays than we once were. Guilt has debilitated so many, kept some from enjoying the life given them. Still, guilt has its uses. It troubles our sleep and pushes us to change. Perhaps we've spent too much time feeling guilty about the wrong things—what we eat, who we love, how much we curse—when we should feel guilty about the fact that others are so poor and most of us are not.

I am grateful for what I have, and I have much. Blessings should not be sources of guilt, but excess should. Sometimes people like Farmer come along to instill in us a bit of guilt, just as Jesus did.

Give away all you have, Jesus said. *Give away your shirt and your coat. Blessed are the poor, and woe to the rich.* Are these words for us? For those of us with plenty? If we are not doing something to help the poor, then we are not following Christ. We should feel guilty about that, and our guilt should help us change. —*Jeremiah Sierra*

Saying Her Prayers

This is another day…If I am to stand up, help me to stand bravely.
If I am to sit still, help me to sit quietly.
If I am to lie low, help me to do it patiently.
And if I am to do nothing, let me do it gallantly.

THE BOOK OF COMMON PRAYER, P. 461

Though people borrow these lines in illness, grief, or in any situation of human wobbliness, this prayer didn't suit Rose. At age ninety-five, she couldn't physically support the heavy book for reading, nor could she memorize the lines, but throughout adulthood, she had relied on beautifully written prayers.

Rose was shocked at the idea of brevity and frankness in conversational prayer. I'd suggested that she might say, "Father," and promptly fall asleep without offending God. "Father" was her name for God so I told her that expressing the relationship in that one word would bring pleasure to the Almighty. Or she could pray, "Help!" Realizing that spontaneity was acceptable, Rose chose these words for six more years, telling people she had finally learned to pray! She also gave gleeful thanks over weekly fast-food hamburgers until age 101.

I often think, "Unto you, O Lord," and trust the Spirit to read my mind and heart. This works well in traffic. If only one moment, "Unto you, praise." Or remembering my brother who is ill, "Unto you, Lord, Ted." God knows the details. And when the day comes that I quite literally run out of breath, I trust God to read my wordless longing, "Unto you, Lord. Amen."

If you have an opportunity, tell prayer book lovers that while written prayers are fabulous, short prayers are significant too. —*June Terry*

Margins

Just before sunrise, the morning sky provides a hint of color announcing the dawn. Muted pinks and oranges, purples and blues unfold, giving voice to an artist no longer silent—speaking, but silent still.

In the din of a world where sounds spill over into almost all of our day, every day, we rarely have a quiet time to be with our Creator God and to be aware of God's presence in the world—that still, small voice. Life can become too full, making it next to impossible without some intentionality to make a space, create a margin, a time with our God and Creator.

My own tradition invites me to begin my days with prayer—to fill the space around me with prayer—painting the background for the canvas that will be my day. I also end my days in prayer as I remember what has been in the space of waking hours and reconcile this with my relationship to God. These margins are not filled with my prayer, but oftentimes are silent as I look about the largeness of creation and humbly realize my small space. There I know the blessings that each day brings to my life and the life of those around me.

These margins are my way of not only making time to be with God, but also having God be at the beginning and end of every day.
—*Debbie Royals*

Are You Up For It?

Early in the morning,
before the restless voices in your head wake up,
be still in the presence of the Lord.

Our first waking moments are a perfect time to be still with God. Psalm 46:11 reads: "Be still, then, and know that I am God." It is in quiet stillness that we experience the soft, gentle voice of the Divine breathing a tender whisper into our hearts. Dawn is a special time of the day. When we first emerge from sleep it seems our receptivity to God is uninterrupted.

Our restless minds never seem to quiet the chatter. Deep thought and introspection are helpful to our walk with God, but when our thinking becomes mindless obsessive chatter, the voice of God is drowned out—even when we don't want to drown it out. Mindless chatter is like an invisible force field effectively blocking the one Voice we seek to hear the most, the very voice of God in our hearts.

Being still in the early morning is an opportunity to find that place of peace within. Once the restless chatter realizes you have awakened to a new day, it will start its assault on your mind. Beginning the day in the quiet stillness of the Lord will help quiet these voices and lead to greater joy and peace throughout the day.

So, why not start the day sitting in stillness before the quiet presence of the Lord? Why not invite that presence into your heart before the restless chatter in your head wakes up?

God is there in your first waking moments, eager to embrace you in a cloud of love. Are you up for it? —*Wilfredo Benitez*

Plundering the Egyptians

And so they plundered the Egyptians.
— EXODUS 12:36

Just before the Israelites left Egypt, they asked the Egyptians for their gold and silver jewelry. The Egyptian people were kind enough to oblige, "and so they plundered the Egyptians." Why were the Egyptians so willing to give up their stuff?

I do not have gold or silver to be plundered, but I surely have an abundance of stuff. I especially love candleholders. Once, when I saw a particularly gorgeous candleholder, I could not buy it because I had no place for it in my home. "You have reached a saturation point," says my son, a tad accusingly.

I cannot justify the indulgence of owning fifty candleholders in an electrified house by calling it a "candleholder collection," because it's not. It is simply an accumulation.

Maybe the Egyptian people also had a saturated supply of stuff. Maybe they realized their accumulated wealth was a benefit of slave labor. They certainly had reached a saturation point with the exploitation of other people. Maybe they decided, when the Israelites were now free to leave Egypt, to help them on their way, making up for all those years of cruel exploitation. So when the Israelites plundered the Egyptians—asking nicely, I hear—they did the Egyptians a favor by helping them to give up stuff that was, in truth, a burden to them.

I still love my candleholders. But if I ever find myself enslaved to my possessions, it may be time for me to plunder my inner Egyptian and liberate myself from spiritual captivity.
—*Joanna Leiserson*

Supporting Role

In the seventeenth chapter of Exodus, the Israelites are engaged in a fierce battle with the Amalekites, and Moses is at the top of a hill, holding up his staff over the army in blessing and intercession. As long as he continues to hold up his hand, Israel is winning, but there's a problem—as the day goes on, Moses' arms grow too tired to hold up the staff, and the Amalekites begin to regain ground. Then Aaron and Hur sit Moses down on a rock, and each of them lifts up one of his arms, holding them steady until the sun sets and the battle is won.

Until she became homebound in the last year of her life, my mother maintained a bulletin board at her church. Every day—and especially on Sundays—she carefully perused the local newspaper for names of members of the congregation, especially young people, who were using their gifts to accomplish something positive in the community. People who were taking leadership roles in civic organizations, or being honored for outstanding work in their profession or years of faithful volunteer effort; kids who won in sports or received scholarships; Girl Scouts, Boy Scouts; performers in music, dance, or theater—all these stories went up on the bulletin board. Just as she'd celebrated the efforts of her children and grandchildren by posting our news on her refrigerator, my mother celebrated and supported the lives and ministries of her church family, too.

If we're going to be a blessing in the world, we need to hold up each other's arms. Look around—who's holding up your arms, encouraging and celebrating your ministries, helping you prevail in your battles? Whose faltering arms can you support? —*Mary W. Cox*

Does This Make Me Look Fat?

We need others to help us see. Any woman who has ever asked her friend, "Do these pants make me look fat?" knows this truth.

Our own perspective is only so helpful.

That's one reason why we human beings live in community. We can see ourselves from only a limited number of perspectives. Those around us—our friends, our fellow pilgrims on the journey—offer us opportunities to look outside ourselves for perspective and help.

Yet often, our fears and doubts of our worth prevent us from having the hard conversations and opening ourselves to others for their loving help. Perhaps we have been hurt by others who assaulted us with so-called helpful advice that cut us even more deeply. Perhaps we have decided our own egos are to be trusted...alone. Perhaps we are afraid the vulnerability of holy conversation is more than we can bear.

Opening ourselves to the honest conversations is scary. We might be hurt. We might see that changes which need to happen will cost us some parts of ourselves we've become quite attached to. We might be called as Christians to trust that the whole life-death-resurrection cycle isn't just about a long weekend in the spring.

We also might find that the new thing God is calling us toward through these conversations is simply awe-inspiring. Waking up to the beauty of resurrection is not a myth. My own life has shown this to be true.

May we have the courage to trust God enough so the eyes of another will let us see ourselves more clearly—so we may follow God more nearly. —*Laurie Brock*

You Are the Music While the Music Lasts

Imagine attending a concert in which the orchestra is about to perform a piece that is particularly dear to you—in my case it might be Brahms' Second Piano Concerto. The audience falls silent, the French horn plays the haunting opening notes, the strings enter, and the pianist sets fingers to the keyboard.

As the music flows into you, at first you may want to be the pianist. You want the music to be streaming through your hands and body, to be singing through your fingertips. As you listen intently, absorbed in the music, maybe you say, "No, I want to be the conductor; I want to stand with open arms, listening with such pure attention that I hear the whole of it, every note and every space between the notes, receiving it all into my body and guiding and responding to it as it takes shape around me."

Then, as your listening deepens, you give yourself even more fully to the moment. You become very silent, very still. You forget yourself and become the music. Moment by moment the music is giving itself to you, and moment by moment you are giving yourself fully to the music. You have relinquished all sense of who you are, yet in that self-surrender you have never felt more fully yourself or more fully alive. Later, if someone asked you who you were, you would have to say, "I don't know. I am Brahms' Second Piano Concerto."

God is always courting us, always luring us to fall in love. Listen intently, give yourself to the present moment with utter sincerity and an open heart, and who knows what God will do? —*Margaret Bullitt-Jonas*

Letters of the Kingdom

Some people in our congregation are sending letters to neighbors around our church. The initial handwritten letter, on stationery created by one of the third graders at Saint John's School, simply says, "Dear Neighbor, we are praying for you; using the enclosed paper and stamped envelope, please tell us what you would like prayers for." We mailed out two hundred letters, with no preconceived idea of the result.

The first response was from a great-grandmother. Remembering how people used to write letters, she made copies of our letter and is now using it to write to her great-grandchildren. Her prayer request: for peace in the world so my precious ones can grow up in a world better than the one I grew up in.

Another neighbor wrote back that her circle of friends has diminished and her family is distant. She is lonely and isolated and had wondered if anyone cared. Our letter reminded her that she is loved and prayed for. Her request: pray for love in the world.

Another letter especially moved me. Written on personal stationery, the second line of this thank you note said, "Please pray for children in orphanages." The neighbor didn't know that eleven years ago my wife and I prayed the same exact prayer. Those prayers dramatically changed our family and the lives of our two adopted daughters, Galina and Victoria. The neighbor reminded me of God's kingdom and the power of prayer.

Seeking God can be as simple as writing a letter, praying for peace, praying for love, or praying for widows and orphans. Seeking God can even be a simple reminder of blessings once forgotten.
—Dave Marshall

Deeply Loved

I'm sort of a Valentine's Day humbug. I like chocolate and flowers well enough, but I most enjoy spreading Valentine cheer by sharing the lore about Saint Valentine, a Roman priest supposedly beheaded on this day around 278 for performing illegal marriages for young lovers. (Romantic, isn't it?) It's not that I'm a lonely and bitter single; even those years when I have a date leave me a little leery about the practice of exalting romance—and just for a day.

I can always use a reminder, though, to prioritize and maintain all my relationships: relationships with a significant other, with family, with friends, with colleagues and coworkers and people from my church—and my relationship with God. While my earthly relationships are all with flawed, broken people, people who will hurt me (and whom I will hurt), God's love is perfect, even when we forget it's there.

Not too long ago, I encountered an important message from the website EXAMEN.me, an Ignatian resource: "You are deeply loved, fully forgiven, and complete in Christ. Walk in that truth today." The words are simple, but this is a powerful reminder. I don't know how you'll celebrate Valentine's Day—with hearts and candy, thoughts of third-century martyrs, or as just another Friday. Whatever you do, remember: You are deeply loved. You are fully forgiven. You are complete in Christ. —*Alissa Goudswaard*

The Extraordinary Ordinary

Some days are special. Some days are divine. While today is not noteworthy on the church calendar, for you, today might be the day above every day, the most important twenty-four hours of your life.

Just after midnight, on February 15, 2012, our son called to say our first grandchild had been born. We had been anxiously awaiting the child's arrival. He may not have chosen the day of his birth, but that day, an ordinary day, became the most extraordinary day for us. After all, in our eyes, he is the "holy grandchild."

Could today, an ordinary day, be the moment when everything changes? Jacob's father had sent him on a holy mission. He had traveled for days. Night had fallen. Weary, Jacob took a stone pillow. He had a mysterious dream. God promised him divine presence—God would never leave him. Awaking, Jacob built an altar using the stone pillow.

Then, on an ordinary day, there in an eastern field, was a well, covered with a stone. In the distance he saw Rachel, bringing her father's sheep to water. Overcome with love, "Jacob kissed Rachel, and wept aloud" (Genesis 29:11). His love was profound. Jacob vowed seven years of service to Rachel's father in exchange for her hand in marriage. An ordinary day had become anything but normal.

What divine thing might appear on this ordinary day? Maybe some holy love will be born this day if we are pregnant with the expectation of God's arrival. —*Gil Stafford*

Up to a High Place

Living in Boston during the construction of the "Big Dig," a major transportation project, was often a frustrating experience. Constant road work caused huge traffic jams. I remember taking off from Logan Airport one morning and, as the airplane gained height, I could see all the different traffic jams, some several miles long. But from this perspective I could also see small side roads that the drivers could have driven down to avoid some of the hold-ups ahead. Of course those poor drivers could not see those roads, because they were stuck in the middle of the chaos. But being lifted up, as I was, gave me a completely different perspective.

There are many occasions in the psalms when God graciously lifts the psalmist, who is often distressed or in the midst of chaos, up to a high place. "He lifted me out of the desolate pit, out of the mire and clay; he set my feet upon a high cliff and made my footing sure" (Psalm 40:1-2).

So often our own lives can feel confused and chaotic, as tangled and frustrating as a rush-hour traffic jam. Where are we stuck right now in our lives, in need of the clarity of a fresh perspective? Perhaps we can follow the psalmist's example and seek a different ground. Taking a few days away on retreat, or literally climbing a mountain or hiking in the hills, can be a wonderful way of allowing God to lift us out of our own version of "the mire and clay," so that we can regain perspective on our lives and see again with clarity. —*Brother Geoffrey Tristram*, SSJE

The Robin's Lesson

A robin provided rich entertainment for me one morning. Our patio table and chairs, right outside my study window, were still draped in their heavy nylon winter tarp. The tarp was worn; long shiny blue threads were unraveling from its edge. The robin wanted those strings for his nest. A strong wind had them dancing wildly, glinting in the sunlight. The robin would chase one around and finally catch it in his beak, then take off with it, but it would yank him up short when he had stretched it taut. Regaining his little feet and flapping his wings in frustration, he'd go right back to it, until after about eight tries he finally gave up.

Aren't we like that robin? Something bright and shiny catches our eye, and we lunge for it. We catch hold and think it's ours, but then discover it's not really ours: it's attached, most often to old, worn habits of acquisitiveness and envy. Instead of building up our nest, it entangles us in disappointment and frustrated desire. These so-called treasures are simply tired trinkets, the unravelings of a false and trivial life.

How different are God's good gifts—home and hearth, families and friendships, learning, rewarding work, the boundless riches of creation. They might not always glitter and dance in our view, but in their richness and abundance we can take off and soar, because there are no strings attached! That, indeed, is the meaning of grace: God's undeserved love, no strings attached. —*Betsy Rogers*

A Scary Story

There is an exorcism story in the gospels (see Luke 8:26-39) that is quite frightening. It could be right out of a movie. Jesus cast out the demons from a man and then sent them into a herd of swine. This did not turn out well for the swine. They rushed down a steep bank into the lake and drowned.

This story is part of a series of miracle stories. The one before it is about Jesus stilling a storm while he and the disciples are in a boat. The ones after it are about healings.

The exorcism story is different from the ones surrounding it. For one thing, there is a negative consequence to what Jesus did, at least for the swine. For another, Jesus did not leave people happy. Instead, they were frightened and implored Jesus to leave.

There is just something different about casting out our demons. Storms and diseases are dangerous, even life-threatening. Demons do not take life away. They hijack it. They take it over, take possession of our lives for their purposes rather than our own, and rob us of living the lives we have been given and substitute something less in their places.

Demons are harder to get rid of, in part because they are quick to protest that they do not need to be gotten rid of at all. They make it hard to distinguish between what is really of us and what is really of them. That's why getting rid of them is messy business.

You can just about guarantee that someone is going to lose a pig in the process, and that someone isn't going to like it. —*Stacy Sauls*

"I Found It"

Several decades ago, a movement swept the church, emanating from evangelical circles. The movement was manifested in buttons, bumper stickers, and billboards which read "I found it." It was a bit of a teaser, meant to trigger questions about what has been found. The answer, I seem to remember, was that the truth of Christianity had been found. Or that a relationship with Christ had been found. Or that eternal life had been found, as if it were a remote control that had fallen between the cushions of the sofa.

I was just a young person when I first ran across these buttons, but I never felt inclined to wear one. In later years, when I reflected on the campaign, something didn't sit quite right with me. For starters, my limited understanding of the nature of the Christian faith was that it is not a matter of finding "it," but rather a matter of finding a person, a relationship. More than that, I knew pretty early on that the progression was backward. My experience of the spiritual journey was not so much that I found something, but that someone found me.

As we focus in this book on what it means to seek God, we will of course recognize that our relationship with God is a two-way street, a journey of mutual discovery, the synergy of grace and gratitude. But the headline, the big news, the billboard message is that long before we were looking, God found us. Thank God. —*Jay Sidebotham*

Callused Prayers

Small calluses are forming on the inside of my right index finger and middle finger. At first I wondered what caused this new roughness. Had I forgotten to use hand cream? Had the water become harder?

And then I remembered...it's a callus from writing so much! It has been so long since my graduate school days, the last time I had this kind of roughness at the bend of my digits. With a secretary or administrative assistant while I was working for so many years—and with the new technologies—I have had no calluses. Maybe cramps in my fingers or threat of carpal tunnel, but no calluses.

I recall studying an older friend's gnarled fingers that were covered with calluses. An esteemed scholar and prolific writer, his right hand represented his years of sitting at a desk—writing, thinking, gnawing on his knuckles. Will mine become as noticeable in years to come, I wondered?

At the end of an afternoon this past week, a new friend stopped by my office to share that his sister had died suddenly, and he was grieving sorely. He was planning to go back to his home country at the end of the week for the burial. We sat together, talking quietly as the sun set, until we needed to turn on lights to see our faces. Mostly I listened while he gave voice to his rambling thoughts, questions, and remembrances. I responded with an occasional gentle question, and ample space for contemplation, silence, tears, and reflection.

We ended our time together holding hands—small calluses on my right hand and all—with heads bent and knees touching, in prayer; calluses forgotten and love remembered. —*Westina Matthews*

Fie, Death

Death is all around us. We see it everywhere, since all living things must one day die. But death isn't just physical. We grieve the grudges that harden our hearts. We suffer when the best of ourselves is rejected. We rage in frustration when our dreams are thwarted.

Perhaps the most daily experience of death is in loneliness. We are all lonely sometimes. In the song "Message in a Bottle," Sting proclaims, "Seems I'm not alone at being alone." If it weren't so tragic, we could laugh at the irony.

We are lonely as we wonder if anyone really loves us. We are lonely as we realize that no one truly knows us, any more than we truly know anyone else. We are lonely as we realize that we don't even know ourselves. Loneliness steals our identity.

Here's the thing: You are not alone.

Whatever your suffering, you are not alone. There is One who has gone before you. There is One who has experienced and broken the power of death. And this One, Jesus, this man who was also God, loves you! Jesus took on the suffering of the world. Jesus surrendered to and defeated death because he loves *you*.

You are not alone. We often talk about Jesus like he's not in the room. But he is.

Jesus walks with you in your darkness. Did you know? Your darkness won't last forever. Jesus has already won the battle. Light is already pouring in. Jesus is even now filling you with life. Love is surrounding you.

You are not alone. In your crying, in your dancing, in your boredom, in your gladness, in your loneliness, you are not alone. —*Kristine Blaess*

Faith, Prophets, and Economics

Wall Street Collapses! Loans Denied! $700 Billion Dollar Bailout! In recent years, we have witnessed increased joblessness, shrinking investments, home foreclosures, and stagnant wages—frightening times in our economic history. Many say these are the results of infectious greed on Wall Street that has trickled down to Main Street, corrupting individuals and institutions alike.

I am not immune to the influence of greed and excess. I have a fairly new car that I did not necessarily need sitting in my driveway, but I was caught up in the cultural tides, compelled to have something more "presentable." In retrospect, I wish I had used my money more wisely and set my priorities within the framework of faith.

Thousands of years ago the prophets warned against the factors that led to our current crisis. Micah spoke out against land barons who were unjust and inhumane, as creditors manipulated the courts and foreclosed on family farms (Micah 2:1-5). Amos spoke out against Israel, denouncing the society's decadent opulence and the smug piety of elites who "trampled the head of the poor into the dust of the earth" (Amos 2:7). Jesus warned his disciples to be on their guard against all kinds of greed (Luke 12:15). These warnings are just as relevant today. They speak to us collectively and individually.

Like the prophets, we can align ourselves with God's will. Like them, we can advocate for a just society that closes the great abyss between rich and poor. We can use the power of the ballot box to demand sensible financial governance. We can re-examine our priorities and explore our life's purpose more deeply, seeking God's kingdom above and in all things. God's love shall endure forever, and with that love we will truly prosper, both now and in the age to come. —*Owen C. Thompson*

Stuck

Did you ever wake up one day and suddenly realize that you are stuck in some way? You're in a rut, perhaps, living mostly on autopilot. Or you realize that you've been withdrawn lately. Maybe you feel some vague dissatisfaction about your life, work, relationships. Maybe you are having a spiritual dry spell.

We all get stuck. It often starts out innocently enough. We're extraordinarily busy, someone has been sick, a family or work crisis has kept our attention and focus for a short time, and then, like the Prodigal Son, we come to ourselves and realize that things are out of whack. We've gotten off the path or stopped in the middle of it, while life has gone on without us.

I had one of those experiences recently. I just felt dull. I decided it was time to take stock and begin to discern something new for myself. I had no idea what that new thing might be except that it would mean getting unstuck.

So I drove to a neighboring town and attended an evening church service that included prayers with a lay pastoral prayer minister in the side chapel. I told her I felt that I needed to discern something new for myself and wished for prayers to begin that discernment.

She said: "God, show Penny who you are, and show her who she is."

The tension in my shoulders released immediately. That was just right. I believe that the way to becoming unstuck is to see who God is and see who I am, and then to begin to work with that. —*Penny Nash*

"*I Have Called You Friends*"

Each time I read those words in John 15, my heart is filled with joy. My favorite way to communicate with my friends is via daily texts. Although I cannot text with God in the same way, I am definitely connected with God all day long. When I was about seventeen, a friend told me, "I am constantly talking with God. We are in a constant conversation." Since then, I have done the same. I shoot heavenly texts to God all the time. And I know God replies.

Me: God, I am feeling down.
God: Cast your burden on me; I will sustain you.

Me: God, please help my friend who is sick.
God: I will take sickness away from among you.

Me: God, please help me find a job.
God: I will fully satisfy every need of yours.

Me: God, I need a parking space; I'm late because of this Houston traffic!
God: Front row!

Some people laugh when I share that I communicate with God as my friend. However, God also promises in the same chapter, "Ask for whatever you wish, and it will be done for you" (John 15:7). Whatever you wish. Parking spaces included. God is very specific and I take God's word for it. Will you? I know it might be a stretch to think of God texting you. However, God says: "I stand at the door and knock!" Or, "I stand next to my iPhone (yes, I do believe God would have an iPhone!) and text!" Let's not make God wait. Let's reply and include our favorite emoticon. I am sure God will send one back. —*Sandra Montes*

The Blessings of Snowstorms

With windy haste and wild halloo the sheeting snow comes down
And drives itself through bush and swale and leagues of stubble brown.
Blessings on the waiting fields when the sheeting snow comes down.

— LIBERTY HYDE BAILEY, "SNOW-STORM"

Liberty Hyde Bailey was an early twentieth-century naturalist, horticulturalist, and writer. He had particular impact on the life of author and agriculturalist Wendell Berry. Bailey's poem reminds us of the blessings of snowstorms. This is something we too easily miss. We mistake the "windy haste and wild halloo" in our lives as merely chaos. We assume that nothing good comes from this chaos, that a well-ordered life is the only life worth living. Sometimes we fall into the trap of thinking that there's a place for everything and everything should be in its place. But that's rarely how life actually happens.

Life comes at us in fits and starts. There is an inherent messiness to life that defies our simple categories and neat boxes. There are snowstorms on days we hoped to travel, rain when we had hoped to go to the park, and sunshine when we are stuck inside for all-day meetings. And of course, it's not just weather. Loved ones die or move away, friends may have a falling out, we may lose our job or our house, and our plans may fail.

We don't look forward with eager expectation or joy for any of those things. But it is in the chaos of the snowstorm that we can discover the blessings of the snow. It is in the chaos of our lives that often, if we are open, we can discover the blessings of God.

—*Aaron Klinefelter*

Lowering the Centerboard

There was plenty of wind, but we couldn't get the boat to go forward. We adjusted both the main sail and jib, pulled them in and let them out, and still the boat refused to go. Then, we realized the centerboard was still lifted out of the water. With one simple push, the boat glided forward, and making the most of the wind, we headed across the bay.

As I approach the season of Lent, I realize the simple but important lesson this teaches. There is plenty of wind to guide me through each day, countless opportunities and sources of inspiration. I need to lift my sails and catch that wind (or spirit), but, as with the sailboat, I might only move sideways. There is a centerboard that needs to be lowered—a simple gesture that gives my boat direction.

This is the season of gestures, those taken and those not, all with the hopes of working with the wind and moving forward. Too often I focus on the wind, on the opportunities and inspiration of life, and not on the other parts that help move me forward. It is not either/or; we need wind just as we need a centerboard, but we sometimes focus on one and forget the other. This is the season of adjustment, to trim sails and lower centerboards, to make sure we are making the most of all we've been given and are heading in the right direction. It is a time to move forward, rather than floating aimlessly in the wind.

This year I am going to focus not on one thing for Lent, but many. I am going to make forty (forty-six, if you count Sundays—which I do) small gestures. I am also going to *not* do forty-six other things in hopes that, together, those decisions will lower the centerboard of my life. This may not seem big, but I have no doubt my spiritual boat will move forward. —*Chip Bristol*

Turning on the Divine Autopilot

As with driving, the autopilot feature of my brain is designed to make the routine parts of my life easier. I can get ready for work and leave home without worrying that I have forgotten my glasses. We can't pay close attention to every little thing all the time.

Sometimes my mental autopilot works too well. I am so accustomed to driving to work each day that on one holiday, I ended up in my familiar parking space before I realized that I was supposed to be somewhere else.

My mental autopilot can also lead my spirituality awry. Spiritual life, even if routine, is meant to be a daily practice, but not a mindless one. A sudden angry outburst, an inappropriate remark, a fit of envy— small or big sins crop up regularly to remind me that I need an overhaul. My mental autopilot needs to be adjusted.

I can trust my mental autopilot to be a faithful guide to right actions only if God is its engine. When I make God the center of my life, then my autopilot will emerge out of God's spirit of love rather than my habits of the world. And with the Divine Autopilot, God is the pilot who guides me straight and true. The Divine Autopilot is mindful, not mindless.

The Divine Autopilot does not take us to the first or easiest place to go. Christian discipleship will lead me to share rather than hoard, forgive rather than hold on to anger, and even to accept forgiveness when I don't want to admit that I've done wrong. It's not easy, but it's the only way to go. —*Joanna Leiserson*

Passing it On

My grandfather was a giant of a man...When he walked, the earth shook.
When he laughed, the birds fell out of the trees.
His hair caught fire from the sun. His eyes were patches of sky.

— ETH CLIFFORD, *THE REMEMBERING BOX*

I raised hogs when I was a boy. I also spent a lot of time with my grandpa. One day, after we fed the hogs, I was impatient. Thinking there was nothing more to see or do, I was ready to go. Grandpa, however, had settled his long, lanky frame back against a tree and was standing there watching the feeding frenzy. He wasn't just watching either; it was like he was *studying* them!

What was there to watch, I wondered. I mean, if you've ever seen hogs eat, it's just a rush of movement and activity and then lots of grunts and smacking noises. However, knowing we wouldn't leave until Grandpa had a notion to, I stood beside him and tried to see what he saw.

Eventually I saw a little. Some hogs would push others out of the way if they thought another was getting more than they were. Some would assess the situation and maneuver themselves so they'd be able to see everything and would even make trouble when another hog changed spots at the trough. Others seemed content to mind their own business.

Still, I wondered, what's the big deal?

Almost as if he could read my thoughts, Grandpa looked down at me, pushed his old sweat-and-dirt-streaked straw cowboy hat back on his head a little, and grinned at me.

"You can learn a lot about people by watching hogs eat, boy." —*Bo Cox*

Listening for the Silence

In my first semester as an undergraduate, I struggled to adjust to life in a new city, a new campus, and a university social culture from which I felt totally alienated. My only real relief from the academic and social pressure came from the hours I spent watching television. Even though I had been a very active churchgoer for as long as I could remember, God seemed further away than ever.

In a few months, I could scarcely stand the suffocating sense of godlessness anymore. So on Ash Wednesday, I picked up my dorm room TV and put it under my bed. Then I made a schedule so that three times each day for an hour apiece I would sit in my room and read scripture or another Christian book and pray in silence. My atheist roommate found it very strange indeed! Nonetheless, I stuck to that prayer schedule rigorously for the rest of the school year.

Long ago, the prophet Elijah learned to hear God not in the wind, the fire, or the earthquake, but in the "sound of sheer silence" (1 Kings 19:12). Like Elijah, it was not in my textbooks or classes or television that I felt the Lord's presence. Only by forcing myself (with God's grace and mercy) to set aside space for prayer and silence every day did I know the closeness of the Holy Spirit. Before long I was looking forward anxiously to my next meditation time. It was like walking from a drafty old basement into the warmth of a perfect summer day.

—*Charles Graves IV*

Dust and Tears—Glue that Binds

Lent is about to begin for the Christian tradition. It begins with a ritual remembrance of death and the imposition of ashes on the forehead to remind us that we were made from dust and someday will be dust again.

Recently I was asked to lead a memorial service for a Navajo/Apache man. He had influenced the lives of many Native people living on the streets and, for many of them, had been the glue that held this community together. We listened to stories about how he protected some of the ladies and guided the men who depended on him for wisdom and advice. I sat listening as everyone shared their relationship to this man. Around the circle there were tears and laughter coming from the memories of joy as well as from the sense of loss and grief. In the end, each person offered a handshake or a hug to everyone else there.

I thought about this man being the glue that bound the community together. And I realized that when we shed those precious tears, remembering happy and sad things along with the dust, a new kind of "glue" is made. Community is such a blessing, and taking time out to connect and reconnect is essential to that bond. Equally important is our willingness to be bound in community. —*Debbie Royals*

A Season for Sincerity

Love righteousness, you rulers of the earth,
think of the Lord in goodness
and seek him with sincerity of heart.

— WISDOM 1:1

What does it mean to seek the Lord with sincerity of heart? Folk etymology suggests that the word "sincere" finds its root in metallurgy. Metal is pure when it is without wax; the Latin word *sina* means without, and *cera* means wax. Artisans might cover up a flaw in a sculpture with a wad of wax to make it look better than it actually is. Builders might fill in gaps of bricks with wax, making a structure less than sound.

The same can be true of our hearts. The call to sincerity of heart points us to the aspiration to be single-minded in our spiritual journey. As philosopher and theologian Kierkegaard said, purity of heart is to will one thing. How often in our spiritual journey do we find ourselves challenged in the sincerity department? How do we deal with the distractions? How can we move closer to purity of heart? One mentor was fond of saying that he never met a motive that wasn't mixed. We admit as much every time we say the confession, acknowledging that we have not loved God with our whole heart and soul and mind. Is there ever a day when that is not true?

How might we move today toward a true sincerity of heart? It starts by admitting we're not there yet. It starts by taking time to remove distractions. The upcoming season of Lent will give us a chance to do that. Pray today for sincerity of heart.

—*Jay Sidebotham*

Harbingers of the Kingdom

There is something pregnant about March. It's burgeoning with all kinds of nascent potentiality. It is round-bellied, almost full-term, teeming with life just under the surface, eager to break out. No, it's not quite spring yet. Not quite. But winter's grasp is weakening ever so slightly. The strength of that grasp is waning just enough in our neighborhood that crocuses are starting to bloom. These small harbingers of what is to come recall to me Jesus' words about the kingdom of God.

Jesus compares the kingdom of God to a mustard seed. A teeny tiny, one-millimeter mustard seed that may grow to be a plant eight to ten feet tall when mature. Birds may even come and nest and find shelter in the full-grown shrub. What strikes me as particularly notable: Jesus is clear that the kingdom of God is like both the seed and the mature plant. All the potential possibilities are present in the seed, but the seed is not fully realized. The seed, like the kingdom, is *now*, but also *not yet*.

In our lives we glimpse the kingdom. We see small harbingers of the world the way God desires it to be. It is a world of mutual love and respect, of peace and prosperity, of hope and new life. The kingdom of God is the rule and reign and way of God that is benevolent, generous, and peaceable. We live in a world pregnant with the nascent potentiality of the kingdom of God on earth as in heaven—and are reminded of this kingdom whenever we see a crocus popping up out of the cold, dark soil. —*Aaron Klinefelter*

And They Will Know We Are Christians by Our—Foreheads?

When I was a kid, I dreaded Ash Wednesday, not because of its holiness, but because it meant my mother would be serving tuna fish on rice for dinner, and I had to go to school with a huge thumbprint on my forehead. I always wished someone would invent a perfectly cross-shaped stamp to dip in the ashes, so at least my peers and curious onlookers would know I was religious—not a kid who didn't bathe.

The church I grew up in had two priests, one of whom was my father. My father had huge hands and wasn't known for artistic skills. The people who went to my father for ashes looked like their foreheads were used as police blotters, while those in the other line had nicely shaped crosses. We always got in my father's line. So I spent the day trying to "accidentally" wipe the ashes off my forehead—removing my sweater several times hoping they would rub off, trying to work up a sweat so they would wash off or I'd have an excuse to wipe my brow.

But even if Picasso himself administered my ashes and autographed his work, I would have been unhappy. The sad truth: I was ashamed to be seen by others. I wasn't comfortable sharing my faith in public.

Our society often sees religion and spirituality as things private and internal that guide individuals but have no place in the public arena. Faith does have its private side; Jesus himself said "Beware of practicing your piety before others in order to be seen by them" (Matthew 6:1).

But Jesus also sent his disciples out into the world and said "Let your light shine before others" (Matthew 5:16). As we begin our Lenten journey, I pray that we won't forget that the mark of the cross isn't temporary. We cannot rub it off no matter how hard we try. It is the mark of love, given to us in baptism, and it marks us as Christ's own forever. —*Owen C. Thompson*

Enter the Wilderness, Enter Abundance

As a college student, I haphazardly attended my Christian university's noncompulsory chapel services, but Ash Wednesday merited special effort. It was one of my favorite services, so silent, somber, still—everything my frenetic student life was not.

On a typically chill and dreary late-winter day in the Midwest, I left my seat and shuffled along the queue snaking across the warm, blond wood of the chapel floor. I stepped toward the elevated central platform to stand in front of a favorite English professor, a volunteer ash distributor. She dipped her blackened thumb into the pot of ashes and looked into my eyes. "Enter the wilderness," she told me, crossing her thumb on my raised forehead. "Enter abundance."

Enter the wilderness.

Enter abundance.

Neither she nor I could know what great wilderness and wild abundance were in store for me—that year and since. Those words, though, that juxtaposition, stayed with me through many seasons and still rings true for me about what grace the Lenten experience holds. It's a fast season, a spare, naked time of wilderness and absence, but it is only by living into that wilderness that I'm prepared for a deep knowledge of the Paschal feast's astonishing abundance.

Marked and mortal, we all must cross the Lenten plain, the Good Friday bridge that points toward Easter—Easter annually and Easter ultimately. It is not easy to travel the wilderness, and it is a privilege.
—*Alissa Goudswaard*

The Whole Picture

With twinkling eyes, the rector threw out a splintered sentence, "All things work together for good." Spluttering, we relied on a credible military veteran to respond: "All? How about World Wars I and II?" The conversation took off.

"All things work together for good" may be scripture's most misquoted, ill-timed phrase when torn from its context. In tragic situations, well-meaning people offer this fragment, leaving out the rest of Romans 8 which helps define "good." The author, Paul, expected his readers to step back, as if to view a painting more clearly, to see the whole picture with the word "good" against a vast background. In fact, if this were a painting, it would require a huge wall: glory-yet-to-come and hope focused on a divine chemist who can make things "work together." Being loved by God, knowing that our Creator is for us, not against us—these all help define the "good." What a wonder: God is for us!

An invisible word becomes clear if our eyes follow the sweep of Paul's brush. That word is "ultimately." God's goodness and power will deprive our trials of their ultimacy, of what today may feel bruisingly final. Such massive truths seem obliterated when pain is at its worst, and we need lots of time even to glimpse ultimate outcomes. Since the delay between pain and peace often calls for a stretch of active trust, we must allow one another plenty of time. And we must give God time.

The friends who followed Jesus on the way of the cross experienced disappointment and hopelessness. Stunned, they watched him die. Ashes to ashes, dust to dust. But it wasn't over yet. —*June Terry*

How'd You Know My Name?

Signs that spring is not that far away: I heard birds singing; I saw my first squirrel; daylight saving time begins tomorrow; the sun rose at 6:20 a.m. this morning; and I no longer need the electric blanket at night, just the heating pad.

Today, I slipped into chapel for a few minutes on my way to meet a friend for lunch, to thank God for the changing season. I was there just in time for the reciting of the Lord's Prayer. It reminded me of the story about the little boy who was just learning this sacred prayer. One night as the boy kneeled by his bed with his parents standing over him, he began: "Our Father who art in heaven, how'd you know my name?"

In Luke 1, we are told that the angel Gabriel came to Zachariah and told him that he and his wife Elizabeth would have a child, and this son would be named John, which in Hebrew means "God is benevolent."

While Wesley and Pat Matthews may have named me Westina, the angel Gabriel has given me a name: child of God. God my Father has many names; but because he knows my name, when I call him, he hears me and he answers, "Yes, my child?"

And he will be called
Wonderful Counselor, Mighty God,
Everlasting Father, Prince of Peace.

— Isaiah 9:6

—*Westina Matthews*

Soul Soil

For many faith traditions, this day marks the first Sunday of Lent. Lent, from an old English word that means "spring," is a season marked by deep gestation and inner growth. The landscape for most of us in North America is slowly, slowly waking from a deep winter slumber. The brown landscape of barren trees and dead grass is returning to life.

Not instantaneously, however. Nature reminds us that regardless of how we may perceive our lawn going from dark and dead to desperately in need of mowing overnight, growth and germination take time.

Soil is nourished with water and decay. Seeds are held within the womb of the earth. Their cells divide and expand. Roots reach downward; stalks strain upward; life pushes forth in tiny increments. Until, finally, creation is reborn.

Lent is a time for spiritual gestation. Our focus on repentance, prayer, study, and devotion nourishes the soul soil that may be thin and depleted. God reminds us that fallow time is a time of replenishment, important for our spiritual well-being.

For the season of Lent, what are the ways you can nourish your soul soil? What are the tiny bits of new creation germinating within you, waiting to be born?

We are called by God in this holy season of Lent to prepare for the life that is waiting to burst forth in Easter.

So tend your soul soil. God has plans for what has been planted to grow into your life and the world. —*Laurie Brock*

Repentance

Jesus proclaimed, "Repent, for the kingdom of heaven has come near" (Matthew 4:17). I have a hard time with repentance.

Maybe the problem is not having a very good sense of what repentance actually means. The word in English means to feel sorry for something you've done, but not so in Greek. The Greek word does not mean to feel anything at all. It means to *think* something. The original concept Jesus is after is to change your mind, to change how you see things. The repentance Jesus is after is not about feeling guilty. Jesus really isn't even after a change of mind in the sense of replacing a wrong opinion with a correct one. Jesus is more after an *exchange* of mind, exchanging God's mind for your own. It is about seeing as God sees, having God's perspective.

Way too often we understand repentance as about how we behave. It is not. We understand it as about how we feel. It is not. We understand it as about how we think. It is not. Repentance is about how we see, about seeing as God sees.

The very first thing we see from God's perspective is exactly what Jesus saw, how near the kingdom of God is if we just reach out and grab it, if we just step out and enter it.

The most important part of repenting is questioning the godliness of the way things are now. It really is impossible to repent without admitting the possibility that God's mind might be different from our own, that God's sight might be different from our own, that God's perspective might be different from our own. Otherwise it is impossible to see as God sees. That is what repentance is all about. —*Stacy Sauls*

Simply God

My sister has Prader-Willi Syndrome (PWS), a rare deformity of chromosome 15. When she was born in 1955, the doctors diagnosed her as a "floppy baby." The following year the first medical reports of PWS were released. Not until 1970, upon reading an obscure article, did my parent's discover a name for Dinah's suffering.

People with PWS have an eating disorder that leads to morbid obesity, straining their abnormally smaller internal organs. They also explode with extreme behavioral episodes of rage. The mortality rate for those with PWS is three times greater than that of the normal population. Having a PWS child dramatically increases the rate of divorce and creates emotional problems for siblings. Depression, chronic grief, and feelings of being an outsider are common among their families.

My sister has outlived all expectations because of the loving care given her by family and devoted caregivers. My parents were happily married for sixty-three years until my mom passed away two years ago on this day. My mother raised us while she taught school and served in the church. She offered classes for mothers of special needs children and was active in the PWS association. My mother never complained. Instead, she loved and served. I asked her how she could be so valiant through Dinah's struggles. "God, simply God," she would say. In her book, *Dinah's Story*, my mother wrote, "Out of difficulty, confusion, and heartache, comes peace, acceptance, and love. Dinah is our Dinah, and God shines out of those blue eyes."

Memorials carved from tears dripping on the stones of the soul cry out to generations yet born. Thanks, Mom.
—*Gil Stafford*

Awesomeness

I saw a nifty photo on Facebook—a person holding up a hand-lettered sign that simply says, "Be Awesome."

"Yeah!" I thought as soon as I saw it. "I want to be awesome! I'm going to be awesome today!"

It didn't take five minutes, though, for the self-doubt to set in. I'm not awesome. In fact, I'm incredibly flawed. I get so much wrong, every day, in my thoughts, words, and deeds. I am so not awesome.

And so once again I fall into the abyss of perfectionism. Because I am not perfect, I am unworthy. I can't be awesome because I am not perfect. It's all-or-nothing thinking, which is paralyzing and stunting. If I don't do anything, then I won't mess up.

Awesome is not the same as perfect. No human is perfect; every human makes mistakes. So by my self-doubting calculation, nobody can be awesome.

Perfectionism is a terrible thing. Every day we have a hundred chances to do the right thing and to be awesome in some way. If life were baseball, and we did three or so things right and almost seven things wrong, we'd qualify for the Hall of Fame. Baseball players and fans know this and rejoice. The perfectionist, however, cannot ever be happy. What about those seven swings and misses? Those seven dropped balls? Those seven fly outs?

"Be perfect as your Father in heaven is perfect," says Matthew (5:48). Right. But maybe this would be more helpful: "Be awesome as your Father in heaven is awesome." If perfect trips you up, then lose it from your vocabulary.

Forget perfect, and just go out there and be awesome today. —*Penny Nash*

The Land Got Its Rest

All the days that the land lay desolate it kept sabbath,
to fulfill seventy years.

— 2 CHRONICLES 36:21

The land finally got to rest. It rested from the tyranny of kings and people who didn't follow the Lord. It rested from the horrors of God's people passing their sons through the fire. The land lay desolate. But the land also abided.

Is that how it is with us, too? We become desolate. The good that we have seen, the fruitfulness that we have enjoyed, is pruned away. We are stumps rather than branches. We are desolate. And we sabbath. We abide. We turn again to our Lord, reconnect, lay quietly because we don't have any other energy, and the Lord ministers to us. The Lord nurtures us, heals us, works the soil around our roots, preparing us in our desolation for the next season of fruitfulness. It may not look like anything is happening, but underneath, where we can't see, preparations are being made. The next season of fruitfulness is already planned, and we are being prepared.

Sabbath. Lent. A time of waiting. A time of reconnecting with our ground and source. The land looked desolate, but it enjoyed its sabbath. Seventy years of sabbath, preparing to welcome her people home.

And at last the word comes from Cyrus. "Let him go up." Then the people of the Lord return to their land which has abided and is now ready for them. Let them go up. Let them build a house in Jerusalem. Let them become God's people, living on the restored land.

—*Kristine Blaess*

Time to Seek

In one ordinary, average week, I talked to several people whose walk in faith had barely begun. One was a recent college graduate who said he was too busy for God because his career was starting and his friends were very important to him. I met with a mom, in her early thirties, with two kids. With swimming lessons, soccer practice, and everything else, she also said she didn't have time to seek God. A couple in their mid-fifties sought a quick route to God. At the peak of both their careers, with a grandchild they loved to visit and a Sunday morning routine that involved coffee and reading the paper, they wanted to see if God could fit into their schedules.

I talked on the phone to a jaded retired man who at every mention of God launched into a tirade about how the church persecutes people and rejects science. And at the end of the week, I met with a hospice patient who could no longer hear or stay awake long enough for a conversation. Her children, desperate to know their mom was saved, called me in; but there was little I could do, except pray that she, whose faith is known to God alone, may have rest in that place where there is no pain or grief, but life eternal.

The prophet Isaiah instructs us to "Seek the LORD while he may be found, call upon him while he is near" (Isaiah 55:6). Perhaps today is the day to seek and find—the scriptures warn us that tomorrow may be too late. I pray it will not be, or was not, too late for the souls I met during that fateful week. —*Dave Marshall*

Walking the Desert

Walking the desert is no easy task. The grim sound of a dark wind surrounds us at night, and the scorching light of the sun in the day is no consolation. The desert is steeped with danger; it is an exhausting place that can drain the soul of its very will to live—and yet into the desert Jesus goes for forty days and forty nights. Did he have a super power that made him immune to the hunger, the thirst, and the predators of the night? Was he indifferent to the cold of nocturnal darkness and the sweltering heat of the day?

When he entered the desert Jesus had no super human power. He had no special status as the only begotten Son of God; he was simply Jesus in all his human vulnerability. In that regard he was no different from the rest of us.

The ordeal of the desert is a reminder that suffering will be our companion sooner or later. None of us will escape it, and for some it may seem to go on forever. The paradox in this is that suffering can lead us to a place of ultimate liberation—as it did for Jesus.

Jesus did not run from the desert experience, and he emerged as the teacher and miracle worker that we know. The desert is an invitation to empty ourselves of any notion that we are masters of our own lives. In our suffering we discover our dependence on God and the gift of grace to sustain us. God's grace is our guide through the perils of the desert.

Why run from the desert experience? The desert leads to liberation!
—*Wilfredo Benitez*

Rush Hour Sabbath

...and God rested on the seventh day
from all the work that he had done.

— GENESIS 2:2

Today I joined the rush hour traffic jam on purpose. I love being in rush hour traffic! I think it's because I love being part of a group all committed to the same goal—getting to our destination and surviving the trip, though, in this case, it is for most people an unpleasant commitment.

The slow pace of rush hour traffic forces me to slow down my internal engine as well. It would be possible, I suppose, to keep gunning my mental accelerator trying to get ahead, but, like my car on a stalled freeway, it doesn't do any good. The futility of impatience is so much more obvious when it's a car and not a brain.

So it makes sense just to accept the flow of traffic and to take time off from the frenzied pace of office life or daily worries. Maybe rush hour is inaptly named for me. I think of this time as a kind of "rush hour sabbath" or a sabbath on wheels, a kind of seventh day that makes me rest from all the work that I normally do.

In the relative hush of stilled cars, I can relax my mental engine that focuses me all too much on me, and even sit idling. As I slow down, I notice something right beside me—my unseen and often ignored passenger, the Holy Spirit. As befits the spirit of sabbath, a traffic jam makes me shift my gears. Why not shift to the real first gear, that segment of time belonging to God? —*Joanna Leiserson*

Yearning for God

The great spiritual leader of India in the twentieth century, Mahatma Gandhi, once said: "We become what we yearn after; hence the need for prayer." Gandhi is not suggesting that we will get whatever we desire in life. Yearning for wealth, popularity, or success does not guarantee that we will obtain them. Rather, what Gandhi is saying is that our lives are shaped by our deepest desires. If I desire wealth above all else, the desire for wealth will shape my values and goals, my interactions with others, and my actions in the world. I will become a person whose decisions and interactions are dictated by the desire for wealth.

"Hence the need for prayer," says Gandhi. Prayer offers us the space, the time, and the perspective to reflect on our desires and motivations, to evaluate them in God's presence, and to choose them (or set them aside). In prayer I can ask myself: What are my deepest, most authentic desires? What are the desires I want to embrace and affirm so that they can shape the way I live? What competing desires will I choose not to embrace?

The goal of the spiritual life is to desire God in all and above all. "One thing have I asked of the LORD," says the psalmist, "one thing I seek" (Psalm 27:5). And again, "Whom have I in heaven but you? And having you I desire nothing upon earth" (Psalm 73:25). Imagine what you could become if you yearned after God; if you desired more than anything else to know, love, and serve God.

—*Brother David Vryhof,* SSJE

Life in the Midst of Death

Occasionally, in the spring, I like to sit in the Trinity Wall Street churchyard. The churchyard is really a graveyard, full of old slate tombstones. At least 11,000 people are buried there. Yet, on a nice day, people will sit in the churchyard and eat lunch or talk on their cell phones; tourists will take pictures or just enjoy the sun.

This proximity of life and death is at the heart of the Christian experience. We are not meant to dismiss death, to pretend it does not exist. This is why we experience Good Friday and Maundy Thursday every year, why we remember death and resurrection every Sunday.

These reminders of death can provide perspective on our short and complicated lives. The gravestones are a reminder, as are the cross and the ashes on our foreheads and the passing of our loved ones. We live in the midst of death, but not without hope and not without meaning.

Christ reminds us that the response to death should not be despair. Death is real and scary, and we are not meant to pretend otherwise, but we are also called to do God's work, to spread the good news in the midst of our fears. The sun shines in the churchyard, and there's always work to be done there, mowing the grass and planting flowers. The tulips bloom and the magnolia trees flower and cover the ground with their petals. Life goes on amidst the gravestones. —*Jeremiah Sierra*

Just Another Poor Soul

An old man sleeps with his conscience at night.
Young kids sleep with their dreams.
While the mentally ill sit perfectly still
and live through life's in-betweens.

—JOHN PRINE, "THE LATE JOHN GARFIELD BLUES"

The young man looked just like any other person leaving a psych hospital; he had his yellow discharge papers crumpled in one hand, a white paper sack full of a thirty-day supply of discharge meds tucked under the other arm, and was holding his personal belongings in a clear plastic bag marked "property."

Just another poor soul leaving the mental hospital; I'd seen it before.

I nodded and smiled, but he didn't notice me as I walked past. He was busy signing papers the patient care assistant was holding in front of him on a clipboard. "Remember to keep your appointment tomorrow with the community mental health center," the worker was saying as I let the door shut behind me and stepped out into the bright sun.

Just as I crossed the street, a pair of shrill screams came from the parking lot I was about to enter. Suddenly two small children burst forth from between the cars and raced past me, so close I had to step aside to let them pass.

"Daddy," they screamed, and I turned to look just in time to see the young man I'd just passed in the entryway set his stuff down as he knelt and opened his arms wide. "We love you, Daddy. We missed you," they said, muffled, into his chest.

"I love you guys, too," he replied into their hair where he'd buried his head. —*Bo Cox*

Eternal Springtime

I was born in Trujillo, Peru—*la ciudad de la eternal primavera* (the city of eternal springtime) and was raised partly in Guatemala—a country also referred to as the "eternal springtime."

With spring come life, newness, and change. We often hear the phrase "spring cleaning." During spring we can also look within and check our spiritual home. What is dirty, unused, cluttered, or simply taking up space? In 1 Corinthians we see something similar: "All things are lawful for me, but not all things are beneficial"(6:12). This reminds me of one of my favorite mottos: "Just because you can doesn't mean you should!" Just because you can fit (squeeze) into size six shorts does not mean you should! Just because you can reach that high note if you scream does not mean you should. Just because you can text, put on makeup, and talk on the phone while driving... Well, you get the idea.

May God help me identify which things are beneficial and I must keep, and which things I must discard, give away, recycle, or replace. As God spring cleans my heart and soul, I can hear: "These jealous thoughts will be discarded. This bad attitude will be replaced with happy thoughts. This perfectionism will be recycled and will be made into tolerance."

How can I keep eternal springtime in my soul? By remembering: just because I can doesn't mean I should! —*Sandra Montes*

Grace Makes Us True

The church calendar today commemorates Thomas Ken, a man who exemplified integrity in its truest sense: matching one's every thought, word, and deed to deeply held, principled ideals.

As chaplain to Princess Mary, wife of William II of Orange, Ken angered William by criticizing, publicly, William's brutish treatment of Mary. Removed from his chaplaincy, Ken returned to England and became royal chaplain to Charles II.

When Charles's mistress visited London, Charles proposed to lodge her, for his convenience, at Ken's home. Ken, again risking royal wrath, refused to board "a woman of ill-repute." Charles bore him no ill will, and a year later named him bishop of Bath and Wells. At his consecration, Ken declined the customary celebratory dinner and instead donated the money to charity.

Still later, Ken stood courageously against Charles's successor James II in his effort to restore Roman Catholicism to England. He was jailed in the Tower and tried for sedition, but then acquitted and carried in triumph through the city's streets.

His dust-up with James notwithstanding, Ken refused to abrogate his oath to James during the 1688-9 Glorious Revolution, and when William and Mary took the throne, Ken would not swear loyalty to them. This decision would not do him any practical good; James was gone. But Ken acted not from self-interest but from principle. He was removed from his See, and spent a long retirement in Wiltshire.

A man of integrity in a world of constantly shifting allegiances, Ken witnessed to the power of grace to make us true—true to our beliefs, true to our commitments, true to God. In Thomas Ken, God has given us a reliable plumbline against which to measure the truth of our own lives. —*Betsy Rogers*

Beside Still Waters

Love is like water. Sometimes it pours into us like gentle rain, softening our hardened hearts, refreshing our desert places, moistening inner landscapes that are barren and parched, turning them green again and inviting birds to sing. Sometimes love springs up from within us, inviting us to open the gates and fling wide the doors, so that love can flow out through our eyes and hands, our actions and words, and quench a thirsty world. Love, like water, is essential for life.

Water is like love. It refreshes when it is pure and when toxins are removed. It gives satisfaction to everyone who enjoys it in sufficient abundance. To maintain vitality and equilibrium, we must take it in daily, by sips or gulps. It needs to be protected, to be used wisely, and to be shared. Water, like love, is essential for life.

In a world in which millions of people have no access to clean, fresh water and almost 2.5 billion people live without adequate sanitation, the pressures of a growing global population and a hotter, more chaotic climate are putting increasing stress on water supplies. Fresh water is more precious than ever.

We long for justice to roll down like waters (Amos 5:24), we yearn to draw water from the wells of salvation (Isaiah 12:3), and we know that Jesus has promised to meet us in every thirsty person to whom we give a cup of cold water (Matthew 10:42, 25:35). Today, on World Water Day, we give thanks for the gift of water and for the opportunity to conserve, protect, and share it, with love. —*Margaret Bullitt-Jonas*

In the Wilderness

O God, you are my God; eagerly I seek you;
my soul thirsts for you, my flesh faints for you,
as in a barren and dry land where there is no water.

— PSALM 63:1

At a time when he led a nation torn by civil strife, Abraham Lincoln famously spoke of being driven to his knees in prayer because he had nowhere else to go. He was by no means a churchgoer, but he was clear about where he would draw strength in the wilderness of those challenging times.

I suspect we all know moments of wilderness. In those times, in those places, what resources are available to us to help us move forward? Where can we discover power beyond ourselves?

Our church recognizes the reality of wilderness in our lives by annually marching us through the season of Lent. It's a season compared to that desert journey, corresponding to those places in our lives that feel barren and dry.

On this Sunday in the season of Lent, how are you navigating that wilderness? Are you sensing that your life unfolds in a barren and dry land? What are the thirsts that you experience? The key to moving forward in the wilderness is to begin by offering those barren experiences to God, asking God to quench those thirsts, to fill those needs, to provide resources. How will you do that today?

—*Jay Sidebotham*

A New Song

In the day when buying a Coke was within an allowance's grasp, we drank from glass bottles. The contents never lasted long, and we were left with empty bottles, which soon became musical instruments. I can still hear the sound we made by blowing air across the mouth of the bottle.

I was reminded of this childhood memory when I was speaking with a group of recovering alcoholics who described themselves as people "with a hole in [their] soul through which the wind blows." I knew just what they meant.

For whatever reason, I have always felt incomplete. Like the character in Shel Silverstein's book *A Missing Piece*, I have searched for whatever was missing. Like the Coke bottle, each time the winds of life blew, I could hear the sound of emptiness.

Like so many people, I looked for ways to fill the hole. Whether with work, achievements of one kind or another, friends, relationships, possessions, drugs, or alcohol, the goal was to fill the hole and stop the sound. Every fix was temporary, and soon the hole returned, seeming bigger than before, and the sound got louder.

Fortunately, I entered a recovery program that helped me understand my condition. We all have a piece missing, a bit of emptiness inside, and the sooner we come to realize this, the sooner we can rely on our Creator to make the sound of wind into a joyful song. The sound reminds us of our need for God, and instead of being a refrain of shame, it becomes a reminder of our need and a melody of authenticity.

Accepting this, and letting God make it into music, invites others to come along. —*Chip Bristol*

The Garbage Jesus

Images of Jesus abound. In one of my photographic walkabouts on the outskirts of Havana, Cuba, I came across an image of Jesus at the bottom of a busted garbage dumpster.

As I was walking, my artist's eye caught a glimpse of Jesus peering from the bottom of a trash bin, his chin resting on a dirty and discarded pinkish flip-flop. God only knows how many miles that flip-flop walked before it rested on the face of Jesus.

The Western Christian world is currently observing Lent. This sacred time in the Christian calendar has given my photograph a special meaning to me. According to the gospels, before Jesus was crucified, he was beaten and tortured then made to drag his own cross to the place of his execution. Golgotha, where he was crucified, was literally a garbage dump outside of Jerusalem. It doesn't get any worse than that for a spiritual master committed to a vision of peace, hope, justice, and love. It was a ghastly end to a brilliant beginning. Jesus walked the talk and paid a hideous price for it. The dark side of humanity reared its ugly head.

I suspect that many in the world of religion would prefer a more sanitized version of the death of Jesus. After all, what is the appeal of a brutalized Messiah left naked to die nailed to a cross in the stench of a garbage dump? There is no appeal in that at all!

Lent is a walk toward Holy Week. Can you draw inspiration from a Messiah who believed in humanity, even when all the evidence screamed against him? Walk the talk! —*Wilfredo Benitez*

Seen and Unseen

For we walk by faith, not by sight.
— 2 CORINTHIANS 5:7

My neighbor and I stood on the rooftop of our building at 6:50 p.m. that chilly evening, looking up at the sky for a sighting of the space shuttle Discovery. This was to be the shuttle's thirteenth and final visit to the orbital outpost. It had undocked from the International Space Station earlier in the day for the last time, as it prepared to make its descent back to earth.

We could see our breath chilled by the air as we looked up in long periods of silence, craning our necks to catch a glimpse of a bright light. Breaking the silence, my neighbor quietly said she appreciated that someone in our building had imagination and would share the moment with her.

Shivering in the near-freezing temperature (with a wind chill of 31 degrees Farenheit), we kept searching for the bright light, having been told that it would "light up the sky" at precisely 6:54 p.m. We saw a lot of airplanes flying overhead, but nothing that looked like the space shuttle. Finally chased inside by the wind and cold, we gave up, never seeing the Discovery on its final mission.

Sensing my neighbor's disappointment, I reassured her, "Well, even though we didn't see it, it doesn't mean that it didn't happen."

As I journey with others during this season of Lent, I think about our aborted attempt that cold evening. Even though I did not meet Jesus when he walked on earth, and even though I witnessed neither the crucifixion nor the resurrection, it does not mean that it did not happen. —*Westina Matthews*

Yelling at the Lord

In Robert Duvall's film, *The Apostle*, there's a scene in which the preacher is praying. Loudly. Late at night. His mother tells a complaining neighbor, "Sometimes he talks to the Lord, and sometimes he yells at the Lord. Tonight, he just happens to be yellin' at him."

Yelling is not usually my style, but I have been known to yell at people I love—my husband, my daughter, my siblings, friends. And I have yelled at God.

When I worked in a parish office, I'd often go into the chapel for a few minutes on rough days. One Lent, a beloved woman in the congregation was dying of cancer; I had seen her in the hospital, wasted and unconscious, and I knew it would be soon. Alone in the chapel the next day, I looked up at the crucifix, veiled for Lent, and yelled, "You do well to hide your face!" Then I sat down and wept. I went back into my office significantly unburdened.

Once I pitched an outright tantrum in the direction of God. My then preteen daughter had to have a medical test repeated, and I was frantic with worry. Alone in my house, I threw myself down on the living room floor, beating my fists on the carpet and kicking my feet, crying and screaming, "I hate this, Lord! I can't stand this!"

Later (after receiving normal test results), I sheepishly told a friend at church about my tantrum. She laughed. "That was probably the most honest prayer you prayed all week," she said.

We know the principal kinds of prayer in the Catechism: adoration, praise, thanksgiving, penitence, oblation, intercession, and petition.

Writer Anne Lamott lists these three: "Help! Thanks! Wow!"

I know there's still one more: Yelling, weeping—and walking away, leaving all that with God. —*Mary W. Cox*

Annie on Lent

Annie is my Labrador Retriever and spiritual director, who counsels me about Lent.

One day, and after Ash Wednesday I might add, she decided to help herself to some rolls left temptingly out on the kitchen counter.

Annie has no trouble reaching most things on the counter and never hesitates to do so, although she tries not to get caught. She has been known to help herself by nudging the donut box open, getting a single donut, and then closing the box back the way it was. She has been known to steal a lunch from my colleague Sam when I take her to the office. I find this highly amusing. Sam does not.

It would be possible, I suppose, to get mad at Annie. It strikes me as wasted energy to get mad at a dog for acting like one.

That brings me to Lent. It also makes no more sense to be mad at ourselves for being human than to be mad at dogs for being dogs, which is not what Lent is intended to do.

One of the things being human means is that we human beings are limited and finite and oh so imperfect. The season of Lent begins with a reminder of that very reality as ashes are smudged on our foreheads: "Remember that you are dust and to dust you shall return." But there is no sin in being who we are.

Sin comes in not when we fail to be more than what we are—that is, human—but when we succumb to being less than what we are. That is challenge enough for us. —*Stacy Sauls*

Worry

So do not worry about tomorrow,
for tomorrow will bring worries of its own.
Today's trouble is enough for today.

— MATTHEW 6:34

Have you ever noticed the body language of a person who is worried? Often times you will notice that the eyes are downcast and the shoulders are rounded over, as if a person is folding in on himself. The reason for the worry is personal and unique to the individual. And just as uniquely, each person carries the worry in her own way.

Jesus tells us not to worry. He alerts us that worry is a part of life's experiences. But what Jesus is really inviting us to think about is a life without worry—a life guided by faith. Trusting that God is at work in the world and in our lives is not so easy, particularly in this world where we are encouraged to think of ourselves as self-sufficient.

If we are honest with ourselves, though, we know what it feels like when the Spirit is at work in our lives. Some call these moments serendipity, synchronicity, or coincidence. The Celts called them "thin places" and in my tradition, the Pascua Yaqui, we call it *yo ania* —the enchanted world where our Creator is present and guiding our every move.

Remember this quote from author and scientific computing pioneer Keith Caserta: "Worry is the interest you pay on a debt you may not owe." —*Debbie Royals*

Be Kind to One Another

Kindness is the practice of mercy: "Be kind to one another, tender-hearted, forgiving one another, as God in Christ has forgiven you" (Ephesians 4:32). Mercy is not often the order of our day. On the news we continually hear reports of people being publicly exposed and condemned. Whether or not we concur that these people ought to be ousted or outed, there is always an invitation for our compassion, rather than our sarcasm.

The word "sarcasm" is from the Greek *sarkázein*, literally "to strip off the flesh." People who are exposed have already been stripped. They don't need our help with that, nor do they need more judgment. They have enough of that, mostly from within their own souls. They need to be reclothed. They need to be shrouded with compassion, which means we suffer with them—because we could so easily be them.

People simply do not wake up some morning and say to themselves, "How can I screw up my life? How can I make things really, really bad for myself and for my family and colleagues?" Life isn't like that. Bad things happen to bad people and good people alike; and even good people are prone to make some very bad decisions. All of this can have terrible, sometimes inescapable, repercussions, like a tsunami of the soul that a person has started but cannot stop.

The theology Jesus confronted in his own day can still surface today: people get what they deserve. I hope not, certainly not for myself. We're told, "As God's chosen ones, holy and beloved, clothe yourselves with compassion, kindness, humility, meekness, and patience" (Colossians 3:12). Let us reclothe one another through kindness, too. —*Brother Curtis Almquist,* SSJE

Stories That Last

Psychologist Milton Erickson says the power of the parabolic metaphor happens in the learning, which takes place within the unconscious. In other words, we hear the story and understand its literal meaning—it appeals to us on a conscious level. But the miracle of the metaphor keeps working on us, even after we have "stopped" listening—like Jesus' stories shaping us for two thousand years.

My grandfather was a storyteller. He told stories about my grandmother, who died before I was born. He told how she raised their four children. How she could transform the meager food they had into a banquet. How she sewed their clothes out of flour sacks. How she picked cotton stride for stride with him. He said that at age fifteen she covered his back in a fight, breaking a bottle and holding off two would-be attackers while my grandfather had it out with a third man. He told me how she fearlessly faced death in her mid-thirties. For years, he hated God in his grief.

My grandfather never told me how to live, how to love a woman, how to care for my family. My grandfather never told me to value hard work. My grandfather never told me one thing I "should do," or "ought to do," or "had to do." My grandfather only told me his stories. Though he died twenty-five years ago, I still hear his raspy voice. I am still learning from his words, something new every day. His parabolic stories had the impact of Jesus' stories in my life.

So, what stories are you telling, and to whom are you telling them?
—*Gil Stafford*

A Different Kind of Opening Day

In 1983, I recruited Kevin to pitch at Grand Canyon College. His talent was like a high-power line—enough voltage to light the city and dangerous enough to destroy. Kevin's gifts led us to our third championship. Days after we celebrated, the Cleveland Indians drafted him. His star rose quickly.

By 1993, Kevin was a prominent figure in the Indians' bullpen. But tragedy struck that spring. Pitchers Steve Olin and Tim Crews were killed in a boating accident. Synchronicity kept Kevin from joining his friends that fateful day. But grief has no pity for the seemingly indestructible. Kevin could not find a release from the grip of loss. His inability to cope frustrated management, so they traded him. "Out of sight, out of mind." Without support from professional baseball, his career was thrown over the cliff. So much discarded trash. He lost interest in living. The drugs he had "played" with now became his escape from reality.

On his third arrest he faced four years in prison. Our two-hour visit went by too quickly. Kevin needed to talk, and I needed to listen. Kevin began to ask the questions of life's meaning. Its absence crawled through his skin like fire. Seeking privacy, we leaned into each other. Somewhere in the questioning, he began to open himself to God. He was found by the God to whom he had paid little attention.

I couldn't cry, for his sake. He could not go back to his bunk in the midst of angry and hostile men showing any weakness. But in the cell of my car, I could unload his despair with my tears.

The anguished wailing of a soul-friend comes from darkness searching for light. —*Gil Stafford*

A Still, Red Light

Once upon a time, a still, red light on a misty rainy night called to me. I had to photograph it. I was drawn by the red glow of its foggy haze, and I could not resist.

Despite the dreary conditions surrounding the light, I found comfort in its stillness and brightness. The night was cold and wet, but it did not matter. I had to get the shot, and I am glad I did.

I often ponder why this particular light on a foggy night called to me. Perhaps it revealed an inner darkness? The truth is, I found the feeling it evoked soothing. I believe that is a sign I have come to terms with my own shadow side.

Lent offers us an opportunity to delve deeply into the scary domain of our shadow side and be at peace with it. Trying to suffocate our shadow side, that side of us we may consider sinful, only magnifies it. Insistence on suffocating it is fear based, and fear can turn our shadow side into an ugly raging beast!

We all have a shadow side; God created us that way, and there is no need to fear it. Grace brings balance to our walk with God, and a healthy shadow is actually a companion on the way. We need not fear our shadow, for it can only exist within the context of light!

Why not befriend your shadow side during this season of Lent, as Jesus did in his desert walk? Even in the apparent darkness of the shadow, God's light will shine—and you will see the light, and it will comfort you, even on a dark, foggy night! —*Wilfredo Benitez*

Cloudy Days at the Beach

I expect too much of life.

I suspected this while in school, came to see it more clearly as I grew older, and now stare it in the face on a daily basis. Awakening at the beach on a cloudy, rainy day, I am reminded of it once again.

There is little in life better than a sunny day at the beach. Looking out at the waves breaking rhythmically as the various birds swoop down can fill my soul like nothing else. Watching as children make sandcastles or play tag with the sea can turn back the years of my soul. But sandcastles wash away, games lose their appeal, and children grow older.

It is tempting to expect life to remain a certain way and people to stay as I have known them, but that's like wanting it to be sunny each and every day at the beach. Today's rain, while disappointing at first, is also an invitation to give my sunburned neck a break, to wear long pants and socks, to explore that independent bookshop down the way. Accepting the change in the weather is the trick. Expecting things to remain the same, the curse.

The lesson is more important than spring break contentment. It's about accepting the changes in life that come as rhythmically as the waves. "To everything there is a season," it has been said. That includes a person, job, or relationship; a creative passion, interest, or calling; one's youth, health, or vitality; financial well-being, network of friends, and family relations; the sense of serenity, joy, and optimism. The sun shines equally on each, but the clouds come as well.

Learning to bask in the sun and dance in the rain is what I most need to learn. Packing bathing suit and sandals, as well as raincoat and shoes, makes for a full vacation—and life.

—*Chip Bristol*

Beloved Community

*Our goal is to create a beloved community
and this will require a qualitative change in our souls
as well as a quantitative change in our lives.*

— DR. MARTIN LUTHER KING JR.

I live in an area where there is strong community spirit. People here, as in many places, literally wear their hearts on their sleeves. They proudly display the name of their favorite community on their T-shirts, jerseys, and jackets.

In a recent commercial, images of citizens, young and old, flashed across the screen. They wore names of beloved communities, cities, and towns which silently proclaimed pride, values, legacy. This caught my attention, and I waited to see if my town was there. It was. There was my community.

In August 1968, Dr. Martin Luther King Jr. stood before the thousands who lined the Mall during the March on Washington. They came to make a peaceful claim for justice, jobs, and dignity. Standing high on the steps of the Lincoln Memorial in sight of the sprawling crowd, King brought to mind the image of Moses on the mountain.

In his "I Have a Dream" speech, King presented an alternate vision of community. It was about pride in belonging. However, he challenged the notion of who could belong. Membership had one important criterion: those beloved of God. And all people are the beloved of God. King's vision of community changed a nation.

The beloved community is like no other community. It is a place of transformation where our souls and lives will be changed. It is a community where everyone can find a place and call it *their* community. —*Karen Montagno*

If You Are Able!

In Mark 9, a dad and his son go to Jesus and ask him to have pity on them and help them, if he is able. If Jesus is able? How often do we say to God "if you are able"?

I love this scripture because it reminds me of a face I make when someone says something that baffles me. When I am incredulous, I emulate Tyler Perry's movie character Madea. I look around and point at myself as if saying, "Is s/he talking to me?"

I wonder if Jesus made a face when people said things that baffled him. *If you are able!* Is he talking to me? Are you saying this to me? The One who gives sight to the blind, makes the lame run, and the mute shout with joy? The One who makes the doubtful walk on water and death tremble? Are you asking me if I am able?

I bet Jesus didn't make a face, because he knew and knows that we are helpless. We forget and are ungrateful. We want to see to believe. Jesus is ever patient and acts. And heals. And calms. And loves. And is.

I have seen God's abilities in extreme ways. I have received the best job at the best time. I have been healed in dramatic ways. Yet I still say to God, "if you are able." May God help me say: I know you are able! Help my unbelief! Oh, that we would not limit God by our little faith, but rather allow God's extreme power to cover us and reveal daily that God is able. —*Sandra Montes*

A Good Thing to Give Up

And can any of you by worrying add a single hour to your span of life?
— MATTHEW 6:27

I gave up worrying for Lent.

I'm mostly an optimist who falls asleep within minutes of laying my head on the pillow. But if I'm not careful, I can twist myself into a frenzy.

I knew it was bad when I woke up in a sweat. I had dreamed that my coworkers won the lottery—and I hadn't put in my two dollars for that day. I tossed and turned for two hours. Instead of dismissing the thought—and the crazy improbability of winning the lottery—I worried that I'd missed my big chance.

It was time to recalibrate. I wrote this passage of scripture on a Post-it note and placed it on my computer screen. When I began to unduly fret, I caught sight of the note, read it again, took a deep breath, and returned to the task at hand. It wasn't easy. Chronic worrying is a hard habit to break.

I have come to see over-worrying as one of my sinful tendencies. When I over-worry, I lose sight of my blessings. I'm not fully present, I'm not thankful for the past, and I don't look forward to the future. And frankly, over-worrying about the little things diminishes the times when real worry is warranted.

By making a conscious decision about worrying, I found that I could sometimes stop the cycle, to use that time for work and play, and especially, when I needed it most, for prayer.

—*Richelle Thompson*

Mulled Grace

Releasing the flavor of mulled cider or wine takes time. You add seasoning or other ingredients to the beverage. Warm it slowly over low heat. Once the drink has cooled, you sip it, roll it around in your mouth. Finally, you enjoy the taste. Mulling over an experience until understanding bubbles to the mind's surface is also like that. Releasing a palatable flavor takes time.

In the book *Mending the Heart*, John Claypool says that we don't learn from experience but from creative reflection on experience; that we're capable of re-perceiving events to assign new meaning for the present and future. I call this "grace-mulling." A friend has been wounded by someone's words, and we are hurt, too. Or a crisis hits. Loss blinds us. Temporary limitations become permanent. In such circumstances, we may become preoccupied, no matter our present activities.

After a year of cancer treatment, I decided to scrutinize everything, looking for grace, thinking it over to re-perceive things. I asked God, "Beyond the obvious treatment and stress, what was going on? What were you up to?" I tried to identify specific graces. Grace-mulling again proved invaluable four years later when I was forced to survive not only something, but to survive someone. Coming slowly out of shock after my husband's death, at least I knew the tracks toward grace-mulling, a process that is leading me toward health.

Many of us are practicing self-examination to prepare for Easter's joy. Perhaps today is a time for grace-mulling if we are discovering our inability to measure up. Since God offers the abundant grace of forgiveness in Christ, today and forever, who am I not to forgive myself?

Mull it over. —*June Terry*

Who Would You Have Me Be?

When I was growing up, one of my mother's oft-quoted scriptures was "Faith without works is dead" (James 2:17). Every day there was some uproar among us siblings. Perhaps this one received more than a fair share of something, or that one bent the rules of a particular game. My mother saw these squabbles as teaching opportunities. She reminded us that loving God was not only about saying prayers at night: loving God should shine through everything we do.

It was hard to believe God cared about our silly fights and petty disagreements. God does care, our mother insisted, because God loves us. God wants us to share in that love by becoming more loving, more giving, and more just. These talks did not put an end to our sibling bickering (sorry, parents!), but they remain a central part of my understanding of the Christian life.

"Faith without works is dead." Ouch. This verse challenges me as much today as it did thirty years ago. Think about it. It is easy to say we love God. But where is this love reflected in our lives? Do our finances and calendars show a real commitment to Christ? Do we treat each and every person we encounter as if we are meeting Jesus himself? Do we forgive when we are wronged or harmed by others? None of us can do these things perfectly. If, upon reflection, we recognize that we are not maturing into people who love God and sharing that love we have been given by God, it may be time to recommit ourselves.

We might begin each day saying, "God, what would you have me do today? Who would you have me be today?" —*Yejide Peters*

Waste Not

If the teacher is indeed wise he does not bid you to enter the house of his wisdom but rather leads you to the threshold of your own mind.

— KHALIL GIBRAN

Around thirty-five years ago, I helped my grandpa build a chimney. We used native stone—more plentiful than grass in parts of southeastern Oklahoma—and mortar, and took it slow. I actually worked with another man while Grandpa watched and guided us as the chimney unfolded, helping us to shape it and make it look like the one he envisioned in his mind.

We used old tools, repaired with handles that didn't quite match or held together with baling wire. When the mortar mix required sand, we dug it from the ground. There wasn't a lot of overhead for new tools and equipment.

Sometimes, in the morning before we started, Grandpa would have me pull rusty nails from old boards. We'd then stack the boards in the dry barn for use later, and he'd even have me straighten the bent nails for reuse. (By the way, if you've ever tried to drive a formerly bent nail, you'll understand me when I say it gives a new meaning to perseverance.)

When we fixed fences, we did it with bois d'arc posts cut from the land, used barbed wire, baling wire, and rusty steeples fished from a rusty can.

When it was near time to get paid, Grandpa'd suggest that I ought to let him hold my earnings so that I wouldn't spend it all.

These days, as I struggle to learn to live with less and be a better steward, I am grateful for his legacy. —*Bo Cox*

Lessons from the Civil War

My Civil War buff husband has resolved to visit the war's major battlefields during these sesquicentennial years. So we've embarked on a series of trips to find them and learn about these bitter and bloody encounters between Americans of the North and South.

These outings are invariably interesting. Learning, of course, is its own reward. But one can't contemplate the Civil War without profound horror. Pondering Wilson's Creek or Vicksburg or any of the war's savage battles, standing at sites like Shiloh's Bloody Pond, reading first-person accounts of corpses lying thick in the fields and the unearthly cries of the dying—one can't help but ask: How could we do this to ourselves?

The unhappy truth is that many, perhaps most of us, are engaged in our own inner civil wars. Our false selves, obsessed with power and position and personal opinion, rebel against the image of God at our core. Though we profess love and yearn for it, so often selfishness triumphs. This conflict within eats away at us. How can we do this to ourselves? And this conflict within creates conflict without, in our homes and communities and across the globe.

Perhaps as we observe the sesquicentennial of our nation's civil war, we might consider our own as well, and pray for the grace to submit our unruly hearts to God's design, to lay down our arms against ourselves and one another, and move into that "day of peace that dimly shines through all our hopes and prayers and dreams" (*The Hymnal 1982*, #597). —*Betsy Rogers*

The Dance of the Dandelion

Every spring my neighbors begin an odd dance. I call it the dance of the dandelion. And just so we're clear, it's a dance that one partner is leading and the other is following. The dandelion is leading—and winning. But that doesn't stop my neighbors from trying to keep up.

It has become common practice in our land of carefully cultivated lawns, professionally designed landscapes, and DIY home improvement to despise the lowly dandelion. The broad-leaved aberrations are bad enough as they proliferate in our Kentucky bluegrass, but when the shock of yellow flower erupts, we can become down right apoplectic. All manner of chemical warfare is unleashed to rid ourselves of this interloper.

But before we depress the trigger on that weed killer, might we consider the dandelion? Surely Solomon in all his splendor was never dressed as vibrantly as a spring dandelion. The simple beauty of brilliant yellow pom-pom sitting atop a stem is stunning. Then there's the overnight transformation from flower to seed head. No wonder children think of these floating white puffballs as wish-making material. Not only might we notice the simple beauty of the dandelion, but we might also savor the abundant usefulness of the thing. You can eat the leaves, brew tea from the roots, and make wine from the flowers.

Perhaps we should dance with the dandelion. Perhaps we might let it lead us into an appreciation of a God who provides. Perhaps we might follow in the dandelion's footsteps of growing where we are planted and trusting that there will be enough. I've never caught a dandelion losing sleep about the worries of tomorrow. —*Aaron Klinefelter*

Fragrance

In my part of the world, the wisteria is blooming now. Wisteria is considered a nuisance by some, and it has been known to take over small buildings and choke out trees. Planted in an appropriate location, however, and monitored and tended, it is magnificent.

Outside our local library is a little park with a fountain and a wisteria-covered structure shaped like an open barn roof. In the summer, the leaves shade the sitting area underneath. Right now it's a blanket of buzzing bees surrounding purple blossoms. It is a blanket that creates a sweet fragrance that wafts all over the park. It's a wonderful spot in which to sit and read or just sit.

The overwhelmingness of the wisteria reminds me of the jar of pure nard a woman used to anoint Jesus' feet. Not everyone thought she should do such an extravagant thing, and yet her extravagance was praised by Jesus. In fact, Jesus himself was pretty extravagant with stuff that other people considered a little suspect, too. That was a lot of wine he made at that wedding, wasn't it? He was pretty free with his healing, as well. His list of dinner companions definitely leaned toward the shady, and not the kind made by summer leaves. He drove out scores of demons, whatever that means. He did things in a big way, and yet there was always a plan.

I often resist the overwhelming. I'd rather things stay more under control. Preferably my control. But fortunately, I am not in control, and so God's overwhelming, extravagant magnificence spreads through the world like sweet perfume. Thanks be to God for that! —*Penny Nash*

Peter's Faith

Jesus prayed that Peter's faith would not fail. And it didn't. Peter's courage failed, certainly. His fear caused him to deny Jesus three times. But even before Jesus' trial and death, Peter knew his role. After he turns back, after he comes back from denying his Lord, he knows that he is to strengthen his brothers.

Strange, isn't it, that the disciple who has the greatest public failure is the one whom God calls to strengthen his brothers? Jesus knew that Peter was going to be the one to fail. And Jesus chose to give Peter the extra gift of faith despite—or because of—it.

It takes someone who has walked through the valley to lead others through the valley. Peter is primed to strengthen the other disciples simply because he's been on the road they are walking. He has been afraid and denied his Lord, and then in returning to him received forgiveness. Peter has walked far enough down that road to know the road leads to the One they love the most. He can give them encouragement, food and water, and strength along the way.

Lord, give me faith today. I want your faith that is perfect. Mine is so weak. Let me trust your faith, and let your faith bring healing in our midst. —*Kristine Blaess*

Saving Gracey

"Gracey's gone under the building," said the cathedral sexton.

It was Good Friday, and the Diocesan Office, where I worked, was closed. Exterminators were scheduled to seal the building and treat it for termites—until the sexton saw Gracey, the semi-feral cat I feed in the parking lot between the office and the cathedral, duck into an open vent, a favorite refuge. Then he called me.

When my husband and I got to the office, the hoses that would carry the lethal gas were already snaking through the door, but the men told us they'd wait while we tried to rescue the cat.

We cut the lock off the access grate to the crawl space under the building, and my husband wriggled in. Soon he was back out, filthy and shaking his head; when Gracey saw him, she'd run further into the shadows. I wept. He crawled back in.

Suddenly one of the exterminators shouted, "There she is!" I saw a gray blur explode from the vent and streak across the parking lot. When I caught up with Gracey, she had ducked under the gate into the alley between the office and the wall of the cathedral garden. She turned and glared at me before disappearing around the side of the building.

"You cat!" I yelled. "We went to all this trouble to save you, and you just run away!"

Then I heard myself. I don't remember if we made it to the Good Friday liturgy after that, but I had caught a glimpse of Good Friday from God's point of view. *I went to all this trouble to save you, and you just run away.*

Yes, we do that. Gracey was back on Monday, and I fed her. God does that, too. —*Mary W. Cox*

Holy Time

Holy Week is filled with ceremonies that are progressively intense. We begin with a time of celebration that quickly turns from joy to a series of actions further compromising our ability to celebrate, once we recognize how easy it is to lose the support of those closest to us. This journey through the week demonstrates the fragility of life.

Pascua Yaqui tribal ceremonies coincide with the Christian tradition of Holy Week. We follow a similar path, holding in tension our need to get past the uncomfortable yet knowing that we can only get there by way of the challenging path before us.

It is part of our human nature to avoid doing that which will cause us pain. We are not inclined to cause pain either, but sometimes we do hurt others unintentionally. And yet, in order to reconcile our deeds and find peace, we have to first acknowledge our faults and seek forgiveness. When this happens, a holy space opens up and we find new life ahead of us on the path.

This week, Jesus leads us down this path, and we are given opportunities to reconcile ourselves to God, our neighbor, and ourselves. Holy spaces replace our burdens, and we see ourselves in a new light.
—*Debbie Royals*

Too Much or Just Enough?

For whenever you eat this bread and drink this cup,
you proclaim the Lord's death until he comes.

— 1 CORINTHIANS 11:26

I had just walked into the house, having traveled six hours to spend a long weekend with my mother. Before I could even put down my suitcase and give her a hug, she was beckoning me from her wheelchair to have a seat. Ninety-three years old, my mother knew that she was on the other side of the mountain sliding down, and her own end in this life was within easy reach.

"It is time to write my obituary," she stated matter-of-factly. "I've been reading obituaries in the weekly newspaper, and I think some of them are just too long. I don't want all that said about me. Get your pen and paper."

As I began to transcribe, it made me wonder how Jesus said that he wanted to be remembered. Was Jesus concerned that we might say too much or perhaps not enough?

In Chapter 12 of John, Jesus speaks about his death and foretells his betrayal. But it is in the Gospels of Matthew, Mark, and Luke, as well as the First Epistle to the Corinthians, that we may find how Jesus wanted to be remembered.

On this Wednesday of Holy Week, we remember that this is the day when Judas Iscariot, a disciple turned betrayer, agreed to show the chief priests where they could easily capture Jesus. Tomorrow, on Maundy Thursday, we will be reminded of how Jesus wanted to be remembered, and how he may have dictated his own obituary—with not too many words, just enough.

—*Westina Matthews*

The Shoe Shine Man

It's funny where you run into Jesus if you're paying attention. I met him once at the airport shining shoes.

"You live near here?" he asked.

"Yes," I answered. "Have you always lived here?"

"All my life. I'm one of eight. My wife is one of eleven." I was strangely not disturbed by this bit of information I'd never known about Jesus before.

"Y'all get together a lot?" I wondered out loud.

"All the time. Someone tells me they haven't spoken to their brother in six years or they don't get along with their sister, I say, get away from me. If you can't get along with your brothers and sisters, well then, you can't get along with me."

I got down, paid for the shoe shine, and tipped Jesus $2.00.

On the night before he died, Jesus washed the disciples' feet. He said to them, "You call me Teacher and Lord—and you are right, for that is what I am. So if I...have washed your feet, you also ought to wash one another's feet" (John 13:13-14).

It's a rather intimate thing, the washing of feet, not so appropriate for strangers or people who do not get along. It's more about brothers and sisters, people who grew up taking baths together, after all. The whole point is about those around the table making room for each other. If God in Christ can do that for us, well then, shouldn't we be able to do that for each other? And if not, it's what the shoe shine man said. "If you can't get along with your brothers and sisters, well then, you can't get along with me." —*Stacy Sauls*

How Shall We Mend It, My Dear?

John Constable is one of the best-loved English landscape painters. His oldest son, also called John, writes about a particular day he would never forget. It was an exhibition of his father's new works, to include the unveiling of a great new canvas. The moment came, the curtain hiding the canvas was slowly lifted, and the new painting revealed. There were gasps of shock, for right across the canvas from top to bottom was a great tear.

All of Constable's children were there except John. He finally came home, looking guilty. "Did you do this?" asked his father.

He replied, "Yes."

What happened next is something the young John would never forget. His father looked at him and said these gracious words, "How shall we mend it, my dear?"

Our world is a beautiful work of art—God's gift to us. Yet we have torn God's canvas from top to bottom. Our greed has damaged the environment, our sin scarred our relationships and divided people of different cultures and races. Constable's son expected punishment, and so might we. But Constable spoke instead these gracious words, "How shall we mend it, my dear?"

And God, instead of punishing us, sent Jesus into the world to save us from tearing ourselves apart. On the cross, with arms outstretched, Jesus was mending a broken world and bringing God and humankind together again. As Saint Paul put it, "In Christ, God was reconciling the world to himself" (2 Corinthians 5:19).

Each one of us is called to share in this work of reconciliation. What are your gifts? And how are you using them to mend the torn canvas of God's broken world?

—*Brother Geoffrey Tristram*, SSJE

Waiting...

Nothing seems to be happening.

I've been exercising for weeks, eating healthier, and I don't see any changes. I've been going to AA for months, and I still want a drink. I thought it would be different by now.

He's been gone for months, yet I still expect to see him walk through the door and throw his coat into the corner every night. When will the pain of grief stop?

Stasis. That time of waiting. Quite honestly, we humans stink at waiting. We want it now, now, now!

Today, Holy Saturday, we wait. All Creation waits. Christ has died. Our wounds are still painful. We want to be healed. We are tired of waiting.

Underneath the layers of dirt, grief, pain, and ennui, life is stirring. At the very core of creation, God is alive, moving and transforming. Transformation, it seems, happens at the very core first, deep within us, before we can even feel the change of God happening. Trust the slow work of God, even when life is in stasis.

And then...

And then the deep light that never truly faded finds a crack, a wound, a break within our selves and souls. And bursts forth.

Rejoice now, heavenly hosts and choirs of angels! Rejoice, the old is falling away! Rejoice, God is still living and moving.

Can you feel it? Can you feel it within your very soul? If not, keep on. You will. God will find a way. Somehow, someway, in a way that will likely be surprising, mysterious, and even uncomfortable.

Because resurrection isn't just a story, a day we celebrate in the church year with hymns and prayers and flowers. Resurrection is real. Amen. —*Laurie Brock*

Look in the Right Place

Why do you look for the living among the dead?
— LUKE 24:5

Broken-hearted women come to the garden on that first Easter morning seeking closure, saying a final goodbye. Things had not worked out as planned, for sure. So they seek to manage their grief, making their way to the tomb, an act of love and devotion.

Upon arrival, grief turns to terror and perplexity, and not yet joy, as two men in dazzling clothes ask what they are looking for. Specifically, those two men, maybe angels, ask pointedly: *Why do you look for the living among the dead?* It's more than simply asking about what they are seeking. It's about whether they are looking in the right place.

The women come with one agenda in mind: to honor the dead, spices prepared for the occasion. What they find is something unexpected. God's power has launched them on a whole new journey. What they expected to be a dead end suddenly becomes a threshold. A tomb becomes a portal to new and resurrected life.

As you come to this Easter morning, the question may be put to you as well. Are you seeking the living among the dead? Has your routine, your religion, been sapped of life? Has the energy, the animation, been depleted? Do you stand at a dead end or a threshold?

The promise of this day is that there is a possibility of new life. The question this Easter morning: are we ready to experience it, to be surprised by it? It's all about whether we are looking in the right place.
—*Jay Sidebotham*

¡Aleluya! Cristo ha resucitado ¡Aleluya!

Yesterday was Easter Day. My favorite holiday. It is the most wonderful time of the year. It is the reason for every season. It is God's triumph over death. Acts 2:24 proclaims, "But God raised him up, having freed him from death, because it was impossible for him to be held in its power." It was impossible for death to hold Jesus.

Has death ever had its grip on you? Does it now? Are you battling cancer? Or maybe some terrible thing short of death? Are you facing divorce? Are you dealing with a troubled son or daughter? Are you nursing an addiction? Are you looking death or despair in the face and trembling? Friend, I dare you to believe that Jesus in you is more powerful than despair or even death! I encourage you to remember that God is always before us, making a way.

God has power over death. What is the death you face today? Unbelief? Jealousy? Fear? Lust? Pain? Death? Whatever it is, it is powerless before God. Will you believe that what is impossible for you is more than possible for God? Will you let go of that which binds you and leads you to the depths of death? Will you allow that which brings you down to go down alone?

Will you shout *¡Aleluya!* and release God's life-giving power today? You are not alone. I am shouting with you! —*Sandra Montes*

When a Leaf Needs to Speak

Today, on Earth Day, I hold a leaf in my hand. If I allow it to speak, I hear three things.

Here is the world in its beauty. This leaf is unlike any other. Spend five minutes examining its stem, veins, color, and shape, and see that it's a very particular leaf. Seeing the leaf with God's eyes, we perceive its preciousness and beauty (Genesis 1:31).

Here is the world in its fragility. This leaf is soft, easily torn, and separated from its tree. It evokes the vulnerability of God's creation, the extinction of species, the alarming discovery that atmospheric levels of heat-trapping carbon dioxide are higher today than they've been for millions of years. We can no longer treat the earth with impunity—drilling, mining, dumping at will, burning fossil fuels at record rates, buying and discarding the next new thing and the next, as if nature were a business and we were holding a liquidation sale.

Here is the world in its need and longing to be healed. The living world beckons, even cries out: "Stand with me! Protect me! Set me free!" Bearing witness to the risen Christ, we proclaim that God can renew the face of the earth. The Spirit inspires us to live more lightly on the earth and to protest the political and corporate pharaohs that make hefty profits as they unravel the web of life.

If I could, I would place this leaf in your hand. We need people who live with grateful awareness of life's beauty and fragility, people willing to take the risk, bear the cost, and share the joy of protecting the creation that God so loves (John 3:16). —*Margaret Bullitt-Jonas*

Emptiness

When entering a church on Easter morning, there are many things on which we can focus: colorful flowers, festive attire, and beloved hymns. Listening to the story, many characters wait to greet us: loyal women, baffled soldiers, and frightened disciples. Of course, there's the risen Lord, but sometimes the brightness of the morning makes it difficult to see him clearly.

This year, the eyes of my heart are drawn to an often-missed feature of Easter morning: emptiness. Like wind, emptiness is hard to see, but it surrounds us. It's everywhere you look on Easter.

It's in Peter's heart as he thinks of his denial. It's in Mary's heart as she thinks of her son. It blows down the alleys and swirls into rooms... anywhere the disciples try to hide.

Emptiness is in the pews as well. It's in the widow sitting alone for the first time in thirty-eight years. It's in the couple trying not to show their marriage is falling apart. It's in the high school girl worrying what her friends will say of her dress. It's in the man whose bank account is full but whose heart echoes. It's in the one who fears she works too much, just as it's in the one who longs for a job.

But there's another emptiness on Easter morning, the emptiness of a tomb. Once filled with the darkness and stench of death, it now holds the light and breeze of resurrected life.

"He's not here!" The words ring out across the centuries, and when the two types of emptiness meet, nothing remains the same. Suddenly the widow and the couple no longer sit alone, the anxious girl and wealthy man are filled, and people of all shapes and sizes find the peace that passes all understanding.

That's the miracle of Easter.

That's the blessing of emptiness. —*Chip Bristol*

Warmed Hearts, Informed Faith

Oh, to have been there on that first Easter! I'd like to time-travel and land outside Jerusalem on the road to Emmaus within hours of the resurrection. Walking there, Jesus might sense my presence, but the people with him might be too absorbed in their grief. They hadn't yet begun to comprehend the resurrection (Luke 24).

When Jesus approached to walk with them, they didn't catch on. Not perceiving who he was, they asked where he'd been and how he could've missed Calvary's catastrophe. He didn't let on that he knew those things as no other human being would ever know them, but he did explain scripture. That evening, he broke the bread at dinner. Aha! Recognition! Later, one asked the other, "Weren't our hearts burning while he was with us?" Running back to the city, they breathlessly reported the miracle.

Like those early disciples, I've been sad, and Jesus has drawn near, restoring hope. I've been as slow to catch on as they were. Like them, haven't we all wondered whether God is aware of local and global catastrophes? And haven't our hearts been strangely warmed, as theirs were, on Easter?

But Luke, a physician, is reporting the facts, as any scientist would (Luke 1:4). He might say that though our hearts are warmed, faith needs to be informed or educated. He wants us to become certain of Christ's death and resurrection, so he gives facts about those who gave evidence, of witnesses who knew Jesus, saw him die, and then walked and talked with him three days later. And Luke might say, "Warmed hearts? Informed faith? Sounds like health to me. Run with it. Run, for heaven's sake." —*June Terry*

Scars and Stories

In her book *Still*, Lauren Winner shares the story of her friend who, preparing for confirmation at age twelve, told her pastor-father that she wasn't sure whether she believed everything, whether she could claim these beliefs forever in front of the congregation. Her father's reply: "What you promise when you are confirmed…is not that you will believe this forever. What you promise when you are confirmed is that that is the story you will wrestle with forever."

This echoes, somewhat, the story of Jacob, wrestling—with whom? The mysterious figure. God? So his new name (Israel) would suggest. Jacob wrestles all night, and winds up with a limp and a blessing. What a deal.

Even the resurrected Christ, God incarnate dead-and-raised, kept the marks of his wounds: "Jesus came and stood among them and said, 'Peace be with you.' After he said this, he showed them his hands and his side" (John 20:19b-20a).

I mean, this is the Jesus who rose from the dead; I'm pretty sure he could've gotten rid of those scars if he'd chosen to—but he didn't, and we know a wounded Christ, a Christ who went through quite a three-day night and didn't leave unmarked.

I think it's a common impulse to want to get through life unscathed: clean, pure, flawless. I know I don't often like messiness. That never happens, though. Life leaves marks. And these marks—these physical or emotional limps and scars—are only perceived as imperfection or weakness. Perhaps, really, they're blessings. They're what make us human, what show that we've really lived. They are our stories, etched onto our selves, indelible and holy reminders.

—*Alissa Goudswaard*

A Planet Named George

When English astronomer William Herschel saw a new object in the heavens in 1781, he planned to name it after his benefactor King George III. This heavenly object turned out to be a planet, so if Herschel had had his way, George would be the name of the planet that lies between Saturn and Neptune. Luckily the idea of a planet named George did not capture the hearts of the astronomical community, so the object was renamed "Uranus."

I think about the importance of names when I reflect on Jesus during the Easter season. The days after Jesus' resurrection were days of mystery and bewilderment, when the disciples struggled to grasp just who Jesus was. What name for Jesus tells us who he really is? God-with-us, surely—Emmanuel. The Son of God? What about Jesus as Redeemer? Savior, Lamb of God, Good Shepherd, Suffering Servant, Bread of Life, and Light of the World?

Each of these names tells us something different about who Jesus is and what he does for us. As we move through this season of resurrection mystery, consider these names as portals through which you might encounter Jesus in all the richness of his glory.

Some of the names might speak to you more than others. Some names may resound in you like a planet named George—unable to capture your heart. Other names may draw you into deeper relationship with and love for your risen Lord. Me, I like the image of Jesus—just Jesus. Jesus who told great stories, who touched us lepers, and who comforted us when we were hurting.

What name for Jesus speaks to your heart?

—*Joanna Leiserson*

Live the Risen Life

On Easter day we cry out "Alleluia!" to the risen Lord. We acknowledge the entirety of our faith as it is culminated in that one glorious day. Soon after, the trumpets grow silent, the lilies wilt, our "alleluias" seem to lack enthusiasm, and life returns to normal as we make way for the long season after Pentecost. Though we cannot stop the swift movement of the calendar, we can and should take more time to revel in that Easter spirit. Easter is more than just a fleeting season—the risen life in Christ is a way of living and being in the world.

So what is the risen life and how do we live it? It is the life the disciples experienced after they saw Jesus risen from the dead, his victory over evil and death confirmed—a life of joy, peace, love, hope, fulfillment, and purpose. In Christ these things are not seasonal or fleeting. They are eternal.

The apostles went out in joy, with courage and conviction, proclaiming the good news of the resurrection, baptizing, healing, raising the dead to life, establishing and building up the church of God in Christ in the world. The risen life is a life lived in faith without fear. The risen life is a life of freedom, where one is free to hope, free to believe, free from the bonds of evil and death. The risen life is a meaningful and purposeful life lived for the glory of God alone. The risen life enables us to look at a world overcome by darkness and despair, fear, anxiety, and death and cry out "Alleluia! The Lord is risen!"

The pages of the calendar will be torn away. The seasons shall come and go, but the one thing that will always remain is God's love revealed through him who died and rose again to new and everlasting life.

The Lord is risen indeed. Alleluia!

—*Owen C. Thompson*

A Lottery We Win

There is an ad campaign underway where I live, complete with white billboards that say "BELIEVE." These got my attention because, as a priest, I'm in the business of "believe." I've now seen this "BELIEVE" motto displayed on construction site barrier walls; in between the boards are images of Neil Armstrong standing on the moon and protesters sitting atop the Berlin Wall.

This ad campaign promotes a lottery, and I heard a brief report on the radio about it. A spokesperson said lotteries are typically patronized by folks in the lowest economic rungs. This campaign is designed to attract middle-class consumers by addressing things that are important to that group. Does it upset you as much as it does me that a lottery would use "BELIEVE" because belief is important to middle-class consumers? All advertising, I suppose, is about manipulation, but for some reason this campaign is particularly offensive and annoying to me.

After the resurrection, Jesus took (doubting) Thomas's hand and said, "Put your finger here...do not doubt but believe" (John 20:27). We seek God with the belief and hope that he offers an abundant life to us, both in this world and in the kingdom to come. It's not a one in a 175 million chance or a contest in which you might be the lucky winner of God's grace while everyone else loses. Rather, there is a "winner-every-time," because God loves all of us.

Jesus came for everyone. The Holy Spirit gives everyone grace upon grace. No lottery; no winning numbers—God's wheel always comes up on love for you and for all. —*Dave Marshall*

Hallelujah, Easter!

Easter comes around every year, marked by fun events such as the Easter parade in New York City where women and men can sport outrageous hats, be silly, and be gay—both in the traditional and modern sense of the word—hallelujah! Kids love to go on egg hunts, while families prepare for Easter dinners. On the religious side, people who normally don't show up at church might make an annual pilgrimage on Easter. It is all happiness and cheer.

Easter seems to be imbedded in popular culture as a time of fun and games, but what is really the point for a world where most people are constantly running from authentic living and the quest for a deeper meaningful life? As I cruise through Facebook pictures, I get the impression that many of us are eager to show off what a good time we are having, but is that forced happiness perhaps masquerading a hidden silent despair, an absence of Easter?

The modern secular interpretation of Easter seems to be about good times; hence the real meaning of Easter is actually lost. The narrative connected to a Teacher who once walked the face of the earth and was brutally executed because he had a vision of what the world could actually be (a place of love guided by our care for one another, without judgment) gets totally lost in the pop-culture narrative.

There's lots of spiritual wealth to be discovered in the Easter narrative. I invite you to check it out with fresh new eyes. Easter is ultimately about the power of life over death, the choice to live an authentic life in the inclusive love of Christ. —*Wilfredo Benitez*

Summoned From the Tomb

"Unbind him, and let him go." These simple words from John's Gospel (11:44) have always stirred my heart. Jesus calls Lazarus forth from the tomb. This friend has been dead, and his family grieving, for four days. His sister Martha is alarmed, expecting the awful stench of decomposition.

The miracle is astounding, but does Jesus say "Behold!" or "Look at this"? No, he simply says, "Unbind him, and let him go." Take off the cloths in which his lifeless body has been wrapped; let him open his eyes and stretch his limbs. He is alive!

Jesus speaks these words to each of us, I think. In the many small and not-so-small deaths of human existence—our loss, our pain, our disappointments, our shame, the hurts we suffer and the hurts we inflict—we are bound. The funeral cloths that enshroud us might be anger or resentment or guilt, discouragement or despair, sadness or fear. Whatever they are, we are truly bound, unable to live the fullness of life that God intends for us.

But Jesus summons us out of the tomb! He calls us forth out of our lifelessness into his abundant life. He penetrates the shrouds of human sin and unhappiness and lets us go, like a caged creature released, to open our eyes, stretch our limbs, and explore the full, God-given freedom of human existence. We are free to rebuild relationships, renew our minds, rekindle our hearts—unbound to live and love and serve.

"Unbind him, and let him go." May we hear these words spoken to us, and rejoice! —*Betsy Rogers*

A Cyclical Faith

Spring in New York feels to me like a gift. The sidewalks I love to walk down, the park benches and the pathways along the river that have been too cold to frequent for months, are mine again to enjoy.

Having come from Texas, where the temperature varies from warm to hot to really hot, the changes in the season still come as a surprise. While the winter has its pleasures, the spring is like the end of an illness, when the nausea lifts and the headache dissipates, and I'm overcome with gratitude for the things I took for granted.

Our life of faith is likewise cyclical, filled with periods of gratitude and engagement and times of cooling and closing down.

For a while last summer, my girlfriend and I weren't attending church as regularly as we usually do. Maybe we just needed to step back so we could better understand our place in the community, or maybe we needed more space in our lives, which were particularly busy at the time. This is not to argue that we should drop out of our communities, but rather that faith is not a continuous upward journey.

Sometimes God will hide; sometimes we will need to stop searching for God or we will exhaust ourselves. A life of faith isn't so much a road but a cycle of seasons, circling around the divine, in and out of the sunlight. We'll have days when we're out in the cold wind of doubt or sorrow, and days when we're open to the workings of God—and on those days the joy and peace of our faith feels like a gift given to us. —*Jeremiah Sierra*

Do You See This Woman?

One day Jesus was invited to dine at the house of a Pharisee (Luke 7:36-50). While they were at table, a woman "who was a sinner" entered the room with an alabaster jar of ointment. She began to wash Jesus' feet with her tears and dry them with her hair. We are not told who the woman was, or what had earned her the reputation of a "sinner," or how she knew Jesus, or why she was weeping and anointing his feet. We see only her simple act of profound devotion.

The Pharisee objected mightily to this woman's presence in his house. He said to himself, "If this man were a prophet, he would have known who and what kind of woman this is who is touching him—that she is a sinner." Jesus turned to him and asked him an important question. He said, "Simon, do you *see* this woman?"

He was not asking if Simon had noticed her; of course, he saw her. What Jesus was asking was, "*What* do you see when you look at this woman? Can you really see *her*, or are you seeing only the label you have affixed to her? Can you look past the label and see her as she is?"

That's the problem with labels, isn't it? When we label others, we stop seeing them. It's important, then, to ask ourselves the same question Jesus asked Simon. Who is it that I have difficulty seeing? Is there a person—or group of people—whom I refuse to see? Can I set aside my labels and take a fresh look? —*Brother David Vryhof,* SSJE

The Wedding at Cana

I wonder, who got married the day Jesus turned the jars of water into wine? Whoever they were, Jesus' mother was intensely committed to ensuring the reception was perfect. Could the wedding have been for one of Mary's other children?

I have performed a fair number of weddings and been to plenty of receptions. The events were joyous occasions with a varying degree of tension woven through the family fabric. Things happen—and most become part of the legend of family lore.

My hopes and tensions for our daughter's wedding were good weather, a perfect ceremony, a joyous party—and for nothing, not one thing, to go wrong. One of the many things my daughter and I have in common is our taste in music. We constantly share new bands and our favorite singer's latest release. I knew her reception would have music for everyone. She even told me about the special song she had chosen for her first dance.

She was gorgeous. The wedding was perfect. Time arrived for the party. The stage was set for the most important dance of the evening. The specially selected song for a lifelong memory began. The lovers were serenaded by the romantic melody. Then, the unthinkable happened. The music stopped in mid-verse. I headed toward the deejay. Before I reached the dance floor, he fired up a new power dance tune. My daughter and her new husband tore into an unforgettable dance routine.

Water from ancient musical jars had been turned into the joyous celebration of rich red wine. Miraculous? Of course. She is my daughter.
—*Gil Stafford*

Shallow Streams and Deep Rivers

In my travels this spring, I crossed many shallow streams and deep rivers and realized I needed to recognize the importance of each.

The shallow streams are narrow and full of activity. The water splashes around the rocks and debris in the streams, causing excitement and wonderful sounds. Eventually, the water reaches the deeper river it feeds, and suddenly the scene is noticeably different. The chaos and confusion that brought so much life to the shallow stream are hushed as the larger, deeper body of water moves toward an even deeper sea.

When I think about my life as an individual and our common life as a community, I see the need for both the shallow stream and deep river. There are the day-to-day concerns of life that sometimes seem to stand in our way like rocks and debris, against which we splash and make noise. There are bills to pay, jobs to do, carpools to drive, and errands to run. The activity is exciting, but it can be overwhelming and distracting as well. Life in the stream is essential, but it ultimately leads us beyond the narrow, chaotic place to someplace else. The bills, jobs, and obligations allow us to reach the place where we can look beyond the day-to-day and swim in deeper waters. As an individual, this is where I see beyond to my life's purpose and to the kingdom of God. In community life, it is where we move beyond rent, cleaning supplies, and websites to the meaning of our being together in the first place.

I sometimes spend too much time in the stream and forget about the deeper river. I also sometimes dwell too long in the deep river and neglect the stream that feeds it. As with so many contrasts, the lesson is in appreciating both and balancing what each has to offer.

May we all learn to navigate the stream so that we may reach the deeper river. —*Chip Bristol*

But I Hate Them!

He prayed to the LORD and said, "O LORD! Is not this what I said while I was still in my own country? That is why I fled to Tarshish at the beginning; for I knew that you are a gracious God and merciful, slow to anger, and abounding in steadfast love, and ready to relent from punishing."
— JONAH 4:2

Jonah is a priceless example of satire and snark in the Bible. Jonah, a prophet, is actually successful. The entire city of Nineveh repents, including the livestock.

What a win!

But Jonah is mad. Furious, in fact. He rails at God, saying, "I *knew* you were gracious and merciful and loving!" He's so mad, in fact, that God is all the things God is, that Jonah just wants to die.

We laugh.

Then perhaps we see ourselves. After all, we love to say that God is loving and merciful and forgiving to all. We put that message on bumper stickers and Facebook posts. Yay, God!

Until we see that mercy extended to those whom we call enemy and those who have hurt and betrayed us. We'd like them to get their just deserts, but God loves and forgives them.

Then Jonah's words ring a bit true.

Loving our enemy sounds great in theory, but living it out day to day? Harder than it looks. The Ninevites were enemies to Jonah. He might pray for them, but, deep inside, he wanted them to get what he thought they deserved.

Jonah, in his raw honesty, speaks truth. Loving our enemies, those who hurt us, is tough. And it is what God asks of us. —*Laurie Brock*

Get Real

As a child I learned to keep quiet in church. Pinching my younger sister was not allowed—neither was wiggling, waving at friends, or climbing over the pews. Although these rules ensured a peaceful worship service, they also reinforced my general impression that God only liked people who were well-behaved.

When I was seven, I wrote God a letter and threw it out my bedroom window so it would fly up to heaven. My mother retrieved the letter and kept it in her filing cabinet. Not surprisingly, the letter was a plea that I be good. For a child who longed for contact with the divine, the only way that I could imagine God was as a giant version of my parents—someone who loved me best when I was "good." I tried to pray accordingly: I dressed up in my Sunday best, offered God my good and holy thoughts, and put my best foot forward. Here was my nicest, kindest self, the self that my parents liked best, the self that I liked best—the self that surely God liked best, too.

But what if God actually longs to encounter not our best selves, but our whole selves? What if God yearns to know not only our warm, loving feelings, but also our anger, sadness, fear, and doubt? What if God welcomes prayer that expresses our true selves, including feelings that we tend to conceal? C. S. Lewis once observed, "The prayer preceding all prayers is 'May it be the real I who speaks. May it be the real Thou that I speak to.'"

When we sit down to pray, God whispers in our ears, "Get real."
—*Margaret Bullitt-Jonas*

Welcome

Whoever welcomes one such child in my name welcomes me,
and whoever welcomes me welcomes not me but the one who sent me.

— MARK 9:37

Welcoming is a gift. For some, it comes naturally. For others, it is so central to the culture of their people that it becomes second nature. When I was young, guests would frequently appear at our home, be invited in, and offered a comfortable seat, water, and often food. Sometimes they would stay for a while and other times the visit was brief. No one asked if the guests wanted or needed a seat, water, or food. It was just offered and always accepted without hesitation.

Being welcomed is also a gift. I wonder how often we see it as a gift, and how often we expect it? You might wonder why it might be important to ask ourselves if we expect to be welcomed when we arrive somewhere.

My relatives teach us that humility is the key to understanding the gift of welcome, and now I am beginning to understand this teaching. When I arrive somewhere and expect that I will be welcomed, I might be disappointed with the quality of the welcome. However, when I arrive without expectations, every welcome is a great gift—no matter what is offered or how it is offered.

I imagine that is why Jesus used a child in this teaching from Mark.
—*Debbie Royals*

The Sick and Tired

My wife met Charles when he was a resident of a state institution. Everything suggested that he could not succeed at the group home she managed, which was intended to lead to self-sufficiency. He had trouble communicating because of a severe stutter. He limped. He had a pretty low IQ. Ginger, however, saw something in Charles beyond all that.

Charles could pray up a storm. His prayers were a lot like sermons. One night we were at Independence House when it was Charles's turn to say the blessing. We bowed our heads.

"Ah-ah-ah-ah, Oh Lord, we pray for the sick and tired." He went on. And on and on and on. Before he finished, he had recited in one way or another most of salvation history. He ended on a note of heartfelt thanks. "And Lord, we just want to thank you for Moses...who cut down the cherry tree. Amen." That would be "Amen" with a long A, not the timid way Episcopalians like to say it.

I thought at the time that Charles had merely interjected an expression he had heard somewhere along the way into a rambling prayer that pulled together a lot of sources. I have come to believe since, though, that imploring God to help the sick and tired had a lot to do with the quality Ginger saw in Charles that most people missed.

Charles was sick and tired. He was sick and tired of living in an institution, of being dependent, of being treated as an inferior. Being sick and tired gave him what it took to change his life despite being dealt a pretty poor hand.

The sick and tired are particularly open to God's salvation precisely because they are sick and tired. —*Stacy Sauls*

Now!

Seek the Lord while he may be found,
call upon him while he is near.

— ISAIAH 55:6

It sounds like timing matters. Isaiah's injunction suggests that there may be a time when the Lord may not be so easily found. There may be a time when the Lord will seem more remote.

In the call to seek God, a vocation that is at the heart of this devotional book, we get the sense that there is some urgency. If you hear God calling, answer the call. Do it now. Don't wait. If you feel led to be a seeker, go looking now. Don't postpone or procrastinate. Saint Paul knew this when he spoke to his beloved, beleaguered Corinthian congregation. He said: "Now is the acceptable time. Now is the day of salvation."

Annie Dillard wrote a beautiful, brief book called *Give It All, Give It Now*. It bore the subtitle: *One of the few things I know about writing.* She talks about the art of writing, but I believe there is spiritual application. She writes: "Spend it all, shoot it, play it, lose it, all, right away, every time. Do not hoard what seems good for a later place in the book, or for another book: give it, give it, all. Give it now."

Today, you will continue, in word and action, to write your own spiritual autobiography. Take today as an occasion for seeking. Seize the moment. Do it now. Dive in. Timing matters. Seek the Lord.
—*Jay Sidebotham*

Stories to Learn By

By the time our son was five, we knew he would carry on the family tradition of storytelling. He could read before he went to school and remember each page word for word. Often when he told a story, we had to ask what new book he just finished.

My wife was a college professor at the time, and our son's first-grade teacher had been one of her students. When my wife picked our son up after school, his teacher remarked to her what an amazing trip we must have experienced the previous weekend. My wife was quizzical, so the teacher went on to repeat our son's story. Obviously, he was a great storyteller. His storytelling was a mixture of his reading and imagination. We did spend serious time helping him understand the importance of prefacing his "made up" stories with an explanation.

Our son's stories were in depth, colorful, and filled with subtle meaning about his life. He could have been telling children's parables, although, as adults, we had to work at deciphering his allegory.

Bruce Chilton, in *Rabbi Jesus*, posits that Jesus used his life experience in developing his parables. I can imagine Mary reminding him to not throw the garden seeds too far. Otherwise they would not find good soil. I can see him carrying home a lost lamb after hours of searching the desert.

Seems though, Jesus' listeners had as much trouble understanding his stories as we did our son's. Maybe if we listened as children we would better understand? —*Gil Stafford*

Love and Mothers

Everybody has a mother. We can all agree on that. But beyond that, the celebration of motherhood in the form of Mother's Day is complex indeed. For some, this is a painful day, for a variety of unhappy reasons. For others, it is truly a pleasure and a joy to celebrate the mothers in our lives.

And yet even in that joy, mothers have different desires for how the celebration should go. Some mothers spend Mother's Day in the company of their children. Others spend it enjoying a day without children.

So to be honest, it's not that easy to talk about Mother's Day.

Mother's Day was founded by a childless woman, Anna Jarvis. Her mother had organized Mothers' Day Work Clubs during the Civil War. Among other things, the mothers fed, clothed, and nursed both Union and Confederate soldiers without distinction.

Miss Jarvis apparently quarreled with her mother just before her death, and soon she decided to honor her late mother by starting the tradition of Mother's Day. But she was quickly dismayed by the growing commercialization of the holiday. She was even arrested for disturbing the peace by mounting a protest against it.

So in the midst of all this complexity, let us simply let love have the last word here. Miss Jarvis wanted to honor the kind of sacrificial love that she saw in the Mothers' Day Work Clubs. She wanted to highlight the power of compassion to change the world.

Compassion changes the world. Let this be our prayer on this Mother's Day: for love to heal all wounds.

—*Penny Nash*

Mom

God could not be everywhere, and therefore he made mothers.
— RUDYARD KIPLING

My mom. There have to have been (and maybe still are) times, considering the two sons she was "blessed" with, that she wondered what in the world she'd done wrong to deserve the pain and heartache we caused her.

In my quest to understand my Creator, I've often used my mother's love as a metaphor: She loved me when I was unlovable, when I didn't want to be loved, and when I desperately needed love.

I can remember when I was a kid turning into a young man, wild and lost and bent on destruction of self and others, how hard she fought to save me. She'd literally knock on the front doors of houses where I'd be inside drinking and doing other drugs. The people I associated with ridiculed me. I thought my mom must've hated me; why else would she ruin my "good times"? Only later did I realize she was trying to save my life.

My wife and I spent some time with my mother yesterday. We went out to eat and when we returned, I mowed her yard. She lives alone and tries to do all her yard work herself, so it was a privilege for me to help her.

Yet, she thanked me. I owe this person my life, many times over, and she thanks me for one small act.

I love you, Mom. I know you may not read this today, but it never hurts to let an "I love you, Mom," loose into the universe.
—*Bo Cox*

A Light on the Stand

"No one lights a lamp and puts it in a clay jar or under the bed. Instead, they put it on a stand so that everyone who comes in can see by the light" (Matthew 5:14-16). This is especially true for God. God has kindled light in us and won't hide it in a clay jar or under a bed. God will put this light on a stand, so others can come in out of the darkness.

God has kindled light in me. Even though I wonder *where* and *how* and especially *if* it will be put to good and full use, I can trust that God won't hide my light under a bushel basket. It's not about showing off, but it is about God putting us in places where we can fulfill our purposes—to enlighten the nations; to offer clarity, safety, comfort, and strength; to bring light for others to see and navigate by; to bring light for us all to work and love by.

Lord, I hope you'll use the light in me to your best advantage. Don't put me under a bushel basket. Lord, I trust that, just as you exhorted your people to use the light that is given them, you'll use me. You'll set this light on whatever stand is best. I will wait, trusting, to see what lampstand comes along. I'll shine where I am right now, too.

All the light we have is just a glow within your already bright morning light. We are not shining in the darkest night but in the midst of the coming dawn. Let your dawn break upon us. —*Kristine Blaess*

God Shines Through

I was mainly concerned with not setting the church on fire as I processed in with the choir at my first Easter Vigil service. Candles plus vestments plus sheet music took the greater part of my concentration. As we worked our way through the liturgy, though, I began to relax, and I glanced out at the congregation and my fellow choir members as the last vestiges of twilight faded from the stained glass windows, and the lofty corners of the building fell into deep shadow.

Now, it is common knowledge that candlelight makes people look good—any women's magazine will tell you this—but that night I saw the friends and acquaintances of my parish literally in a new light. In her novel *Gilead*, Marilynne Robinson (speaking as the Rev. John Ames) writes, "Wherever you turn your eyes, the world can shine like transfiguration. You don't have to bring a thing to it except a little willingness to see. Only, who could have the courage to see it?"

For just a moment, I had the courage. I saw the broken, haphazard, holy people with whom I shared Eucharist every week, candlelit and shining—the saints and ministers who inspire and uphold and challenge me. Some I knew better than others, some I hardly knew at all, but in that moment I felt a remarkable intimacy and connection with every one, and in their illuminated faces God shined through.

Moments like this are not the norm for me, but I know these little transfigurations are always glimmering just under the surface. They might break through at any moment; I hope for the courage and willingness to bear witness. —*Alissa Goudswaard*

Practice Resurrection

Poet, essayist, farmer, and contrarian Wendell Berry has a stunning poem entitled "Manifesto: The Mad Farmer Liberation Front." In the poem Berry invites us to:

> *Ask the questions that have no answers.*
> *Invest in the millennium. Plant sequoias.*
> *Say that your main crop is the forest*
> *that you did not plant,*
> *that you will not live to harvest.*

As we sit at the beginning of another growing season, I wonder what Berry's advice would do to us. How might we ask questions that have no answers? Is it even possible to invest in the millennium? And just how does one go about planting a sequoia?

This long view of history and time shifts something important in us. We've become so conditioned to think of the quick profit, the microwaved meal, the instant gratification, and the silver bullet solution that we often forget that there is another way. It is the way of Jesus. It is the narrow road that leads to life (Matthew 7:13-14).

Berry concludes his poem with the words, "Practice resurrection." We would do well to heed his words, for we are an Easter people. We are a people engaged in the ongoing, long-term reconciliation project of God. —*Aaron Klinefelter*

Out of the Mouths of Babes

Our young friend Abigail, age four, was recounting a Bible story from Sunday School to her father. Hers was a highly imaginative version, which diverged in some key respects from the biblical account. Her dad questioned some particulars. "Daddy!" she replied emphatically. "This is the New Testament."

Out of the mouths of babes! Of course we don't rewrite the Bible to suit our whims, but Abby's rejoinder can remind us of an important truth: that in Christ, God has done something completely new. "Behold, I make all things new" (Revelation 21:5), Jesus tells us. We are a new creation. We are renewed, day by day. No matter our past; God has fashioned a new future for us. Christ was raised from the dead "so we too might walk in newness of life" (Romans 6:4).

There is an excitement to the gospel! In Christ, God promises that we are no longer chained to our old, tired, unproductive habits and ways of thinking. What does this mean for me on any average morning? Of course I can't begin to imagine all that it means, but I can know this: that God is breaking me open to new truth, new ways of seeing this beautiful world and all its people, new opportunities to be God's new creation. My task, I think, is to open my eyes and my ears and my heart to receive new understanding, new hope, and let it shape me.

How might we walk, with Abigail, in newness of life today?
—*Betsy Rogers*

Acts of Kindness

A young man in thick eyeglasses, dressed proudly in a too-large baseball jacket, with obviously limited mental ability, boarded the train with me and sat directly across from me. Each time the conductor walked through our car, the young man would inquire excitedly about how much further before his stop.

When the conductor called out the next-to-last stop, the young man jumped up and began to gulp down his hot dog and soft drink, trying to keep his balance as the train sped over the tracks. He swallowed the last bite just as the train pulled into the station, brought down his duffle bag from the rack over head, and started to move to the nearest exit. I wondered if this were the correct stop for him, but didn't say a word. Nor did anyone else.

Suddenly, a woman stood up, crossed over her seat mate, and ran after him. "If you want the main station, you don't want to get off here," she said gently. He thanked her profusely for her unexpected act of kindness and sat down, red-faced from the embarrassment of almost getting off at the wrong stop.

But it was I who hung my head in shame. Why didn't I say anything? Why did I decide to mind my own business, when he clearly needed a little extra assistance?

A widely quoted saying encourages us to "be kind, everyone you meet is fighting a hard battle." Perhaps I will need to do two acts of kindness a day for the rest of my life as penitence for the conscious and sometimes unconscious acts of kindness not taken for strangers, as well as for friends who are fighting their own hard battles.

—*Westina Matthews*

Old Mountain, New Earth

On a lovely spring day in May, Mount St. Helens on the west coast of Washington state exploded and sent tons of ash flying eastward across the country. I lived hundreds of miles away, but right in the path of that black cloud. As the cloud plunged the day into darkness, everybody scurried inside and watched the ashes rain down on the earth.

The next day, we awakened inside an ashtray. Cities and towns were smothered in fine, gray ash—a few inches or a few feet, depending on how close you were to that volcano. Everything was gray. Everything was also eerily quiet. Life does not belong in an ashtray. The world was dead.

But the world was not dead. Eventually the ash buried itself in the ground and gave its mysterious nutrients to the earth. Life started over and even flourished. The mountain became green again. Farm crops and garden flowers grew again, healthier than ever. It turns out that those dreadful ashes did not kill the earth but actually nourished it. The old mountain gave of itself, to seed a new earth.

So it can be with us. Sometimes I need a jolt to renew a flagging creativity. Maybe I am suffering a kind of spiritual fibrillation, my spiritual heart beating aimlessly and getting nowhere. Maybe I am just distracted by old issues or worries. Or maybe I just need to be surprised by a new energy to fertilize my spirit like the volcanic ash fertilized my gardens.

As the volcano surprised the earth with new life, so may we be surprised by life's unexpected graces. —*Joanna Leiserson*

Hobbits and Adventures

"Hobbits don't like adventures" is how the speech began. What followed was a message about finding the courage to leave the Shire and trusting that the adventure in that will outweigh the comfort of the familiar. Yes, there will be mountains as well as valleys, companions as well as dragons, but, in the end, the Hobbit will be changed in dramatic and special ways.

It would have been a good graduation speech on its own, but it came from a boy who, two years ago, was completely and utterly lost. Diagnosed with Asperger's Syndrome at a very late age, he did not know if he even wanted to live anymore. And yet, in that very dark place, his mother found a special school far away. It would mean leaving his "Hobbit hole" and going on an adventure. Like any normal person, it meant leaving the known for the unknown. Because of Asperger's, however, the fears were larger, mountains higher, woods darker, and dragons more ferocious.

But somehow, he rose from his bed and got in the car. He survived the first day, then the second, before realizing there was such a thing as hope. In two years, that lost child was found, or, as the Bible puts it, "He was dead and is alive again" (Luke 15:24).

On graduation day, that boy stood before his classmates—faithful companions and dragon-slayers, one and all—and delivered a commencement address I will never forget. I am not over it yet—perhaps I'll never be—but I give thanks for the courage he found, the companions he walked beside, and the opportunities he seized.

He will never be the same, nor will his father.

—*Chip Bristol*

Believe Less

If you find yourself rather scattered or confused, or if you've lost your spiritual anchorage, try believing less. I'm not suggesting willy-nilly discarding a verse from the Bible, or a phrase from a creed, or an historic Christian doctrine you don't fancy. I'm not suggesting tossing, but rather reclaiming. Go deeper to the bedrock of your soul where you're not confused.

To believe is not to wrap your brain around some existential concept. To believe is to embrace something with your heart, as if your life depended upon it. The English word "believe" comes from the same etymological root as the word "belove," which means to hold dear, to love deeply. Believe; belove. So go deeper. Get out of the confusions of your head and go deeper into your heart. Conform your life around the practice of loving God with all your heart, soul, and mind, and loving your neighbor as yourself.

Start with what is most immediate: yourself. Get on good speaking terms with yourself. You're not able to love your neighbor any better than you love yourself. And the love of God will become very present and very real as you sort out these other two loves: for yourself and for your neighbor. Who you are, what you are, however you've gotten to be the way you are, God knows. And God loves, and God desires…you.

In the scriptures we are called "children of God." There's no reference to "adults of God." We're consistently called "children of God," and God loves children. Children don't reason and wrestle, but tend to act straight from the heart. Trust in your heart that God believes in you; God beloves you.

—*Brother Curtis Almquist,* SSJE

Backlighting

In John's account of the resurrection, there's the dramatic moment when Mary Magdalene turns from the tomb, sees Jesus—and mistakes him for the gardener. What? How could Mary not recognize her friend and teacher, the dearest person in her life?

Yes, she was weeping, and it was clearly impossible that Jesus, whom she had seen die so horribly, could be standing there; but as I picture the scene, I see something else: backlighting.

When I first got a digital camera and was learning to use it, I didn't realize for a year or more that there was an option to override the camera's automatic flash settings if I thought the shot needed more light. During that time I deleted many pictures in which the backlighting from a door or window turned the people I thought I was photographing into unrecognizable silhouettes.

Picture the moment when Mary turned from the darkness of the tomb and saw a figure standing in the garden, backlit by a blaze of daylight. In that light, Jesus was a silhouette that might be anybody—the gardener, perhaps. And then he spoke her name, and she knew him.

Often we fail to recognize our risen Lord when he appears in our lives, because he is backlit by the flames of our anger, the lightning flashes of our fears, or the neon dazzle of the world's enticements. Against those lights, he's only a silhouette, a shadow; but listen—he'll call your name, and you'll know.

"Rabbouni—teacher!"

> *Backlit by sunrise,*
> *risen Jesus, shadow, speaks,*
> *calls my name—alive!*

—Mary W. Cox

Give God a Little Credit

If you had sat on the floor with me today, eight puppies scrambling everywhere, you might've laughed, too. And if you've watched squirrels skittering in the chase, or if you've seen a giraffe licking its lips, maybe you chuckled. I want to give credit to the originator of smiles, laughter, humor, and play. Why wait until the end of the show? Roll the credits. "Laughter in this drama provided by God."

On May 23, I will celebrate someone's birthday. In 2006, I had to work hard to keep a straight face while my husband sneaked away to bring in her birthday cake. Unaware, our friend sat with me. Simultaneously, she was turning seventy-four and watching my chemo drip. Finally, nurses, patients, and family members sang "Happy Birthday." What a treat to see her speechless, soon delivering cake to anyone who wanted it, and smiles all 'round.

For months, my friend, the nurse, and I comprised the threesome that through sheer nonsense made the toxic chemicals seem less objectionable. So many ordinary things became grist for our humor mills that we had to be careful in case patients around us needed quietness. And sometimes we were quiet, but often everyone entered in, apparently relieved.

If you want an example of humor in hardship, read chapter 38 of the Old Testament book of Job. God's response, even in Job's troubles, is funny. We give God credit for many things, but how long has it been since you thanked our source of joy for the blessing of smiles, laughter, humor, and play, as gifts? And who has more cause to laugh than graciously forgiven people on the way back to health through-and-through? —*June Terry*

New Every Morning Is the Love

My mother is eighty-six years old. Sometimes I drive her to medical appointments. One afternoon we sit in a surgeon's office, waiting for a consultation as we weigh her choices. She shows me her aching foot, the bent toes, and fragile skin. Aging is taking a toll on her body, yet her spirit remains as fresh as a child's.

"You know what?" she says. "The other day I stood by the window and remembered your husband's remark: how unlikely all this is! I mean, here we are on a planet spinning every day on its axis at a thousand miles per hour, while at the same time it rotates around the sun at something like 67,000 miles per hour. When you stop to consider that, how unlikely it is!"

We grin at each other, marveling at the way of things. Even as my mother girds herself for the next round of tests, the next series of decisions, the next intervention to slow the inevitable process of physical decline, we pause to acknowledge the wonder of it all: Here we are! How unlikely!

Wonder has power to cut through dread, power to dissolve the conviction that nothing good lies ahead and we're headed pell-mell into darkness. Especially in fearful times, we can cultivate a sense of awe and wonder about the sheer miracle of being alive, the gift of this unlikely moment. Even in a windowless doctor's office, where it's impossible to deny the reality of suffering or the inevitability of death—even here, wonder springs up, bringing news of a larger reality. And we smile, sensing the Love that set the planets in their courses, the embracing Love that never dies. —*Margaret Bullitt-Jonas*

Today the church commemorates Nicolaus Copernicus and Johannes Kepler, Astronomers, 1543.

No One Will Notice

Yesterday I was at the grocery store, and out in front there was a volunteer collecting donations for a well-known charity. The group for which he was fundraising is not a charity I normally donate to, so I walked right by. But as I opened the store's front door, the volunteer walked up to me and asked, "Hey, aren't you the one I've seen preaching at the church downtown?"

Suddenly I recognized him. "Yep, that's me." I winced, embarrassed and feeling guilty. He must have seen me at their Tuesday evening service recently. It wasn't bad enough that this guy unmistakably saw me look at him, look away, clearly ignore him, and keep moving; it was even worse that he remembered my face and knew me as the preacher. "If anybody was willing to help," I thought, slinking away into the store, "it should have been me."

After shopping, I donated a little money on my way out of the store, mostly because I still felt guilty. I hate to admit it, but if the volunteer had not recognized me, I would have given nothing at all.

Sometimes when we've done something that harms others, or failed to do something to help, we get a feeling that nobody is paying attention and maybe we've gotten away with it. It's a trap, every time. C. S. Lewis once famously said, "Integrity is doing the right thing, even when no one is watching." Often I find that the one whom I hope will not be watching is not another person at all. Instead, it is God who taps me on the shoulder saying, "Hey, I remember you!"

Thanks, God, for always loving me enough to catch me.

—*Charles Graves IV*

Sunday in Ocean Grove

When I was a little boy, we would go to the beach in a small town of Methodist heritage called Ocean Grove. It had strict rules about keeping Sunday completely free of work or entertainment. It was illegal to drive a car on Sunday or even ride a bicycle. All the stores were closed. There were no boardwalk amusements. On Sunday in Ocean Grove, the only thing you were allowed to be was bored.

I saw Ocean Grove as old-fashioned and restrictive. Now I see it as revolutionary and liberating, as encouraging freedom to understand more deeply. Ocean Grove liberated me to *be*—not necessarily to be what I wanted to be, but to be who I already was—a human being, a child of God.

That is the purpose of sabbath. It is more freedom than restriction. It restricts what we do in order to free us to be who we are.

We resist sabbath because it interferes with the illusion that we are somehow essential to the world's functioning, an illusion to which we are too deeply attached. It is an illusion pretty basic to the way we live, as if we were in charge, as if we were in control, as if God were irrelevant.

Sabbath is what keeps us human—a once-a-week reminder that the world suffers no major damage if we aren't running it. It is a revelation perhaps unflattering to our egos, but very much in the service of our freedom—because it happens to be the truth.

—*Stacy Sauls*

Co-creators with God

I never feel quite so connected to myself and the world as when I'm creating something, whether it is an essay or artwork or liturgy. It's at these times that I can let all my anxieties go, or at least make something out of these anxieties and fear, find some truth in them.

"The purpose of life is co-creation of the world around us," said Joan Chittister, OSB, at a conference about Christian living that I attended. Evolution teaches us that creation is ongoing and incremental, she said, that it involves mistakes and experiments. That we are part of it.

I spend so much time consuming that sometimes I lose sight of what I am made for. I watch television and I play games on my iPhone. I enjoy these activities, and passivity is sometimes a relief for an introvert like me from the need to do and interact, but still these activities often leave me feeling empty. It is when I'm making something out of my life, my experience, and my connections to others that I feel whole.

God is a God of creation, a creator. We are called to be the same, to participate and change our lives and the world we have been given. Our gifts are not simply handed to us for us to enjoy or to fill us with gratitude (not solely, anyway). To do so is like being handed crayons and construction paper in the second grade and hoarding them under our desks, remembering every now and then to say "Thank you." Instead, we are called to make something with our gifts, to change the world, to do the work, to create. —*Jeremiah Sierra*

How Does Your Garden Grow?

I love gardens. That love of gardens seems hardwired in us. The first thing God did after creating the light and dark and stars and animals and people was to plant a garden and put people in it.

Gardening is often a prayer activity for some people. Planning, planting, feeding, tending, and finally enjoying the fruits mark the seasons of a gardener's life. Getting into the dirt, doing basic cleanup, sniffing fragrance are all ways of tending to our own souls by tending to the earth and making room for beauty.

Gardens are prayer places for nongardeners, too. It is not a coincidence that the creation and maintenance of more green space in urban areas improves the quality of life for urban residents. Gardens connect us with something primal—the earth, the mysteries of how things grow—and provide food and shelter for animals, food and spiritual nourishment for people.

I find it fascinating that gardening is both a mystery and the application of well-known techniques. We know all about germination and the benefit of fertilizing. And yet the products of our technical application can still be a surprise. Something way more beautiful than the simple sum of spading and watering grows up to delight us.

So it goes with our lives. We spend much time with the technical applications: eating, sleeping, exercising, working. But if we do those things with love, then our lives become something greater and more beautiful than a simple collection of activities. We become love and beauty in the world. We are continuing God's creation and God's work of being love in a world that desperately needs to be loved.

—*Penny Nash*

Extravagant Love

Which one of you, having a hundred sheep and losing one of them,
does not leave the ninety-nine in the wilderness
and go after the one that is lost until he finds it?

— LUKE 15:3-4

The parable of the lost sheep is the first of three stories Jesus told in sequence, all having to do with things that are lost then found.

In Luke 15, we first read a short parable about a wandering sheep, discovered and carried home to great rejoicing. Then we read about a woman who loses a coin and turns her house upside down to find it. Upon finding it, she throws a block party. After that comes the story famously known as the Prodigal Son, a story which ends with extravagant celebration. Once again, that which has been lost is found.

Each one of these stories makes the point that seeking is often extravagant beyond reason. Truth be told, if I had a hundred sheep and one wandered off, I'd cut my losses and stay with the ninety-nine. That doesn't seem to be what Jesus has in mind. These parables suggest that Jesus or God or the Holy Spirit are the ones who look for the sheep, the coin, the son. God seeks us, with extravagant, perhaps irrational, ardor.

That's good news for all of us, for sure. But in the power of parables layered with meaning, maybe there's a call for us to mimic that mode of seeking. In the spiritual quest, we are invited to extravagance, beyond cost-effective thinking. We are invited to go to any lengths to discover God's life. As you seek God's life today, can you do so with extravagance? —*Jay Sidebotham*

Emmanuel, God With Us

Then he led them out as far as Bethany,
and, lifting up his hands, he blessed them.
While he was blessing them,
he withdrew from them and was carried up into heaven.
And they worshiped him, and returned to Jerusalem with great joy;
and they were continually in the temple blessing God.

— LUKE 24:50-53

Today is the Feast of the Ascension, which falls forty days after Easter Sunday and ten days before Pentecost. Most images of the Ascension show Jesus's feet peeking between clouds and the disciples looking upward, gawking and amazed, probably confused.

I also think of the Ascension as Jesus stepping through a thin place. In the Celtic tradition, a thin place is a holy place where the realm of here and now and the realm of God are separated by, well, a thin place. Thin places are next to us, as close as our own skin. They are not some place far away. They are part of our world, those holy places where the breath of God moves across our face, stirring our soul.

Our faith reminds us that Jesus is with us. Emmanuel—God with us. Not far away, not over us, watching at a great distance, but *with* us, next to us, as close as our own skin.

Perhaps the Ascension image Jesus yearns for us to embrace is not that of the Holy One's feet peeking from the clouds above us, but the real presence of our beloved Savior with us, who simply stepped through a thin place to remind us that God is never far from us.

Emmanuel, God with us, is as close as our own skin. Always. Forever. —*Laurie Brock*

Impossible Things Before Breakfast

Alice laughed: "There's no use trying," she said;
"one can't believe impossible things."
"I daresay you haven't had much practice," said the Queen.
"When I was younger, I always did it for half an hour a day. Why,
sometimes I've believed as many as six impossible things before breakfast."

— LEWIS CARROLL, *THROUGH THE LOOKING GLASS*

Reflecting on my childhood faith in an attempt to write my spiritual autobiography, I realized that in early years, it was my imagination that brought me closest to God. This is not to say that being raised in the church, with the flannel boards and Bible verses and silly songs, was a bad thing—it just wasn't the most prominent thing. What shaped my theology and spirituality most profoundly were the imagined or invented worlds I found in beloved books and in my own head.

I had a vibrant imagination as a child, and I never really lost that gift—thanks be to God—but it was a long time before I allowed imagination and creativity back into a faith that had become heavily intellectual. Imagination seemed too childish, too subjective, too untrustworthy a place to find God.

A faith without imagination is destitute indeed. Allowing imagination back into my spirituality offered a revival and a renewed forward momentum. It is with this creativity that I can imagine a future for the church, and imagine my future ministry and role in that church. It is through playful imagination that I can approach an understanding of metaphor and story, which are integral to understanding and living into the Christian story.

—*Alissa Goudswaard*

"If It's Still in There..."

I often take for granted that I was blessed with being able to carry a baby to full term. I have met many women who are not able to have children. I have worked very closely with three who have been blessed with a baby after trying for years. One of them said, when I asked about the baby's progress, "I am going to the doctor to have an ultrasound to see the baby...if it's still in there." I assured her the baby was well, but I also realized I never questioned Ellis being in me. Although I prayed over Ellis daily along with many other people, the prayers were for him to be healthy, and not for him to still "be in there."

Elizabeth and Zachariah were childless. An angel spoke to Zachariah to tell him his prayers had been heard, and they would have a baby. Mary, Elizabeth's cousin, was also with child. And when Mary went to visit Elizabeth, the baby leapt inside her. Elizabeth was filled with the Holy Spirit and proclaimed Mary was going to *dar a luz...* give light, give birth...to our Savior. Mary, probably scared, needed this confirmation from someone who knew her. And so she began declaring, "My soul magnifies the Lord, and my spirit rejoices in God my Savior, for the Mighty One has done great things for me" (Luke 1:46-47, 49).

The Mighty One has done great things for me! And I am sure the Mighty One has done great things for you—and will continue.
—*Sandra Montes*

The Old Man by the Sea

The church's calendar today remembers Justin, a converted pagan whose teaching and writings helped form the young second-century church.

Justin told a curious story of his conversion. Born in Palestine, Justin received a Greek education, then set about finding a philosophy that suited him. He tried first the Stoics, then the Aristotelian Peripatetics, then the Pythagoreans, and finally adopted Platonism.

Some time later, as he walked near the sea, he encountered an old man who began speaking of God and the Old Testament prophets. This man said, Justin later wrote, that "There existed...certain men more ancient than all those who are esteemed philosophers, both righteous and beloved by God, who spoke by the Divine Spirit....They are called prophets. These alone both saw and announced the truth to men."

Justin continued: "Straightaway a flame was kindled in my soul; and a love of the prophets and of those...who are friends of Christ, possessed me." Justin went to Rome, started his own school, penned influential early Christian writings, and was martyred under Marcus Aurelius around the year 165.

Who was the learned old man by the sea? How did he speak so convincingly to this erudite young philosopher? What happened to him after God used him so effectively to form one of the early church's great minds?

Truth be told, our lives are filled with people like him. They are both unassuming and unafraid. In their words and in their lives, they show us the truth of Christ. They are among our friends, our neighbors, our coworkers, our children. Can we see them? And will we pay attention when the flame is kindled in our souls?

—*Betsy Rogers*

Stepping Out in Faith

On my way to run errands one day, I watched with horror as a young bicyclist flipped entirely over and landed on her back. Thank goodness she was wearing a helmet. Without thinking, I ran out into the street to stop traffic, while calling out to the woman to see if she was all right. Dazed, she remained on her back for a few anxious moments as she caught her breath. Two other cyclists stopped, came over to move her bike out of the street, and asked if she needed assistance. Thankfully the young lady seemed more shook up than hurt, and finally got up to begin walking her bike home.

I think of her often when I come up to the many crosswalks in my city. I watch the younger pedestrians step out fearlessly—seemingly unconcerned—trusting that the cars will stop and give them the right of way. In some ways, I envy the self-absorption, sense of entitlement, and swagger of the youth.

I, on the other hand, come to the crosswalk waiting, looking both ways, then looking again. Perhaps because of age and experience, I have learned that people do not always follow the rules and often try to find a way around them. So instead, as I approach the intersection I seek eye contact with the driver. *Do you see me? Will you stop? May I cross?* I wait for a nodding acknowledgment, raise my hand in a silent "thank you," and then step out.

Ah yes, youth is wasted on the young. And I wonder, what would I do differently if only I had such fearlessness? —*Westina Matthews*

Breaking Boundaries

Then he took a little child and put it among them;
and taking it in his arms, he said to them,
"Whoever welcomes one such child in my name welcomes me,
and whoever welcomes me welcomes not me but the one who sent me."

— Mark 9:36-37

Now we might think this is such a quaint story. Isn't Jesus just the nicest guy? Look how he loves kids! I mean, that would be a great bit to add to Jesus' eHarmony profile, "Jesus bar Joseph: loves kids, plays games, all sorts," assuming Jesus was looking for a wife, but that's a whole other story.

But his disciples—well, they were sure he'd lost it! You see, children then weren't the objects of unadulterated affection that they are today. Certainly it behooved you to have a fair number of children; they were your life insurance policy. They carried on the family trade and name and took care of you when you were old. But all that was after they had come of age.

For Jesus to show this kind of boundary-breaking hospitality to a young child was not the norm. He was breaking with convention and society. It was not the status quo. But that's not what Jesus does. He welcomes them and tells his disciples that they should do the same. By welcoming the children—the least of the least among them—the disciples and Jesus' followers are welcoming not just him, but the One who sent him. —*Aaron Klinefelter*

Learning War No More

With the seventieth anniversary of D-Day coming in two days, I have been thinking about my time as a volunteer chaplain during my seminary years. I served in a Veterans Administration hospital that was taking in wounded from Iraq and Afghanistan with brain injuries, prosthetics, spinal damage, and ocular injuries. The men and women I had the honor to serve remain deep in my heart and soul.

One day I watched three Vietnam veterans, all in wheelchairs, teaching a twenty-eight-year-old how to use his chair, a new black one. It still had plastic covering on the wheels—that matched the fresh bandages on the soldier's head and hands. Another day, I stood by helplessly as a nineteen-year-old, still in desert fatigues, ran through the hallway with her head down because a flash of sunlight on her medication tray triggered her mind back to the day an IED took three of her friends, her right arm, and her sanity.

A fifty-five-year-old, tough-as-nails Marine wept as he saw the wounded coming in. He choked out, "It was my generation; the sins of my generation; we were supposed to be it. And now this. It's happening again. We didn't stop it."

Seeking God, at times, means holding fast to the promised words of Isaiah, "God shall judge between the nations...they shall beat their swords into plowshares...nation shall not lift up sword against nation, neither shall they learn war any more" (2:4). Seeking God, at times, means praying in thankful remembrance of the many who died for our freedom. Seeking God, at times, means holding on to the hope of God's kingdom where love and peace reign supreme.

—Dave Marshall

The Universe Inside

Nature is the art of God.
— SIR THOMAS BROWNE

Thirty years ago a man came to prison with more time than he could possibly do. At first he was moping around and thinking his life was essentially over and there was no reason to hope or believe or do anything but be morbidly depressed. One day, he was walking on the yard, head down, and the warden stopped him and said, "If you're going to make it, you've got to take time to stop and smell the flowers."

"Yeah, that *sounds* good, but you're crazy," he thought to himself, and went on.

Not long after that, the man stumbled into a prison AA meeting, mostly because, in his words, "There was free coffee." His first identification came when someone spoke of powerlessness, and he could recall sitting on the cold, concrete floor of the county jail that first morning, thinking his life couldn't possibly get any lower. These folks told him that was a beginning spot, not an ending spot.

Years later, participating in a photography program, he was shooting a flower with a telephoto lens. Focusing on the intricate middle of the flower, he was startled to see a small bug emerge from under one of the petals. Almost immediately, a tiny spider appeared to grab the bug and retreat to its hiding place.

"Well, I'll be," he thought. "There's a whole world right inside that one flower." As he sat and let that sink in, the words of the warden came back to him.

He is one of a handful of men who helped me grow up and begin a spiritual awakening in a place not necessarily known for growth and renewal. —*Bo Cox*

Sour Grapes

In those days they shall no longer say:
"The parents have eaten sour grapes, and the children's teeth are set on edge."
But all shall die for their own sins; the teeth of everyone who eats sour grapes
shall be set on edge. The days are surely coming, says the LORD, when I will
make a new covenant with the house of Israel and the house of Judah.

— JEREMIAH 31:29-31

Have you ever eaten something that is so sour it sets your teeth on edge? The sensation may be so strong that your cheeks pucker. Your eyes water. You hold it in your mouth because it is just too hard to swallow.

The prophet Jeremiah speaks to the people of Israel, now fallen from glory, exiled in Babylon. The prophet makes an important point. This familiar proverb attributed present suffering to the sins of the parents. But Ezekiel puts a difference spin on the proverb. The people cannot blame their predicaments on the sins of others. Ezekiel's message is one of hope, challenge, and good news.

The hope is that the people were not simply victims of the actions of their forbearers. People do have some role to play in the circumstances of life. As Eucharistic Prayer C tells us, we are blessed with memory, reason, and skill (*The Book of Common Prayer*, p. 370).

There is also the reality that we turn against God and one another. The result is often a feeling of being exiled from God. Violence, broken relationships, political upheaval, and our economic and ecological crises are examples. The good news is, God does not leave us exiled. God is always calling us to return. Through the beauty of creation, friends, family, and loving strangers, we can find evidence of divine covenant and abundant love. —*Karen Montagno*

Blackened Baby

When Michael and I married, we bought an ebony wood nativity that was made in Africa. I love it for its sleek, dark figures.

Last year baby Jack also came to love the set—particularly baby Jesus, who is the size of a pinkie finger. Jack played with the baby often, always returning it to its cradle—until one day he didn't.

Over the next weeks we looked high and low for the baby; how many places in a house can baby Jesus hide? We finally decided that Jesus was gone, and our nativity would no longer have a baby.

Easter came, and as we celebrated the empty tomb we laughed about our empty manger. Then the night before Pentecost, as Michael made toast, the toaster burst into flames, the fire licking the bottom of the cabinet above.

When our hearts quit racing, Michael pulled the bread out of the toaster and noticed something—a giant crumb, perhaps?—sitting at the bottom. Digging around, he came out with something dark and ashy. It was our baby Jesus. Our baby had been in the toaster for months. Who knows how many times he had been toasted? But he still looks good; the char doesn't show unless you look for it.

During Advent, we anticipate the coming of baby Jesus. But we also look forward to the second coming of our risen Lord—Jesus who at Easter saw and defeated the fires of hell. We are reminded throughout the Advent season, and again on Pentecost, that Jesus who comes to us as Lord turns our lives around. He lights fires in our hearts and under our feet. He challenges and changes us, seasons us with fire, and brings us home into his glory. —*Kristine Blaess*

Windows into Heaven

The fiery Holy Spirit has lit on many heads over the centuries, blazing up brightly in some hearts and burning into a deep and persistent bed of coals in others. In some, the Spirit has produced the "sheer holy boldness" to confront and transform worldly injustice or to dream unimagined possibilities.

Pentecost in many places means glorious music and exuberant additions to the divine drama of worship—kites and banners, balloons, and even birthday cakes! In some medieval cathedrals the reading of the great story of the tongues of fire was accompanied by showers of rose petals falling from tiny windows in the ceiling.

As the spirit falls afresh on us, what are we receiving through that window into heaven? What fire is being lighted in you, what passion, what gift for transformation? How will that fire join with others to light up the world with possibility?

The creative and mysterious gift of language is often a window for discovering the interrelatedness of many human tongues and the varied insights on the world they offer—like the fact that *beloved* and *believe* both have roots in what we "give our hearts to." It works in Latin, too: *credo* is that which I give my heart to. *Creed* is not so much about wrapping our minds around impossible-sounding ideas as it is inviting the heart to let the Spirit work within.

May the window open wide enough for a sparking spirit to set the tinder in our hearts alight. —*Katharine Jefferts Schori*

A Friendship Firmly Planted

She is over sixty-five; I am under forty. I am black; she is white. She is a grandmother and a widow; I am a single woman who does not have children. Our politics are vastly different, we live in different regions of the country, and we are members of different denominations. For all practical purposes, our lives have few intersections.

In a world in which such differences divide, our friendship has nonetheless taken root. In the deep soil of our Christian faith we have found more than common ground—we have found that mysterious something that makes a lifelong friendship.

There are times when our differences mean we don't understand one another. I am remembering the period after her husband's death and her profound grief that I could neither relieve nor fully comprehend. Who was I to speak on forty years of love and friendship now ended? I found myself searching for the right words. They rarely came, for there are few words one can share that will truly comfort the brokenhearted. Instead, in the silence of the unsaid, something I can only call a small pentecost happened, and my friend heard exactly what she needed.

These moments, though sometimes uncomfortable, bring such grace. Because when you know who you are in Christ, you do not have to be afraid of what you don't know or understand. And because, without fail, they leave me with a deeper understanding of the One who has drawn us together. I feel the presence of Christ in our conversations, even the difficult ones. I feel it in the way we listen to one another before speaking and in the way we hear (and are heard) with what can only be called "the ear of the heart." At the center of this true friendship is the bottomless well of Love, a true gift of the Holy Spirit.

For this, and for so many blessings, I am thankful.

—*Yejide Peters*

The Blessing of Babel

The diocese where I live and worship has the blessing and challenge of great diversity. We literally do not speak the same language. At the Diocesan Convention Eucharist, the gospel is routinely read not only in English, but also in Spanish, French, Creole, Portuguese—sometimes in Malagasy, the language spoken in our companion diocese in Madagascar.

This twenty-first-century Babel can be a source of friction, a barrier to understanding, a frequent inconvenience—and a great blessing.

During the past decade of change and controversy, our diocese seems to have experienced less turmoil than some other parts of The Episcopal Church, perhaps in part because we have no expectation of agreement on *anything*, except our mission, "to make known to all people the transforming power of the Gospel of Jesus Christ." Disagreement—and sometimes misunderstanding—are a normal part of life in our diocesan family. We shake our heads and smile, as we do at the opinions of a sibling or cousin or "crazy uncle." There is Babel, but there is love.

Jesus warned us that his words would cause family feuds, and they do. But in a family that regularly assumes words to be lost in translation, it can sometimes be easier to get past language to our shared experience of Christ moving among us.

I'm a writer, and I love to talk. Words are essential to me, yet I have learned as a monolingual *gringa* in a polyglot church that sometimes Pentecost comes not with tongues, but with a shared wordless silence, a smile, a hug, and God's gifts at God's table.

—*Mary W. Cox*

Mutual Blessing

The words "suspicious lump" are guaranteed to capture a patient's attention! As a friend sat with me awaiting the ultrasound, she was considering ways to support me, and I was visualizing a comforting picture of the prayer companionship within our church and beyond.

Later, when the diagnosis was confirmed, my husband and I considered how open to be with people. Being open about illness is tough, and updates would require mutual trust throughout chemotherapy and radiation. We began with a few Christian friends who had well-established habits of prayer. We needed their prayers like a cushion to rest upon, and we wanted their trustworthy company in prayer's mystery and effectiveness. Our trust gradually developed until we were supported by countless people.

Settling for email reports would have been easy, but we each needed eye contact and an arm around the shoulder. We can't see Jesus' facial expressions in the gospel reports of healing, but on God's behalf, contemporary believers offered verbal and nonverbal communications that warmed us. In practical matters that didn't appear "spiritual" on the surface, such kindness registered in our hearts as specific acts of divine origin. John O'Donohue writes, in his book *To Bless the Space Between Us*, "At the deepest level of reality, intimate kindness holds sway. This is the heart of blessing." At the deepest level of reality? God! Through God's children, blessing.

Asked later to write along these lines, I wrote, "Stroll a while, tell me your story, and I will tell you mine. Let's seed the soil with trust. Let's listen well, for listening signifies love. Come, tell me your story, and I will tell you mine." —*June Terry*

A Wet and Soggy Bed
Is a Lonely Place to Sleep

"What we speak becomes the house we live in.
Who will want to sleep in your bed if the roof leaks right above it?"
— HAFIZ

Gossip is a terrible thing, and we are all challenged in our daily living by the words that come out of our mouths. Jesus often encountered the wrath and judgment of zealously religious Pharisees who valued a literal observance of the law over the practice of living an inclusive love where no one was an outsider. His actions in the direction of love, healing, and justice were often met with words of opposition. Quite often even his closest disciples misunderstood his message and murmured words among themselves in a manner contrary to the message of Jesus.

Our faith journey calls us to self-examination. How often do we fall into the trap of saying too much? And how often do we entertain those who engage in this practice? James in his epistle warns us: "The tongue is a small member, yet it boasts of great exploits" (3:5).

Our Baptismal Covenant calls us to respect the dignity of every human being; it is a radical call to love. It is only through the practice of this love that we can even begin to stop the roof leaks above our beds. A wet and soggy bed is a lonely place to sleep. Why not resist the temptation to engage in idle gossip, or even worse, destructive and hurtful gossip? Why even add fuel to the flames?

God calls us to live in a house of beauty and grace. What comes out of our mouths will determine whether we have accepted God's invitation. —*Wilfredo Benitez*

This is God Calling

I love summer! I love the warm (okay, hot) muggy days of summer that wrap around me like a blanket. I love the balmy evenings when the lightning bugs and the stars twinkle together—God's fireworks display. Some of the stars spin rapidly and "leak" radiation as they spin. Here on earth, scientists used to wonder whether these pulses of energy were messages from other inhabitants of the universe, calling us. Now we know better about these neutron stars, but I still think they are messages—messages from God.

The lightning bugs remind me of my answering machine that blinks whenever I have a message waiting for me. It is as if the bugs are saying, "This is a message from God." When I am tempted to complain about the summer heat, the message may be: "This is God calling. Have you checked the weather from Venus lately? The current temperature there is 900 degrees. Be thankful you don't live there!"

But most of the time, the message is: "This is God calling. Come and meet me."

God calls to us all, not just through lightning bugs and neutron stars but in the everyday blessings of life which come from God, and especially in the blessing of Jesus who, while on this earth, probably himself looked up at the stars and looked around at the bugs and thanked God for these simple blessings.

God loves sending messages to us and getting messages from us. God only asks that we keep the line open with a minimum of busy signals. Have you checked your messages lately? —*Joanna Leiserson*

Like a Little Child

I recently spent half a year working as a nanny to a seven-year-old and one-year-old. The seven-year-old was usually leaving for school just as I arrived and returned only a couple of hours before I left, but the one-year-old and I spent the whole day together. I'm the youngest in my family, and most of the babysitting I had done was for older children. This was the first time I'd spent so many hours with a baby.

The one-year-old was just beginning to take his first steps when I began watching him. By the time I left the job, he could run full-tilt without falling. I watched him learn to stack blocks, feed himself, identify animals, and take the child-safety locks off cupboard doors. Every day, he learned something new, launching himself into the world with vigor and a touch of wild abandon. He fell down a lot and cried sometimes, but he always got back up and tried again—and as he kept trying, he got better.

When I try something new, fail, and fall down (usually only figuratively, these days), my first reaction is not to get up and try again. I prefer to nurse my wounds and move on to something else, thank you very much. Any number of interpretations can be pulled from Jesus' injunction to become like little children (Matthew 18:3-4), but perhaps one thing we can learn from the pint-sized among us is a lesson in tenacity and in the joy that can come with passion and persistence.
—*Alissa Goudswaard*

Enough Is Good

Does anyone ever feel good enough?

Trying to make sense of my morose feelings, I sip my morning coffee and look for a way to make it through another Father's Day. This holiday causes me to look in the mirror with abundant judgment and compare myself to other fathers with cascading inadequacy. I should be used to it by now, but the feeling is as fresh as ever.

Growing up with Hollywood's rendition of the perfect father, with characters like Atticus Finch and Mufasa, it's no wonder that many of us sit wilted when this day comes around. With a wonderful father of my own, who died before I could know anything but the legend, the wilting continues. And then, of course, there is my own record...the times when making a name for myself made work more important than my children, when expectations caused disappointment on vacations and family gatherings, and then a divorce that allows weekly visitations rather than daily encounters. There are good times, too, but the holiday spotlight shows cracks and scars with a vengeance.

I'm wise enough to know that Hollywood tells only part of the story, and that my father was as human as he was wonderful. I can probably even get to a place where I can embrace the good of my own fatherhood as easily as the bad, but I think the lesson in all of this lies beyond specific examples and more in the way we all look at life. We have been taught that only the best will do, that perfection is achievable, and have become blind to what lies on the way to extremes.

What if we embrace the less than perfect, the cracked as well as the polished? I suppose my greatest wish for all fathers, mothers, wives, husbands, sons and daughters, executives, students, artists, and athletes is to know that *enough* is good.
—*Chip Bristol*

The Wisdom of Wounds

There is a crack in everything. That's how the light gets in.

— LEONARD COHEN, "ANTHEM"

Last year, I fell from my horse and broke several ribs. After healing for over a month, I got back in the saddle. Literally.

It was with a mixture of fear that I would fall again, doubt about my riding skills, and excitement that I was finally back to riding horses. I wish I could tell you the first ride was magical. It wasn't. My muscles were weak and my technique was rusty. I felt loose and awkward. My second and third ride were slightly better.

And then.

And then I had that ride where I felt my soul ride. I felt my body in position, my backside in the saddle, and every part of my body, mind, and spirit riding.

I also felt my ribs still a bit tender.

I will never again be a rider who hasn't been hurt. That rider ceased to be on a March afternoon. I am a rider who has felt the pain of brokenness. I think, however, being the wounded rider actually makes me a better rider. I can't quite explain how. It's just something I feel deep in my soul.

As we live life, we fall, get broken and wounded. However we may try, we can never return to the person we were before.

What if, instead of reaching backward to who we were, we were present to who we have become because of our wounds? To what awarenesses we may have now, what empathy we may experience now, and what wisdom our scars bring us.

How has our brokenness allowed a new light to shine through us? —*Laurie Brock*

Fire

The summer in the desert Southwest is hot. So it might make sense to you that the element associated with summer in my Native tradition is fire. Fire is known to be both creative and destructive and can exist without fully destroying what it engulfs. In its creative nature, it is known to cleanse and purify. Truthfully it does not destroy at all but recreates another substance—reducing something that was burning to ash or coals.

Spiritually, fire is symbolic in many traditions—an image creating sacred space for prayer. Whether we are meditating with burning incense, marking the beginning of a prayer time by lighting a fire or candle, or reading sacred texts, we have opportunities to reconnect to God in creation through the element of fire.

Our Native women's Talking Circles begin with the lighting of fire. We burn herbs (medicines) and bless ourselves with the smoke. Our senses are stimulated, and through them the sacred space for prayer takes shape. At times we symbolically burn away those things that we might need to let go of or have been carrying. I often think about Psalm 141:2:

> *Let my prayer be set forth in your sight as incense,*
> *and the lifting up of my hands as the evening sacrifice.*

Fire helps us to pray because it helps us to reconnect to creation itself—all our relations—and the One who created it all.
—*Debbie Royals*

Waterloo

When people hear the word "Waterloo," some probably think of the pop band ABBA and their hit song or of a city in Iowa. But for the English, Waterloo was Sunday morning, June 18, 1815, in present-day Belgium. Napoleon was taking over the world. The Duke of Wellington was sent to make this Napoleon's last stand.

Across the English Channel, communication occurred by means of flashing lights, but the night was foggy when a light on the French side blinked out "Wellington" with a long pause. Then, "Defeated." Panic ensued throughout the English countryside. But as the day passed, the fog cleared and the message flashed again. "Wellington," pause, "Defeated," pause, "Napoleon."

A Bible commentary that I read recently suggests that the story of Waterloo is pretty close to what happened on Good Friday. The message sent out from Jerusalem that Jesus had been crucified could have been something like this: "Jesus," pause, "Defeated." On Sunday, it would have been sent again: "Jesus," pause, "Defeated," pause, "Sin and death."

Many times in life, the fog of despair rolls in, sometimes along with the fog of misunderstanding or an incomplete picture that obscures our vision of the truth which could otherwise set us free. Sometimes people call our faith "blind" because we cannot see all the way, as in June, 1815, when the English could not see all the way across the Channel. But some waited and listened. And they received the good news.

Like the women who faithfully went to Jesus' tomb and found that he was alive, like the faithful English who waited on the shore for a sign of good news from the battlefield, may we also have the faith to wait patiently for the Lord, for he has Good News.

—*Dave Marshall*

Fishing with Mattie

The arrival of summer entices my thoughts to fishing with my son Matthew when he was younger. For me, fishing is a good excuse to goof off. It was never so with Mattie.

For Mattie, there was great risk every time he put the hook in the water, the potential for success or failure. There is nothing like the excitement on the face of a small boy who has just caught a fish. The disappointment is equally evident when nothing is on the hook. When Mattie caught nothing, he was one forlorn little boy. That is why when he didn't catch any fish, I would take him to the trout farm—which is a little bit like carrying your fishing pole to the fish counter at the grocery store.

Many stories about Jesus involve fishing, like the day he told Simon to row out into deeper water and let down his net for a catch after a night spent with no fish to show for it. Having known Mattie's disappointment, I am amazed Simon could be coaxed back out into the lake. Maybe it was Jesus' final words that did it. "Do not be afraid," he said. Nothing motivates little boys like calling them chicken. And of course, once they tried again, they hauled in a miraculous catch, so many fish that the boat began to sink. It could never have happened without overcoming the fear of disappointment. Nothing can. I wonder if that isn't what Jesus was up to.

Try again. And do not be afraid. It's how little boys—and everyone else—learn how to hope and love. —*Stacy Sauls*

Smile

I have a bad habit of sometimes not watching where I am going when I am walking, because I am lost in thought and staring hard at the sidewalk. Sometimes I'm frowning or even scowling.

Sometimes people speak to me as they pass by, suggesting that I smile, because it all can't be that bad.

Most of the time they are right. It's not that bad. It's just that life is complicated, and thinking is hard work when one is on the go. I'm definitely a walking thinker, and often what I am thinking shows up on my face.

On the other hand, sometimes it *is* that bad. Sometimes life is really, really hard, and my face shows it.

I think it makes us anxious to see people who look sad or hurt in public. We would rather folks look cheerful. We might even quote scripture: wash your face and put oil on it and don't look like you are fasting (or whatever), but keep that stuff secret and you'll be rewarded in secret (my loose translation of Matthew 6:17-18). Their anxiety brings out our own anxiety.

But I'm not sure the best response is to blithely encourage folks to cheer up and smile. That's a reaction that's about *us*, not a response to the person who looks sad. Perhaps a simple smile from us to them would be better. Perhaps a smile would engage them in a way that reminds them of the goodness of the world, in a way that an admonition to "cheer up!" just doesn't.

Perhaps a smile is an example of incarnational presence and ministry in a hurting world. —*Penny Nash*

Search the Scriptures

In moments of candor, people will ask me: What's the point in reading the Bible? Why do we pay so much attention to a book written so long ago, marked by internal contradiction and often used to beat up on other people?

In spite of challenging questions, our tradition finds many ways to hold the Bible at the center. As disciples, it's helpful to note the ways that Jesus approached the sacred text of his day. Well before the New Testament was assembled, he made reference to the Hebrew scriptures, often interpreting them in new and provocative ways. At one point in a tense encounter with opponents, Jesus said: "You search the scriptures because you think that in them you have eternal life; and it is they that testify on my behalf" (John 5:39). With that, he gave a clue as to how we might regard the scriptures, how to use them in the spiritual journey and in our common life.

Our scriptures, our sacraments, our religious institutions are not an end in themselves, not objects for us to worship. As Evelyn Underhill wrote in a letter to the Archbishop of Canterbury about the spiritual lives of clergy, the most interesting thing about religion is God. Scripture, sacraments, and liturgy are resources given to help us to know God in some new way, to follow Christ more closely, to experience the power of the Spirit in our lives. They are instruments in the process of our seeking.

How do we see them as such? How do we use them in our lives today? —*Jay Sidebotham*

God Is in the Details

One morning, years ago: I am racing around, frantically trying to get my seven-year-old ready to arrive on time for his first day of summer camp. I've prepared his lunchbox, put extra clothing in his bag, and located the sunscreen. Soon I'll search for a towel, and surely his bathing suit is around here *somewhere*. Just then, Sam gets it into his head that the shoelaces in his sneakers are too long. What he needs, he insists, are the shoelaces that are now in his hiking boots. So here we are in the hallway, the two of us peering down at a hiking boot as I hurriedly try to loosen the knot and pull out the shoelace.

Suddenly I breathe and slow down, overtaken by happiness. Here is this son whom I love so much; here are my hands, involved in a useful, simple task; here is a brand-new morning, full of possibilities. A seed of gratitude is suddenly planted in the field of an ordinary day.

If someone were to ask, "How big is God?" I could wave my arms about, make large, sweeping gestures. I could answer, "God is huge! God fills the heavens and the earth! Our minds can't encompass the enormity of God!" And I would be right.

But God is also very small. Scientists have discovered a particle so small that it passes through the earth without bumping into anything, so small that it passes through our bodies without touching us. God can be that humble, a self-emptying Presence that we miss unless we pay close attention. God can be as tiny as a seed, taking root in every moment of gratitude. —*Margaret Bullitt-Jonas*

Bestow Your Love

One leg, a wife, three children, two sisters, seven nieces and nephews, six hogs, four piglets, and a dog—all living under one roof, sharing three rooms and a pig pen.

Juan and his large extended family live in a two-toned, pink-colored home in Cartagena where they are "house sitting." His family—like the other almost two million people displaced by violence in Colombia—was a victim of the paramilitary battling the guerrilla. Juan lost four brothers in the turmoil, he reports to us matter-of-factly, balancing himself on his crutches and volunteering that he had lost his own leg to a propeller in a motorboat accident when he was a fisherman back home.

With loans from an international organization, Juan has grown his businesses: buying more hogs, replenishing snacks and fruits, purchasing a bicycle taxi which he rents out, and creating a savings. Through his diversified businesses, this family of fourteen lives on less than $250 U. S. per month, or on about sixty cents per day for each person.

As we stand on the front porch to say good-bye, I am asked to pray for the family. What can I possibly pray? Bowed heads gathered on the porch, we are all huddled in a group. A staff member translates as I begin with "Holy Father, may you continue to bestow God's love on this family."

Juan spontaneously groans in acceptance of this blessing. My voice cracks as I hold back tears, awed by the resiliency and deep faith of this amazing family, and I continue:

"Holy Father, may you continue to bestow love on each and every one of us." —*Westina Matthews*

My Soul in Silence Waits

I used to live in a small town north of London, through which flowed the Grand Union Canal. I loved to walk along the canal and watch the various narrow boats and barges as they chugged slowly by. Best of all, I liked to watch these boats enter into the locks.

These intricate nineteenth-century locks were built in order to lift boats up, perhaps five or six feet, to the water level of the canal that lay ahead. The lock gate would open, the boat would slowly enter into the lock, and then the gate would be closed. What the boat would have to do next was shut down and remain completely still. And then, slowly, very slowly, and rather wonderfully, this huge boat would be lifted up by the rising waters. It needed no engine, no movement at all. It simply remained still and waited to be lifted up to a new level.

For me, this is a perfect image for prayer. So often we wonder if we are praying the right way, saying the right words, sitting or kneeling in the right position. Those narrow boats remind me that God's word to us is simply, "Be still." Come into the presence of God. Close the door of your room—the lock gates—and turn off the engine and wait. Simply wait for God to lift you up.

This kind of prayer is a wonderful way to start the day, to be lifted up and strengthened by God. —*Brother Geoffrey Tristram,* SSJE

An Outward Silence

When I first moved to New York from Texas, before I had made many friends, I'd frequently take long walks around my neighborhood in Queens or around Manhattan, especially on sunny days, listening to the sounds on the sidewalk and reflecting. These walks were somewhat meditative, without a goal or destination.

Recently, I've found myself filling up every moment with noise. I listen to music or the radio while I commute, I turn on the television when I'm at home. I'm not speaking, but neither am I listening.

I was reminded of this while reading Dietrich Bonhoeffer's *Life Together* with some friends from church. Bonhoeffer advocates meditation and silence every day. "The silence of the Christian is listening silence, humble stillness," he writes.

This silence is not meant to be an inwardly directed silence. Not navel gazing, as I am prone to do, but looking outward into the world, like a walk through the neighborhood, like the quiet moments writing and creating. Silence is not the same as not speaking. It's a directed silence, not toward a goal, but oriented toward God.

Perhaps this is what Jesus means when he says we should love God with all our heart and souls and minds: That we should direct our thoughts outward, toward love and doing God's work in the world.

—*Jeremiah Sierra*

Choosing Compassion, Choosing Life

Out of an awareness of my own brokenness
and the wounds of the world,
I choose life for myself and for others
by being a compassionate presence
wherever need touches my heart.

This simple statement hangs above my computer. It is adapted from the mission statement of the order to which my spiritual director, a Roman Catholic nun, belongs. I put it there, where my eye would fall on it often during the day, as a reminder of my daily prayer that God will fill my cold heart with compassion.

Compassion and I are often strangers. Confessing this is humbling and embarrassing...and true. But as I move inexorably toward old age, I see ever more clearly that compassion is the very heart of the gospel. Jesus doesn't offer doctrines or institutional structures; he doesn't judge those who are suffering; he doesn't harangue sinners.

He responds, invariably, with compassion. The sick are made well. The blind see, the deaf hear, the lame walk and leap for joy, all through the boundless compassion of our Lord. He meets need with compassionate presence. Incarnate Lord, enfleshed, he feels deeply the wounds of the world. My spiritual director and her order know this about Jesus. They aspire only, through their own brokenness, to feel deeply the wounds of the world and to serve as he served, to respond to need with compassion.

Truly, the world is awash in God's compassion, if only we'll open our eyes to see it, our hearts to accept it and our hands to share it. Thus we choose life. —*Betsy Rogers*

Shout!

Have you ever been asked to be quiet when asking for something? Have you ever been told to let someone alone, that they can't be bothered? I love the passage in Matthew 20 where the blind men started shouting as soon as they heard Jesus was passing by.

Passing by. He was not there for three days or for a week-long appearance. He was just passing by. They knew something others might not know. They knew that Jesus could heal. They knew Jesus could do something for them nobody else had done or could do, and they were not going to allow this opportunity, this Jesus, to pass them by. Obviously they had heard about Jesus. Jesus had a reputation. Healer. Teacher. Compassionate. They shouted even more loudly when they were sternly ordered to be quiet.

Do you know what Jesus can do? Do you know, as the song tells us, there is power in Jesus? If Jesus was passing by today, what would you do? Would you be quiet? Or would you shout? Louder? What would you answer if Jesus asked you, "What do you want me to do for you?" What is it that you need today? Healing? Strength? Faith? Peace?

Shout! Don't let anyone tell you to be quiet! Nothing is too little, nothing is too big, nothing is too insignificant, nothing is too difficult. Shout! "This is what I want you to do for me, Jesus!" Jesus will be moved with compassion for you.

But...there is one more step. After Jesus restored their sight, the blind men followed him. Will you follow? —*Sandra Montes*

Are We There Yet?

"Are we there yet?"

I can't help thinking that the question, so familiar to family travelers, is an inborn genetic trait triggered one hour after the car leaves the driveway. Sometimes children even make a repetitive chant out of it, thus increasing its output a hundredfold before the parents put a stop to the noise, if not to the wondering itself.

On my family's first trip to Disneyland, after the timing of the questions reached every five minutes, my father finally told us, "When you see Sleeping Beauty Castle, you'll know you're there."

What a relief to know how to recognize our destination! And he was right. A few interminable hours later, Sleeping Beauty Castle loomed up to our right, and we knew we were there.

I sometimes wonder about salvation. Are we there yet? How can we tell if we are there? The Bible suggests that the mark of salvation is the opposite of Sleeping Beauty Castle—that luxuriant palace with people sleeping away, waiting for a prince to wake them up and fix their problems.

"Are we there yet?" Salvation is a soup kitchen filled with generous cooks and destitute guests sharing a meal together.

"Are we there yet?" Salvation is there when we are at home praying and meditating, just talking with God.

"Are we there yet?" Salvation is there wherever forgiveness is offered and received.

Actually, we are always there. "The home of God is among mortals," says Revelation 21:3. Because God has chosen to dwell with us, we are always in the right place. We don't need Sleeping Beauty Castle to know we are "there."

—*Joanna Leiserson*

Master of the Universe

*At bottom, the whole concern of religion is with
the manner of our acceptance of the universe.*

— WILLIAM JAMES

This spring has been wet. After being in a moderate-to-severe drought for several years and struggling to help keep green things growing, it's a piece of good fortune to hear thunder and rain and see four inches in our rain gauge.

Last summer didn't get especially hot, but there was literally no rain for months. Hundred-year-old trees died. Everything was brown. Wildfires raged. Animals foraged for food and water. Almost everything we tried to grow died.

The year before there was a little rain but it was hot. Temperatures over one hundred degrees reigned throughout the summer. Almost everything we tried to grow died.

Yesterday I was mowing, and the grass was as thick and luscious as a carpet! I don't believe I've ever seen grass that rich; certainly not in our yard. And, thing is, it was growing in the same areas that had been brown the years before.

Before long I was congratulating myself on how well I had done in making this grass grow. Full of pride, I'm pretty sure I was grinning as I mowed. Then it dawned on me that I'd not done anything different this year from the previous several years; the only thing different was the amount of rain.

After that I was still grinning, but now it was at my arrogance and amnesia because I had forgotten once again who was in charge of the universe. —*Bo Cox*

Strength of Presence

As a teen, I noticed in restaurants that couples often ate in silence, and I wondered why they had so little to say. Then I became friends with a couple who had been married for thirty years. They often sat, reading, in what they called "companionable silence" or "strength of presence."

Some of us cultivate God's "strength of presence" in prayer and reading before we walk into daily activities. Others focus on God in a silence described as "centering." What about being reminded of God's presence throughout the day? After all, we find ways to remind ourselves of less significant things. Remembering God's presence might be like my driving the car with a friend as passenger. To show that I'm attentive as she talks, I glance at her quickly, but focus on traffic. If I'm talking, I glance to observe her response. How can we learn to enjoy similar glimpses of God?

For years, one person I know has increased his awareness by trying to thank God for something every time he walks through a doorway! He sometimes forgets, but the habit takes little effort, and he's now more aware of God's attention. A woman matches the tune of her clock's Westminster chimes with the word "Alleluia." After many attempts in which she forgot most of the time, she says that praise has begun "to come out of nowhere" while she focuses on the computer. Even when she consciously missed the chimes, they call her like a church bell.

Why miss out on graced moments of awareness? If noticing doorways or chimes doesn't suit you, what would it take to set up a "tickler" to be reminded of giving God an affectionate glance?

—*June Terry*

Bare Feet

I have a friend who likes to take off her shoes. Family members joke about her habit and roll their eyes each time she sends another picture of her feet resting comfortably on the banister of some deck, a picturesque sunset in the background. True to form, the signature photograph for her blog is of her feet (and those of close friends)...up, crossed, and utterly relaxed.

This summer I have had my shoes off a bit, and each time I do, I think about my friend and her perpetual bare feet. It's about more than comfort. For me, it represents a view of life—and my hope is that, with or without shoes, I can hold that view more often.

Many years ago, a man named Moses was minding his own business when he encountered a bush that was burning but not being consumed by the flames. Startled, he quickly realized it was an encounter with something, or someone, greater than he. He was instructed to remove his shoes, for the ground on which he stood was holy. Moses, like my friend, took off his shoes.

It's hard to stay busy and down to business when your toes are free to wiggle about. It's hard to think about all that you need when a breeze swirls around your infant-like feet and reminds you of all you have. When looking out at a sunset or sunrise, watching children playing tag on the lawn, or talking to a long-lost friend, bare feet are helpful. They remind us that the ground on which we stand is holy. It was, way back when. It remains so today. —*Chip Bristol*

Traveling Hearts

God has set our hearts on pilgrimage. He has given us traveling hearts, hearts that are moving, hearts that have left security behind to follow love. Pilgrim hearts travel lightly—we can't carry much through the desert. We carry in us the Word of the One who has set us on this journey. We carry memories, but not too many, because they get heavy. We've had to leave our book of debts behind. The side of the road is littered with these books of accounts, abandoned by hearts that don't need to keep score anymore.

Each night we lay our heads down wherever we are. There's a freedom in the traveling, a wildness, a looseness. Each day we eat what is provided. We trust there will be food when we hunger and water when we thirst. But we also know this is desert business, and we're not going to get fat on our journey. We travel in the company of fellow pilgrims. We share what we have with them.

And as we travel, the parched valley becomes a place of springs. It is not our power, but it is, somehow, our being there that causes the land to pour forth the life that has been withheld. As we travel, we move not from strength to weakness, becoming weaker through the travails of travel, but from strength to strength.

We travel, pilgrims of the heart, pursuing the Word we've been given, until finally we appear before God in his home. We arrive in his courts, and our pilgrim hearts finally find their home.

Better is one day in your courts, dear Lord, than a thousand elsewhere. —*Kristine Blaess*

Temperance

I saw a video that sent shivers down my spine—a twenty-one-year-old Tennessean videoed himself being stopped at a checkpoint by a tired and easily annoyed police officer. Video subtitles tell how his constitutional rights were violated, including an illegal detaining, a falsified drug "hit" by a canine team, and the subsequent vehicle search that ended when the officers saw his camera. The video highlights the law enforcer saying, "You have no constitutional rights at a checkpoint." It ends with a black screen and the words, "Happy 4th, America."

The next day, coming home from Grandma's, my family was stopped at a checkpoint. It reminded me of the video and more shivers ran down my spine. After watching the video, my dad calmed me with his wisdom. He said both parties in the video overreacted. The driver refused to cooperate, which escalated the conversation. He pushed his rights in a highly charged situation, and then the officer, working late at night and not knowing what awaited him, also overreacted. If both parties had shown temperance and mutual respect, the event would not have escalated.

Jesus told about a man who was robbed, beaten, and left by the side of the road. Two people walked by and did not help. A third man stopped and helped. Jesus asked which of the three was a neighbor. A lawyer responded, "The one who showed mercy." Jesus responded, "Go and do likewise."

Mutual respect and temperance are, it seems to me, the origin of showing mercy. Perhaps a good way to celebrate freedom, as Americans and as followers of Christ, is to show mutual respect, temperance, and mercy. —*Dave Marshall*

Jesus Is Lord

If you confess with your lips that Jesus is Lord
and believe in your heart that God raised him from the dead,
you will be saved.

— ROMANS 10:9

In the political context of the first century, confessing "Caesar is Lord" meant safety, acceptability, and patriotism. The early church, instead, insisted "Jesus is Lord," which made them dangerous, unacceptable, and less than patriotic. Which, I admit, is not a very patriotic thing to say on the Fourth of July. But there it is, and we've got to deal with it. It's a bit like that crazy uncle everyone talks about, but when he shows up for the cookout, he always sits right next to you.

Who or what is Caesar for us today? Those living in the Roman empire of the first century understood that Caesar was more than merely a political ruler; he was also venerated as divine. To confess Jesus as Lord was to stand in contrast to society at large. What might it mean for us living in a democratic society in the twenty-first century to say, "Jesus is Lord"? Is it still dangerous, unacceptable, and less than patriotic? Or have we domesticated the message of Jesus? Might we understand ourselves as living responsibly in our country of origin, but not venerating it above Jesus? Might we proclaim that Jesus is Lord by our lives and our actions that set us apart from the dominant culture and ways of the world? —*Aaron Klinefelter*

Warrior Spirits

You might be thinking about patriotism, given the calendar date. However, there are spiritual attributes that you might also want to hold up in your thoughts and prayers. Warrior Spirits are a way of describing the spiritual strength and well-being needed to be a warrior. And a warrior does not have to be a person engaged in war. Warriors might be people who are defending their family, their community, or a cause they are particularly focused on in their life.

How we care for ourselves is important. We concern ourselves with our physical bodies by choosing our food wisely and exercising all our moving parts. Mentally we remain sharp because we stimulate our minds as well. Emotional wellness requires our constant care, so we engage in healthy relationships and behavior. We understand ourselves to be part of a larger whole in creation. We know our spiritual connections to our Creator God and all that God created is essential to a balanced life.

Balanced living creates a firm foundation for anyone who is facing challenges. Warrior Spirits have a life so balanced that when they face adversity, they are able to remain strong and balanced in the process. Warrior Spirits are focused and intentional in their lives. Their energy is not diluted by distractions to things that are out of balance. We need Warrior Spirits. Are you one? —*Debbie Royals*

Hindsight Miracles

Confession: I've seen every episode of *Joan of Arcadia*. This prime time family drama from the mid-aughts about a troubled teen receiving messages from God is not exactly artful television, but it raises some interesting questions and ideas about faith. I like the priest character, who only shows up a few times but says some pretty smart stuff. At one point, the mom in the show asks him if it's okay to pray for her paralyzed son to be healed. The priest responds, "I think prayer can never hurt, as long as you understand you might not recognize the answer right away. Most miracles occur in hindsight."

Have you ever hoped, yearned, and prayed for something, only to be frustrated when those prayers seem to go unanswered and unnoticed? Sometimes it seems like God is deaf, or absent, or a cruel trickster. When an answered prayer doesn't match the answer we would choose—however right and fitting that answer may seem to us—the answer can be difficult to recognize.

One of my favorite short stories, Katherine Vaz's "The Birth of Water Stories," embraces unexpected miracles, and includes the amazing line: "What are your miracles, and how are they different from the ones you planned for? Please tell me. You must tell everyone." Sometimes, unplanned-for miracles feel an awful lot more like curses than blessings, but when we see them for what they are, we see God at work.

What are your miracles? How are they different from the ones you planned for? Where is God at work in your life? Please: tell everyone.
—*Alissa Goudswaard*

Stepping Out

The sky was a rare beauty of Irish sunshine and mild summer breezes, perfect to begin walking Ireland coast-to-coast, 360 miles in twenty-three days.

Pilgrimage is indeed a spiritual journey. Not to find God, but to be with God. Committing to walking hours each day through the Isle colored in forty shades of green, I was anticipating a holy experience, a presence of the seen and unseen, a connection of the conscious and unconscious. I had no idea what I would encounter. My past experience had taught me that I could gain the knowledge of something fresh in my soul, in my spirit, in this place where the mystical is breathed in like the smoke of an ancient pipe.

Leaving Marlay Park, I started the 1,600-meter climb out of Dublin. The ascent was gentle, winding up the lush sides of the Dublin Mountains. Looking back, I could see a spectacular view of the bay of Dublin, the entire city splashed in rare sunlight.

The sun gave way to a cloudy mist, draping around me like a protective wrap. The trail crawled over a long rock path cut across the barren landscape, a treeless mountainside covered with a dark green impassable shrub growing in the bog. The journey continued across the top of the Glencree Mountains through thick black forests. Ravens arrived at a most needed time to offer encouraging words when I seemed uncertain of which trail to follow.

Before leaving home, a holy woman told me I was at a "Y" in the road of my life. She said I would not know which road I would take until I faced the choice on my pilgrimage with God. Indeed.

—*Gil Stafford*

Trust, Live, Pray

In prayer it is better to have a heart without words
than words without a heart.

— JOHN BUNYAN

"I don't think I'm praying right."

I hear this observation frequently as a priest. That critical voice we hear in our selves and souls about how we fall short in prayer because we can't spill forth perfectly formed narrative structures like those we read in books.

Truthfully, I think we spiritual beings can't pray wrong. We've just lost the ability to trust our heart.

When we laugh, we pray. When we weep, we pray. When we are so overwhelmed with life we can't even speak words, we pray.

When we run barefoot through the grass on a summer day, we pray. When we are awed by the beauty of a flower, we pray. When we are taken away by the luscious taste of summer berries or elegant chocolate and are thankful for the deliciousness of life, we pray.

When we have a quirky thought about life and a friend says the same thought aloud and we both realize the wonderful odd connection of human relationship, we pray. When we sing with gusto or awkwardness, in perfect harmony or completely off-key, we pray.

When we sit in silence and simply *be* for a few moments, we pray.

When we give ourselves fully to express the authentic feelings of our heart, we pray.

In fact, each moment of our life is a form of prayer. The real difficulty in life actually is *not* praying. We do pray without ceasing because we are prayerful souls, exactly as God created us to be. —*Laurie Brock*

Through the Wilderness

Lions and tigers and bears, oh my! Poverty, hunger, and war, oh my! Iraq, Afghanistan, and, Pakistan, oh my! Economic distress, foreclosures, and joblessness, oh my! Environmental degradation, global warming, and species extinction, oh my! Oh my! Oh my!

It really is a jungle out there; thick with the underbrush of evil, brokenness, despair, and sin. Things seems so dire it has become more and more difficult to see our way through the thicket where one can get lost or overcome by the "wildlife." There are times when one feels like a safari explorer without a guide, complete with pith helmet and machete, hacking aimlessly in the hopes of finding clearer ground.

The good news is that we have a guide in Christ Jesus our Lord who is in the wilderness with us, having been there for forty days himself. Fully human and fully divine, Jesus experienced uncertainty, fear, loneliness, and temptation. Yet, scripture tells us that Jesus met his tempter and endured his circumstances with faith, using the Word of God as a tool to withstand the pressures and deprivation.

Jesus is the way out and the way forward. Through Christ and the Holy Spirit we are given the tools we need to navigate our way through the wilderness, to resist the temptations and withstand the forces of evil in this world. And through the church we are given directions and the vehicle with which to navigate our way, though many of us stop attending after the Easter alleluias have faded. Now all we need is the will to endure the journey through the wilderness. May we journey together in faith, hope, and love with the knowledge we have a Savior who journeys with us.

Thanks be to God, who knows the way out and the way through the lions and tigers and bears!

—*Owen C. Thompson*

Unexpected Mercy

As a child, I was the difficult one. Not bad, exactly, or deliberately disobedient, but curious, daring, dangerously creative. Being punished was as much a part of my life as perpetually scraped knees.

One night I did the stupidest thing I can recall from my childhood: I talked Mikey Adams into getting into my wagon with me and riding it down the steeply sloped driveway that led to the garage under his house. What made this the stupidest act of my childhood was that the metal garage door was closed, and we both were totally aware that it was closed, when I pushed off the sidewalk at the top of the driveway.

I have no idea what law of physics my six-year-old self expected to bend. What did happen was we hit that door at top speed, with a metallic thud that resounded through our neighborhood. The wagon tipped over, we tumbled onto the ground, not particularly hurt—but while I was lying there, I saw the enormous dent the wagon handle's hinge had punched into the door. I panicked, and ran home.

As I was running in the door, Dad was coming out, a sledgehammer in his hand. News traveled all too fast in our little cul de sac. I froze, thinking "A spanking isn't enough; he is going to beat me with that hammer," but Dad walked on by, without saying a word. When I heard the series of ringing thumps, I knew Dad was pounding out the dent, fixing what I had foolishly broken. Then he came home, put the hammer away, and went back to reading his paper. That was the end of it.

I imagine that this is how we often look to God—like foolish, daring children who find endless ways to mess up our world, to get ourselves in trouble. And each time, God follows behind us, making things right again—forgiving us without a word but with infinite, boundless mercy we cannot begin to comprehend.
—*Janet Rehling Buening*

An Interval of Gladness

Settling into my seat on a recent cross-country flight, I was dismayed to realize that just behind me and across the aisle was a young girl, perhaps ten years old, speaking incessantly in a loud voice. Sigh. Trying to be unobtrusive, I peered around for a quick look and discovered a developmentally disabled child, slim and pretty and clearly very excited about her trip. Indeed, that very excitement might have brought on the endless stream of high-volume chatter.

I was exasperated. I had expected to work on this four-hour flight. Would I be able to get anything done?

God promptly reminded me of my daily prayer for a compassionate heart. Thus nudged, I asked myself: "What would the compassionate response be in this situation?"

By God's grace, I found myself listening with interest to this youngster—not to her words, because she spoke rapidly and incomprehensibly to my aging ears and I really didn't care to eavesdrop, but to the sound of her voice. And what a voice! It was clear and musical, with a beautiful bell-like quality. And it was filled with joy! This child bubbled over with excitement and an infectious gladness that soon had me smiling and enjoying my flight.

It was a real grace moment: by nudging me to compassion, God had given me a great gift, an interval of gladness at 35,000 feet. God's grace peals around us wherever we are, if we'll just listen. —*Betsy Rogers*

A Healthy Disillusionment

There was a period when I wanted my birthday to be perfect. It was my special day, after all. Of course, it was never perfect, and I'd find small things inordinately upsetting. When I grew up and finally let go of the illusion of a perfect birthday, I began to enjoy my birthdays much more.

Our expectations can ruin perfectly good and healthy things, including Christian community. "Innumerable times a whole Christian community has broken down because it had sprung from a wish dream," writes Dietrich Bonhoeffer in *Life Together*. Fortunately, "God's grace speedily shatters such dreams," bringing us a freeing disillusionment, allowing us to understand each other as we really are.

People in my religious community occasionally disappoint me, and the liturgy doesn't always go smoothly. My community doesn't always give me the good, peaceful feeling that I wish it would. I can only be present when I let go of the expectation of a perfect community that exists to make me happy.

Community, Bonhoeffer says, is a reality, not an ideal. We have to push past illusion to the difficult reality of each other, broken and disappointing and in pain, but also filled with a love that can keep us from falling apart at the seams. Because all of us are close to falling apart, as I am reminded at my church each Sunday, when people offer their prayers aloud. You can hear the varieties of human pain and fear welling up, but also love. Afterward, as we spend time together, there are awkward moments, as there are in any community, and misunderstandings, but we also know that we are joined together with something stronger.
—*Jeremiah Sierra*

Nowhere to Lay Her Head

Foxes have holes, and birds of the air have nests;
but the Son of Man has nowhere to lay his head.

— MATTHEW 8:20

One morning I got up early to be at the laundromat when it first opened. The doors automatically unlocked at 7:00 a.m. and locked at 10:00 p.m. Imagine my surprise to find a young woman already in there. She called out a cheery "Hello," and I responded with a "Good morning."

And then I noticed. She was busily organizing numerous shopping bags around her grocery cart. I must have caught her just as she was washing up in the community sink. After layering a skirt over her slacks and a sweatshirt over her blouse, she sat down to eat an apple for her breakfast.

I was impressed that she had found a safe, warm place to sleep that night. As 8:00 a.m. approached—when the dry cleaners opened on the adjoining side with the internal entryway—she hastily left the laundromat with shopping cart in tow.

I sometimes forget that Jesus was homeless. He lived in community, relying on the hospitality of others for food and sheltering, owning little more than the clothes on his back and the sandals on his feet. If he were alive today, I am certain that Jesus would be found living and walking among the many invisible and often ignored faces of the homeless—the mentally ill, the physically disabled, the victims of domestic violence, the veterans, those with HIV, the young runaways, the families with children, the unemployed.

Where did he lay his head at night? —*Westina Matthews*

Nothing Is Ordinary with God

The church calls the time after Pentecost Sunday "Ordinary Time," but I'd like to share a little secret with you: there really is no Ordinary Time, for with God every day is an extraordinary opportunity to draw closer to the throne of grace. God's beauty and grace surround us, even in the midst of external and internal noise. Why not draw near to the throne of grace and discover the extraordinary connection that you, as a child of God, have within your soul?

The present day will come with a multitude of challenges and unexpected hurdles. These seem to arrive inevitably on a daily basis. Nevertheless, in the midst of this rests the possibility to dance our way to the throne of grace and allow our true God-nature to experience the extraordinary brilliance of the light within.

Hafiz, a wise Persian poet, once wrote: "Complaint is only possible while living in the suburbs of God." If we reflect on the wisdom contained in this brief statement, we will soon come to the realization that we often live in the suburbs of God, creating unnecessary distance between God and us. Ironically God is never distant and always present.

What keeps us from drawing nearer to the throne of grace? What prevents the dance between the Blessed Trinity and us? A dance where the Blessed Three melt into each other and our souls?

It's time to expose the secret. There is no Ordinary Time—all time with God is extraordinary time, and you are being called to draw near to the throne of grace where God's light will become brilliant in your very heart! Rejoice, draw near! —*Wilfredo Benitez*

Griffin: Another Name for Grace

Our family had the incredible blessing of a yellow Labrador Retriever named Griffin for almost fourteen years. She was the perfect dog. Almost.

There was that time she ate a newly installed vinyl floor in the laundry room. There was that unfortunate time biological necessity intervened when I was trying to speak in front of a room full of teenagers. And there were a couple of passive-aggressive tactics she would use to get her way.

The only really bad thing about dogs is the inevitable end. One summer day we found out that time was coming soon. We were able to keep Griffin comfortable and happy for several weeks with medication. She went to our diocesan camp to hang out with the campers, who lavished attention on her, one more time. She could occasionally trot, if not run. She felt up to an occasional foray into the kitchen garbage.

Finally, though, it became too painful even to walk. It was as if the spark went out of her eyes, and when she looked up at us, there was a different message. We knew what she was asking. We were with her at the end. I kept my face in hers as she slipped away. We buried her in a pink blanket.

In all the years of her life, and even on the day of her death, Griffin made God easier for me to believe in. Even on the days when God seemed most distant, if not absent, Griffin was a glimpse into the reality of the goodness of creation, of the meaning of faithfulness, and, perhaps most importantly, into divine sense of humor.

One of the first things I hope to say to God one day is that dogs were a good idea. I'm sure God already knows.

—*Stacy Sauls*

Of Turtles and Skunks

My needlepoint, an alert turtle in profile, has a story. The friend who stitched it had laughed with me about our differing personalities as we discussed Keith Miller's book, *Habitation of Dragons*. Miller wrote that he sometimes resembled a skunk in its readiness to give off an angry odor to keep others away, and he saw someone else as a turtle, ready to hide within its shell. The needlepoint turtle gave me a message: choose courage over retreat.

Through this gift, God has reminded me to stay out of my shell, but more credit must go to Isaiah: "Do not fear, for I am with you, do not be afraid, for I am your God; I will strengthen you, I will help you" (Isaiah 41:10). My old Bibles have smudged corners on Isaiah's pages because I rechecked these promises so often. Now I read the passage less often because the "turtle's head" is out. Years have passed since the day when I began a sentence, "In my humble opinion," and someone who knew me well interrupted and laughed, saying "When did you ever have one of those?"

For forty years, my friend who used to frighten people, skunk-like, has served as a patient advocate for the voiceless and disadvantaged, has worked to help people overseas, and has guided internationals in the United States. Those early energies have been redirected and her gracious life, honored.

We've both been changed. God minimized many of our fears, dissolved some of our defensiveness, and gave us the courage to face outward and to serve others. What am I saying? That God can transform us all? Yes. —*June Terry*

What Do I Want?

Do not be conformed to this world,
but be transformed by the renewing of your minds.

— ROMANS 12:2

I visited the art museum and immersed myself in the colors and shapes of the masters. Over the course of a leisurely afternoon, I wandered from painting to painting, from room to room, gazing at everything with a quiet eye. I was filled with wonder and delight. Before heading home, I decided to stop at the gift shop and to take a quick look around. I walked from counter to counter, staring at reproductions of classic art on neckties and handbags, on posters and scarves. I felt increasingly irritable. I wanted to want something. I wanted to want that necklace, that mug. I wanted to want that shiny or charming object, but I didn't. More and more frustrated, I kept saying, "That's not it! That's not what I want! I wish it were what I want, because here it is, available for sale, and I've got money to spend, but I don't want it."

Increasingly restless, even angry, I finally stopped in my tracks and asked myself, "What's going on? What do I really want?" The answer came instantly: "I want to gaze. I want to appreciate. I want to savor the beauty in this room without grabbing or possessing it." So for a while I explored the aisles of the gift shop, gazing without grasping, as if released from a spell, as if awakened from some evil enchantment. The truth was that I had everything I needed. I wasn't empty now, but full.

Thomas Merton notes: "We have what we seek. It is there all the time, and if we but give it time, it will make itself known to us." —*Margaret Bullitt-Jonas*

Enciende Una Luz...

My dad does not like people looking at his feet.

He has had a tough life. He ran away from home when he was seven. He lived in the streets, often without shoes, for about ten years. He does not like people looking at his feet. I love looking at his feet. Even the rough, unmanicured parts.

I read in Romans that the feet of those who bring good news are beautiful (Isaiah 52:7; Romans 10:15). Papi's feet are beautiful. His news? *God saves, God forgives, God heals, God provides, God can!* Good? Indeed!

There is a song by Marcos Witt, anointed Christian artist, that says, *Enciende una Luz y déjala brillar*...Turn on a light and let it shine. It is not just any light, however. The song continues—*la luz de Jesús que brille en todo lugar*...may Jesus' light shine everywhere.

The song talks about the beauty of the feet of those who bring good news. The song is about my dad. The song is about his feet. *Hermosos son los pies*...beautiful are the feet—of Alejandro, Marcos, Katharine, Teresa, Billy, Alex, Andy. Will you add your name to this list? With your ingrown toenails or perfectly manicured toes. Regardless of how your feet look, will you allow God to make them beautiful as you share good news? —*Sandra Montes*

Conspicuous Othering

We have this amazing propensity, a talent really, for making "others" of people. If we have surplus resources, we call others poor. Or if we are under-resourced, we look longingly, or spitefully, and call others rich. If we feel beaten-down by others, we call ourselves oppressed and others the oppressors. If we have a certain color skin, we make assumptions about others with differently colored skin. You get the idea.

Us/Them	You/Me
In/Out	Black/White
Conservative/Liberal	Christian/Non-Christian
Gay/Straight	Republican/Democrat
Rural/Urban	Rich/Poor
Slave/Free	Citizen/Immigrant
Male/Female	Jew/Gentile

We are conspicuous otherers. We love making our group the "In" group and the other group the "Out" group.

The gospel writer Luke records Jesus' sermon in his hometown (Luke 4). Jesus is announcing the inauguration of the kingdom of God among us. He reads from the prophet Isaiah and proclaims, "Today this scripture has been fulfilled in your hearing" (Luke 4:21). Jesus is breaking down these barriers we construct between others and ourselves. He intentionally and unapologetically dismantles the In-group/Out-group mentality between Jew and Gentile for his hearers—and almost gets thrown off a cliff.

Which makes me wonder, am I to follow in Jesus' steps? What In-groups need outsiders brought in? What walls in my life that prevent me from truly seeing the other need to be torn down? —*Aaron Klinefelter*

Making All Things New

I once lived next door to a young couple whose hobby was collecting antique furniture. On Saturday mornings they would head off to local flea markets to see what they could find. I was amazed by what they would bring back: old beat-up dressers, broken chairs, dilapidated furniture. It looked like junk to me. I couldn't imagine why they wanted it.

But then they would set to work, realigning drawers, securing wobbly legs, scraping off layers of paint, and applying coats of varnish. The results were stunning. Soon they had a house full of treasures, looking as beautiful as the day they were made.

I found it nearly impossible to imagine what this "junk" could become, but they could see it. This couple had a gift for spotting the potential in a piece of used furniture. They could see possibility and a future, while I could see only its present state of disrepair.

There's a saying that "God doesn't make junk," and I believe it. I think God sees potential in us beyond what we can imagine. When we look at ourselves, we are often so aware of our deficiencies, our faults, our shortcomings. But in God's eyes we are full of beauty, potential, and possibility. God has no difficulty loving us as we are, but God can also envision what we could be, even when we are too blind to see it. And it is God's work to "make all things new." So God sets to work in us, loving us back to health and wholeness, teaching us, forming us, guiding us, saving us.

You are a beautiful work in progress. —*Brother David Vryhof,* SSJE

Disguises

You know that sometimes Satan comes as a man of peace.
— BOB DYLAN, "MAN OF PEACE"

A friend and I ride mountain bikes on a somewhat regular basis. The state park where we ride is awash in flora and fauna. Every trip we see squirrels, birds, occasionally wild turkey, and deer, in addition to the thousands of species of plant life.

All of this amazes me. Even though I live not far from there and the habitat at home looks a lot like the park, it's like being immersed in a faraway place once we enter the trees and begin peddling. However, the thing that amazes me the most are the deer and the way they react toward us when we're on the bikes.

As long as we stay on the bike—we can even stop and put a leg down but not dismount—they are more curious about us than afraid. The minute we change our silhouette by stepping off the bike and putting two feet down, that's when they recognize us as potentially dangerous and, with a flick of their big white tails, turn and bound into the woods.

Oklahoma, like lots of other states, has scores of deer hunters, and even though I'm not one, the deer can't tell the difference between me and someone intent on harm. But as long as I stay on the bike, they find me curious, not dangerous.

One day, staring into the large brown eyes of a deer, I wondered how often I let potentially dangerous conditions walk up on me while I stare them in the eye, finding them curious. —*Bo Cox*

Faithful and Forgiven

Today is the feast day of Mary Magdalene, the first witness of the resurrection and sometimes called the Apostle to the Apostles. All of the stories about her in the Bible portray her as a faithful disciple of Jesus who loved and followed him to the very end, even after everyone else had deserted him.

And yet traditions grew up painting Mary Magdalene as a fallen woman. She became the Hester Prynne (the women who wore The Scarlet Letter in Nathaniel Hawthorne's novel of the same name) of the New Testament, a woman who personified sin. She became conflated with the (actually unnamed) "woman caught in adultery." She was considered a prostitute. The stories about her were embroidered, shaded, even twisted, turning her into a singularly bad woman instead of a sinner of Christ's own redeeming, just like Peter and James and John and all the rest of us.

I wonder what makes us want things to be so black or white. I wonder why someone or something must be all bad or all good instead of the mixture we all are. I wonder why we must reduce things so much that they go beyond simple into caricature, exaggerating one feature out of proportion. I wonder why a woman like Mary Magdalene seemed threatening to the early church fathers. Are we really not able to navigate the wonderful (if perplexing) complexity of human life?

We, in all our complexity, are called to be faithful followers of Jesus Christ. And we are all sinners of Christ's own redeeming. None of that is simple, or simplistic, and I am grateful for the mystery of faith shown through the life of Mary Magdalene. —*Penny Nash*

For the Sport of It

...and there is that Leviathan,
which you have made for the sport of it.

— PSALM 104:27

"For the sport of it"—I love this reminder that God enjoys creating! The Creator has such a good time making the sea and everything in it that he throws in a sea monster (a whale? a crocodile? a plesiosaur?), just for the fun of it.

We understand the sheer joy of making something; God's image in us makes us creators, too. It doesn't have to be a world-changing invention, a symphony, a painting, or a poem; we make birthday cakes, birdhouses, backyard gardens, dinners for neighbors who are sick or sad, silly jokes, stories for children. Most important, we make relationships.

We've all experienced that moment when everything comes together—the idea, the desire, the work of our hands—and the whole is so much more than the sum of the parts. Maybe we just smile, or maybe we shout out loud, "Yes! Wow! Got it!" I think that's how God felt about the Leviathan—and everything in creation, including species now extinct and ones that haven't yet appeared. I think that's how God feels about us, in all our chaotic variety. God created, and is creating, "all that is, seen and unseen," for the sheer joy of it.

We pray for those being baptized to receive "the gift of joy and wonder in all [God's] works." This is a crucial gift in a time when we're seeing the disastrous effects of our failures as God's co-creators.

How would it change our relationship with every other creature to think of God's delight in making it? How would it change us to live every day as creatures made to share the joy of creation? —*Mary W. Cox*

Praying Shapes Believing

It's been said that praying shapes believing. In other words, we grow to believe in what we pray for. We follow our heart. We live into our aspirations.

With that in mind, think today about a particular prayer, found in *The Book of Common Prayer* on page 386. It asks prayers for those who seek God or a deeper knowledge of God. That is a prayer that can apply to any of us, wherever we are in the journey. There is always a way to grow more deeply in our knowledge of God. We never come to the end of that search.

Take this day as an opportunity to think about what you will do to seek a deeper knowledge of God. How will that search unfold in your life? What specific action will you take, so that your prayer will be realized in your life? It will be worth the effort, because this prayer on page 386 concludes with a marvelous hope: "Pray that they may find and be found by him."

Seeking works both ways. Isn't that how any relationship works, at least any relationship marked by love? It suggests that our journey will be one of discovery on our part. It also says that in the process, we will come to realize that we have been found.

As you offer this prayer today, with your own journey in mind, let it shape your belief, your confidence, your hope that the search will bring you into deeper relationship with the living God. —*Jay Sidebotham*

Adjusting the Knobs

When I drove across the country with a friend years ago, radios had knobs. One was for volume, the other for sliding the little red bar across the numbers in search of a strong signal and perfect song. When I found a song we liked, we sat back and enjoyed the music while looking at the incredible landscape passing by. All was right with the world.

It wasn't long before the first bit of static was heard, then more, and I had to adjust the knob so we could hear the song clearly. Again, static and more adjustments. Eventually we had to find another station.

"We should just park the car and listen," my friend suggested in frustration.

"Or just wait out the static and see if the song returns," I replied.

The experience is similar to my life of faith. I have been blessed to travel a dramatic and wonderful road, and along the way I have found good and strong signals, ones that make me sit back, look around, and give thanks.

But my journey has also had lots of static. It starts slowly and then cannot be ignored. I have learned to adjust the knobs to stay connected, but I have also had to change stations. I've been tempted to park the car and stay where the signal is strong, but that would mean ceasing to travel. I have also been stubborn and tried to wait the static out.

Adjusting the knobs and changing the stations is part of the spiritual journey. Contrary to what some churches say, the signal can be found on more than one station. The point is to find a signal and keep it clear. But the signal is there. It just needs to be found.

It doesn't move; we do.

May we find the signal and adjust the knobs to remove the static as we travel to our ultimate destination.

—*Chip Bristol*

Sleepless Bird

I woke up early this morning—very early. It is three o'clock in the morning, and I can't sleep. Outside, a bird sings. Don't birds sleep at night? Maybe she can't sleep either.

Especially during anxious times, sleep does not come easily to me. So I am used to sleepless nights. But that does not mean I always like them. I am not a night owl. Nights, to me, are for sleeping in bed. Tossing and turning belong to trampolines.

But God does not always keep perfect time with us according to our schedule. Nor, as it turns out, do the birds. This particular bird will sing in the dark, as if to challenge the morning. She refuses to abide by the rule—be quiet at night. It's time to sleep, not to sing.

But it is quiet. And this quiet time is a gift, an unbidden gift—just like the Holy Spirit, who also often comes unbidden at this hour. This is a time when the mind wanders freely without being reined in by me—or at least by my mental treadmill that in the daytime helps me to get things done but also crowds out the song of the Spirit. Lying sleepless at night, I can often hear this song.

So I'm with Sleepless Bird. She sings to welcome the morning, whenever it will come. And she sings to welcome the Holy Spirit, whenever she will come. Sometimes "nighttime" is just overrated.

—*Joanna Leiserson*

Paddling Upstream

One day Michael and I took the kids canoeing. We are not experts; we are happy if we paddle in a straight line.

We decided to go down a small river. The river is shallow—eighteen inches or so, and we hardly had to paddle other than to steer. Shortly, the grade got steeper, and the river broke into small riffles. It was all great fun.

Michael and I belatedly remembered that we would have to paddle back up this accelerating river. Knowing that we had work ahead of us, we turned around. We paddled as hard as we could, hardly making any progress and soaking the kids, who were now crying. Our family outing had turned into a miserable trial. In defeat, we decided to portage back to the dock.

We nosed the canoe close to shore, and I jumped out to pull us in. But as I pulled the canoe, I discovered how ridiculously easy it was to pull upstream. The water was shallow, and the canoe felt light as I pulled it through the riffles, around the corner, and back to the lake.

Why had we struggled so hard to paddle up the river when it was so easy to pull the canoe? As we admitted defeat and surrendered our plans, we discovered a better way.

Our lives are filled with all sorts of these surprises. We struggle; we become exhausted. It is only when we give up our ideas of how things should be, when we surrender *our* way of doing things, that we are open to God's way. We can trust that God is eager to show us his way. —*Kristine Blaess*

Love Grows

For God so loved the world...
—John 3:16

Tomorrow I will remember, but today I recall the worry that I wouldn't be able to love enough.

Our second child was born on July 29. The day before, as I had many times throughout the pregnancy, I fretted. I loved our daughter, our firstborn, more than I ever imagined that I could. Her long toes and inquisitive eyes, her corn breath in the morning and the curl of her blonde hair on a summer afternoon. Like many first-time parents, we delighted in her every move, chronicling it with videos and pictures and loopy cursive in the scrapbooks.

How could I love another as much? Was it even possible?

And yet the moment the nurse laid our son in my arms, it happened. The capacity for love that I feared was finite expanded, and as much as I loved our daughter, I loved our son too.

That's the mystery of love, I suppose. It can grow and move and transform in ways beyond our imagining. Love defies the laws of science; it confounds logic. I know I'll never be able to fully comprehend, to understand the expanse of God's love, but I catch a glimmer every once in a while in the way that I love my own children.

With God, through God, in God, I experience this boundless love. And I am forever grateful. —*Richelle Thompson*

Jesus Is Real

On the stretch of interstate between my home in central Indiana and my parents' home in West Michigan, there's a large black billboard with white text, which I almost always notice on the trip out and the trip back. One side of the billboard reads, "JESUS IS REAL." The opposite side reads, "HELL IS REAL."

I have my thoughts about what the creators of this billboard intend, and I suspect they and I might disagree on a point or two. Nevertheless, this billboard has become for me a little reminder of the gospel message.

Yes, hell is real. I see it on television, in the newspaper, online. Hell breaks through into every day—it colors the world we live in, and so often, breaks into our own lives. Perhaps you're living through your own hell right now, your own valley of the shadow of death. Perhaps someone you know is. This hell that we encounter is ugly and painful and difficult.

The good news is, Jesus is real. *Jesus is real*! Alleluia! What is this if not gospel truth? We know the hell of poverty and despair and starvation and depression and terror—but we may also know the risen Christ, who loves us and redeems us, who empowers us to resist the powers of darkness and live into the kingdom of God.

JESUS IS REAL. Amen! —*Alissa Goudswaard*

Christmas in July

When you think of Christmas, normally stories about the birth of the Christ child, hymns, and presents come to mind. Have you heard the expression "Christmas in July"? It puts a different twist on how we think about July.

Christmas in July usually refers to the midsummer retail extravaganza! In July when things are slow, many retailers offer special deals. Many bargain hunters wait all year for this shopping opportunity.

I have a friend who anticipates Christmas in July. By summer's end, she proudly announces her shopping is done. She avoids all the frantic anxiety of the holidays.

It's true. July is the time of leisure, rest, and play. Unless we await a child of our own, we are not anticipating the rigors of birth. In July we are not seeking a place for the Christ child. So what might Christmas in July really mean?

Christmas in July can be a reminder that this season, like every season, is a time of promise. The change of pace is an invitation to notice how God continues to come to us—and in new ways. Now we see God's finger creating again and again as the earth bursts forth lush and fragrant.

In "The Summer Day," poet Mary Oliver celebrates the work of God's hand in creation. She says:

> I don't know exactly what a prayer is.
> I do know how to pay attention, how to fall down
> into the grass, how to kneel down in the grass,
> how to be idle and blessed...

This is the gift of Christmas in July!
—Karen Montagno

God of Words

Every night before we went to bed, my parents would read to us—children's books, then C. S. Lewis, and later Tolkien—my dad often nodding off midsentence. Was this what made me love stories so much, or was it hearing the gospel every Sunday? In any case, I find reading some books to be as illuminating and exhilarating as liturgy and music can be, as if I've begun to scratch the surface of reality to see the meaning of the world.

As the Rt. Rev. James Mathes, bishop of the Diocese of San Diego, said at an Episcopal Communicators Conference I attended, "We know that God moves in and around and through words." After all, "the Word was with God and the Word was God" (John1:1).

Words and stories are how we know ourselves and make sense of our history and our faith. We connect the dots as best we can with words, telling a story to ourselves about cause and effect, how we got from there to here. Life is complex, and stories are one way we can encompass even a fraction of it.

God seems to me just as complex. In the Bible, God is oblique, sometimes inscrutable and surprising, transcendent, like the best stories.

Perhaps this is why scripture contains more stories than edicts, and why Jesus taught most often through parables. Proclamations are liable to oversimplify the message. A story leaves us usefully confused, reminding us that words are just the beginning, a lens to help us see a world that we can only begin to understand, a gateway into the deep and complicated reality of God. —*Jeremiah Sierra*

Hostage from Love

There are hundreds of billions of galaxies in the known universe, each containing two hundred to four hundred billion stars. The vastness of our universe is mind-boggling. Cosmologists are of the belief that we humans don't have sufficient imagination to even consider all that is out there. We are all born of the cosmic dust of the universe and into that dust is infused the miracle of Love. Where does that ultimate gift of God come from? How did it weave itself into the DNA of our consciousness? Is it possible that the engine driving the formation of our universe is the explosive and uncontainable power of God's Love?

Love is the engine that powers our known universe; it is the engine that binds our connection to God, and it is the most powerful force in the universe even when it remains hidden from view. Our story of faith is a story pointing in the direction of Love, a Love higher than our own limited human egos.

Jesus was and remains the full expression of divine Love Incarnate in human form. As believers we affirm that the power of his Love was already present at the moment of the "Big Bang" that gave birth to the universe and creation.

Are you holding yourself hostage from Love? Are you missing the gift of Love? Angels are whispering into your ears: "Don't be held hostage from Love; it is all around you and it is the very core of your being." Indeed Love is what birthed and shaped you from the moment our infinite universe was created. God's Love was woven into your DNA. Don't be a hostage from Love! —*Wilfredo Benitez*

Lifesaving

I was making sandcastles with my dad and my son Ethan at the beach. The waves and rip current kept most surfers away, but we noticed two men with rental surfboards, one white and one blue. They entered the surf and were quickly carried dangerously to the north. The lifeguard jumped from her station and hit the sand running with a bright red flotation device. She sprinted a hundred yards and pointed at the man on the white surfboard, shouting something. He immediately paddled to shore. She ran through the waves and instantly was next to the surfer on the blue board. Without slowing down, she placed herself between him and the jetty and towed him around to the other side. Five minutes later, she came jogging back to her post with no fanfare, no reporters, and no picture in the paper.

My dad walked over to the station to talk to the lifeguard. Dad asked, "Did you save that surfer's life?"

Catching her breath but keeping her eyes fixed on the shoreline, she replied, "Yes, I did."

I wonder how many lives get saved on a daily basis, unnoticed. Everyday heroes make a big difference with little or no fanfare.

One day Jesus noticed an ordinary man named Nathanael. Jesus pointed toward him and exclaimed enthusiastically, "Now here is a genuine son of Israel—a man of complete integrity!" (John 1:47). There were no reporters, no pictures in the paper, and no standing around in glory. It was all part of a day's work for Jesus and another unsung hero.

May all of us become the everyday heroes that God intended and be as surprised as Nathanael when the Lord recognizes us.
—*Dave Marshall*

Poured Out

Have you ever read Marge Piercy's wonderful poem "To Be of Use"? When I first encountered it, I was taken by the opening lines: "The people I love the best jump into work head first...and swim off with sure strokes almost out of sight." That describes my dearest friends and many of the people I admire. They are decisive; they commit to a thing, go all-in, and head for deep water without second-guessing.

But as I came back to the poem, it was the last lines that held me: "The pitcher cries for water to carry, and a person for work that is real."

I have long been attracted to pitchers of all kinds and sizes, without quite knowing why. I've bought handmade vessels at craft shows, pottery pieces in the Southwest, and crystal ones at yard sales. Piercy's poem made me realize it is not just the design or shape that calls me, but the potential for usefulness—the inherent ability to do something necessary, useful, and meaningful.

Isn't this what we all seek in some way? To be filled up and poured out, over and over? To find a purpose in our lives, something we can do that matters, that makes a difference, that helps our corner of the world?

Isn't this what Jesus taught us with loaves and fishes, mustard seeds, and stories of good shepherds and Samaritans? To feed, to heal, to love. To be real. Certainly this is what he modeled for us with symbols at the Last Supper and with suffering hours later at his crucifixion: "For this is my blood of the new covenant, poured out for many for the forgiveness of sins" (Matthew 26:28).

The work Jesus gave to his disciples then and to us now, to do in memory of him, is to become pitchers—constantly filled, emptied, and refilled—of love and service, poured out for each other and the glory of God. It doesn't get any more real than that.

—*Janet Rehling Buening*

Clutter

Clutter fills our lives. We are surrounded by the remains of things that once were useful, and we continue to fill our lives with things we are told we cannot live without. Our lives can also be filled with spiritual clutter—practices, incomplete thoughts, and indiscernible motions.

We often consider spring to be the season for cleaning, but I would suggest that summer might actually be the time for taking inventory, establishing the difference between our needs and wants, and then acting on them to design a well-planned, streamlined spiritual life. Why summer, you ask? Summer generally includes a time set apart for taking a break, to visit with people close to us, and to rest. So in addition to going on an intentional retreat, summer might be the best time to identify the clutter and set a plan in motion to clear it out.

Spiritual clutter keeps us from knowing God and knowing ourselves. My elders often remind us of that fact. I have a new mantra that might help. "You do not know whose you are until you know who you are." When we are well-cared for, when we understand the difference between our needs and wants, we begin to recognize the clear path that leads us again to our God and Creator.

I hope you have had a rest this summer and time to clear out the clutter. —*Debbie Royals*

With You Always

Remember, I am with you always.
— MATTHEW 28:20

For many of us, it's in learning to pray the whole range of our feelings that we encounter most fully the tenderness of Christ. Even if we feel utterly lost or abandoned, we are not alone.

Years ago, my husband and I were in a neonatal intensive care unit, bending over our newborn daughter. After a four-hour struggle, she died in our arms. I was filled with grief and rage. For weeks thereafter I spent long stretches of prayer simply sobbing and pounding a pillow on the floor as waves of feeling passed through. There was no other way to be real in prayer. It was here or nowhere that I would find God, here or nowhere that God would find me.

One afternoon, boiling with anger, I imagined hurling my fists against a wall. But then the image changed: I realized that I was beating my fists, not against a wall, but against Jesus' chest. I was raging and pounding within his embrace. The anger was still there, and the fierce need to express it, but everything had changed: I was feeling it now within the embrace of love. Like a canopy, love enclosed and embraced all that was in me. All that I felt and needed so urgently to communicate—all this was received, accepted, understood, and blessed.

Yes, I was still angry, but now I was also amazed, surprised, and grateful. Love had found me in my anger. The part of me that was most raw and violent, even to the depths of despair, had been met, held, and touched by Love. Healing had begun. Healing was here.

—*Margaret Bullitt-Jonas*

Transfiguration

Then from the cloud came a voice that said,
"This is my Son, my Chosen; listen to him!"

— LUKE 9:35

Watching *Antiques Roadshow* on public television is a witness to transfiguration, in a way. That odd bowl that great-grandma would never allow anyone to pitch into the garbage, even though everyone in the family tried, turns out to be a rare example of pottery from a long-forgotten women's religious community. And it's also worth quite a bit. Nothing changed, really, about the bowl itself. It's still an awful shade of green that matched the whipped pistachio salad Aunt Gertrude made for Thanksgiving each year. But now, someone showed us the real value by explaining what it was. Someone showed us a value we ourselves may have been incapable of seeing.

When Peter, James, and John go with Jesus to the mountaintop, Jesus doesn't change. He goes up the mountain the Son of God. And he comes down the mountain the Son of God. Yes, his face shone and his clothes became a dazzling white, but who Jesus is—the Son of God—is the same. But in this moment, along with Moses and Elijah, God has explained, in a particular way, who Jesus is to those who will hear.

God's son. God's Chosen. The one we should listen to.

God shares the deep value of Jesus, a value of which we may be unaware at times. We'd rather listen to our own egos, our own agendas, even our own fears. God, however, reminds us the source of real wealth in life.

In the unexpected and odd, God shows us the wealth of our lives in Christ. —*Laurie Brock*

Transformation

On this day, in 2012, I would finish my 360-mile pilgrimage across Ireland. Black Valley rests under the watchful eye of the Macgillycuddy's Reeks. The reeks are a "black stack" of glacial rock. Walking here was like moving through the history of Irish civilization. Long-abandoned rock structures, once small, rustic homes to eighteenth-century farmers, stand alongside the modern houses of fourth-generation sheepherders.

The ascent began at an active farmhouse. A tall, grand stone from an ancient people stood proudly, yet as commonplace as the barn. The fifteen-foot stone was a reminder of the Irish interweaving of the ancient and the postmodern—though I doubt the people living in this valley are aware they are traveling in a transitional, post-Christian world. If told, they would simply raise an eyebrow.

Having climbed above the farmhouse across the hill of black rock, I sat down for a drink of water. My eyes fell on three standing stones not twenty-five yards away. There in the flow of human time, I was alone to marvel in another's belief, culture, ritual, and the mystical cycle of life.

There was some odd justice that the final day would be my longest. Twenty-three days of mystical exhilaration compressed into the exhaustion of twelve hours. Pilgrimage is more than a walk—it is a way of life to be embraced with every morsel of being, the personal renaissance of the inner beautiful, the haunting, the frightening, the hated, the adored, the soft, the cruel, the humorous, the damaged, the hilarious, the pitiful, every sliver of our conscious and our unconscious, to be claimed as our own.

Pilgrimage: the journey of who we are, and who we are being transformed into. —*Gil Stafford*

The Runaway Bunny's Mom

One of my favorite books to read to small children is Margaret Wise Brown's classic, *The Runaway Bunny*.

In recent years I've seen the book criticized as a dreadful parable of the worst sort of helicopter parenting. I shake my head. This book is for toddlers, who need to know that Mom is near as they begin to explore. But I secretly think this book is for all of us.

Years ago I went to a reflection day in a crabby, rebellious mood; things had not been going my way that week, and the day of silence and contemplation just wasn't working for me either.

I sat there, inwardly wailing, "Lord, I don't love you at all! I don't love my husband or my daughter or my parents or my friends or poor people, and I really, really don't like myself!"

And God spoke to me. I didn't hear an audible voice, but I was completely aware of the words and of a tone of tender parental amusement: "Don't worry. I'm not going to let you get away."

Just like the Runaway Bunny's mother, saying, "If you run away, I will run after you. For you are my little bunny."

If you know the story, you know the mother promises that if her child becomes a rock on the mountain, she'll climb to him; if he's a flower in a hidden garden, she'll be the gardener; and if he's a sailboat, she'll be the wind. In the end, he decides to stay home, and she gives him a carrot.

Does that sound familiar? Doesn't God seek us, tend us, feed us? Isn't the Spirit the wind in our sails?

We don't have to worry—God will always find us. —*Mary W. Cox*

Sitting Down

Then they came to Capernaum;
and when he was in the house he asked them,
"What were you arguing about on the way?"

—MARK 9:33

This gospel reading is perplexing. Here we find Jesus retreating with his disciples. They have just come from a crowd where Jesus cast out a demon. He wants to spend time alone with his disciples, teaching them. But what he teaches them sounds crazy! He tells them that he will be betrayed and killed, and then will rise from the dead in three days. I mean, what kind of teacher says that?

Naturally, they have no idea what he's talking about. They are confused, uncomfortable, stuck in that awkward moment like junior high school boys at their first dance. They just don't get it. They are afraid to ask him what he meant. You can imagine the awkward silence that follows. They keep walking down the road a bit. Then from the back of the group an argument breaks out. Soon everyone is involved. They are arguing about who is the greatest.

So, what does Jesus do? He sits down. Now that seems to me to be significant. He sits down. He doesn't chastise the disciples, yell at them, or berate them. He sits down and calls them over. Then he says, "Whoever wants to be first must be last of all and servant of all" (Mark 9:35). First being last, last being first? It just doesn't compute. You can imagine the disciples' confusion, because it matches ours.

What might all this mean for us today? Where do we find Jesus sitting down with us? Where are we called to serve, to be last instead of first? —*Aaron Klinefelter*

226

The Things We Cannot Hold

"Water is something you cannot hold," writes Ann Carson in her essay, "The Anthropology of Water." She continues, "Like men. I have tried. Brother, lover, true friends, hungry ghosts, and God." I don't quite understand these lines, but I like them. This is how I often feel when I read the work of Carson, but I keep coming back to it. This passage hints at how difficult it can be to hold on to each other and to God, how if we hope to grasp each other completely, we'll fail. Complete understanding is impossible.

Which is fine. I participate in many things which I cannot quite understand. Praying, for example, and kissing. There is some part of us that is drawn to certain mysteries, that yearns for touch, to hold each other. Poetry and prayer (and kissing) might be perfectly understandable to some, but I feel that they are somewhat mysterious, like the Eucharist, like so many of Jesus' words, like much of life.

This used to bother me. I wanted some systematic way to make sense of the world and my faith, but the tighter I grasped at understanding, the more it slipped through my fingers. Fortunately, at some point I stopped worrying and just decided to participate, to be a part of a community, to pray sometimes, and to read poetry and recognize that it moves me. The mystery draws us in. The mechanics will take care of themselves. —*Jeremiah Sierra*

Attitude of Gratitude

Even after all this time the sun never says to the earth, "you owe me."
Look what happens with a love like that.
It lights up the whole sky.

— HAFIZ

Given what you know about me, you must find it startling, maybe even astonishing, that I would have days or moments where I forget to be grateful.

Usually gratitude is a constant companion; so much so that sometimes my coworkers make comments about me going above and beyond. It's not that I'm trying to be employee of the year but, rather, because I occasionally realize I have been granted a life wonderful beyond description. So it's natural to pay that gift forward by making a little effort beyond what's required of me. Sometimes I'm not even conscious of it; I'm just happy to be there, and when I am, it shows.

When I get out of this mindset, this state of grace, is when I begin to focus on me—what's in it for me; my rights; don't you know who I am? These are all dangerous attitudes for me, and despite the fact that I have every reason in the world to be grateful, just let me start to view the world through those filters and I can find something wrong with it.

I'm fifty. My contemporaries are working on retirement and are paying off their second houses. I have a long way to go. There are jobs that are out of my reach because of my past. My car's old and plain. This list can become endless.

However, so can this one: Every moment is a gift I am not guaranteed and can't earn. —*Bo Cox*

The Woman Bore a Sinister Son, and Named Him Ellis

The story of Samson is powerful. Samson was blessed with supernatural strength and performed great feats. In Judges 13, we learn that the boy grew and the Lord blessed him.

Although my son Ellis has never wrestled a lion or destroyed a temple, and doesn't derive power from his hair (though he had it very long at one point), I know he is blessed and possesses great strength. How else can I explain the fact that when he was just fifteen, he began cooking, exercising, and lost almost a hundred pounds? That he knows Latin, Greek, and is learning Chinese? That when he was seventeen, he moved to Boston to begin college? That at twenty, he received two college degrees, and at twenty-one moved to Chicago to pursue a master's? Surely God's supernatural blessing is the cause.

Ellis is the biggest blessing and most precious gift God has bestowed upon me. I never imagined carrying that beautiful, left-handed boy for nine months would lead to twenty-one years (and counting) of joy, pride, and valuable lessons.

Clearly, I am a very proud parent! So is God! If God was on any social network, the posts would be filled with pictures and stories of *you*! God knows how many hairs are on your head and named you! God is proud to be your parent! God might not have Facebook, but God definitely has a Faithbook where you can read how God sees you: important, valuable, and precious enough to die for you.

By the way, *sinister* is the Latin word for left-handed.

Happy Lefties Day, Ellis! —*Sandra Montes*

The Ladies Who Let Their Light Shine

My mother was a nurse. Beating the odds as a black woman in the 1950s, she graduated from Meharry Medical College, taking the Nightingale Pledge. But as a child, I had a great fear of doctors, hospitals, nurses, thermometers, and needles!

Over the course of my life, I observed my mother's sure calling. There were times when her keen eye resulted in someone seeking needed medical attention. I have seen her calm a person's wild-eyed fear with a touch of compassion.

During times of illness, she would keep her vigil, peering through the dim of lamplight. I felt the presence of her quiet, confident hands checking, arranging, and soothing. These were the hands of a nurse.

Florence Nightingale, the pioneer of nursing, was born in 1820 into a wealthy family who expected her to follow social conventions, marry well, and raise a family. However, from a young age, Florence had a calling to acts of mercy, attending to the poor and sick. By her teens, against her family's wishes she began to educate herself to pursue nursing. It was during her ministry to soldiers during the Crimean War that her reputation was established as a trainer of nurses and advocate for patient care and sanitary hospital conditions.

Florence became known as the Lady with the Lamp because of the nightly rounds she made carrying a lamp, keeping watch over her patients. In her later life, despite ill health, she remained a widely respected health care advocate and prolific writer until her death on August 13, 1910.

I have heard both of these women called extraordinary. Their lives invite us to consider where God is calling us to lift our lamps with dedication and compassion. —*Karen Montagno*

Riding Waves

"No, not this one."

"No, wait, the right wave is coming."

Suddenly the dark shadow on the ocean's surface grew until it became a big, perfect wave, and my son and I rode it all the way in to shore.

Every summer I was fortunate enough to live at the beach, and, more than any other activity, riding waves was my favorite thing to do. I loved the excitement of seeing a wave coming my way, committing to it, and then feeling the moment when you know you have caught it. Just writing about it gets my heart beating more quickly, but it was not something I was good at from the start. I have missed more waves than I've caught, been tossed to the bottom—"boiled" as we called it— more times than I can count, and impatiently took waves that did not end up delivering a good ride.

Like every memory and experience I've had, there's something to learn from riding waves. To this day, I long for the perfect wave, the one meant for me, that will carry me to the shore—but it's not as easy as it looks. Maybe there's nothing like a perfect wave. There are waves that look promising but never develop, waves taken because of misguided enthusiasm that aren't the right ones for me. There are also those that have minds of their own and throw me to the ocean floor. But even in the waiting, the missing, and the throwing, there is joy just to be riding waves. Maybe that is the real lesson in all of this.

Happy last days of summer. —*Chip Bristol*

Lord, Let Me Trust You

"It is a good land that the Lord is giving us," the spies reported. It *is* a good land. Our God, the one who brought us out of slavery and provided for us in the desert, is giving it to us. Right now he is giving it to us.

And the people were afraid. In the midst of promise, in the midst of blessing, they cried out, "Why does God hate us?"

I am not alone in crying out against God in the midst of blessing. I am not alone in mistaking favor and grace for something else—abandonment, challenge perhaps? The Israelites cried out against the Lord, and for a whole generation they lost the opportunity to enter the land. God waited to show them the land again until all the faithless had died in the wilderness. The wilderness seemed more like blessing to them than did the land, flowing with milk and honey.

Lord, where did we pick up the habit of turning to you with hard hearts? I can feel the hardness in my own heart. Please soften me and redeem me for another day. Remove my fear and my struggling against you. Let me be soft, broken, and whole for you. Lord, give me faith. Let me trust you as we move into this new land you are giving us.

Thank you for letting us see your favor. We praise you and glorify you. You are our Lord. —*Kristine Blaess*

Live Without Fear

Live without fear: your Creator has made you holy,
has always protected you, and loves you as a mother.
Go in peace to follow the good road
and may God's blessing be with you always. Amen.

— SAINT CLARE

How many times each month/week/day do you act (or react, or not act) out of fear? If you're anything like me, the answer is more than you'd like to admit. Fear of failure, fear of conflict, fear of the unknown, fear of being alone, even fear of success—these fears can easily become prisons.

A life in Christ, though, is not a life lived in fear. Christ "came that [we] may have life, and have it abundantly" (John 10:10b). Fear doesn't really lend itself well to abundant living. Abundant life is living in the knowledge that we are loved and accepted by Christ. We're reminded that "there is no fear in love, but perfect love casts out fear" (1 John 4:18a). There is no fear in love. There is no fear in God.

What might you do if you could conquer your fear? How might your life be different if you approached it fearlessly? Living without fear is not a one-time decision or a sudden change; it is a process. That process, though, undertaken with intention and persistence, has the power to lead into an abundant and fearless life in Christ.

—*Alissa Goudswaard*

Busy

Everybody is busy. This seems to be a given, although to be honest, sometimes I say I am busy because I don't want people to think I'm slacking off. We seem to worship busy-ness in our society. And truly, many people really are very busy.

But all this being busy makes it much harder for us to grow spiritually. Our souls begin to dry up when we are always going without ceasing, when we can never stop to smell the roses or sit with a friend and gaze at the sunset or simply be. Just as the body cannot develop without adequate nourishment and a combination of rest and activity, so the soul cannot grow without soul food and a combination of soulful rest and soulful exercise.

The soulful exercise Saint Paul recommends is praying without ceasing. Praying without ceasing doesn't mean being on our knees in church or beside our beds 24/7. We pray without ceasing even while we are living our lives in the world. Praying without ceasing is being always aware of our Creator and in constant awe of God's creation. It is loving our neighbors near and far, even while we are out doing our daily business. It is paying attention to how we live our lives, ever aspiring to be faithful every day, connecting our shopping and our bill paying and our volunteering and our working with who we hear God calling us to be.

And so, if we must be busy, let us be busy in prayer, in rest, in reflection, in being, and in living love. —*Penny Nash*

Becoming a Presence of Peace

In her book, *Walk in a Relaxed Manner*, Joyce Rupp describes seven weeks of walking five hundred miles across Spain on El Camino de Santiago, an ancient pilgrimage route. As armchair participants, we might picture saints, faces aglow, lost in lofty thought, but the walkers who take on this challenge are human beings like us who face the nitty-gritty of their own limitations.

A friend of mine who walked the Camino told me about the lack of privacy in hostels, the fifteen-pound backpack limit, the discomforts that could grind the walk to a halt, and the situations in which she had to let go of expectations. Wise choices were necessary, and the most significant underlying choice was to trust God—both in a general sense and in the specifics.

Our own lives may seem humdrum in contrast to walking all those miles, but in daily life, I believe the choice to trust God in concrete circumstances is similar and can propel us forward in faith. We will be changed for the better.

Each morning, I borrow a line from Joyce Rupp's pilgrimage prayer: "Strengthen your love within me that I may be a presence of your peace..." God alone can strengthen love within me and create peace that isn't just for my comfort, but given in God's generosity as a presence for others. My peace can sometimes be elusive; then I pray yet again, "Strengthen your love within me."

Becoming a presence of peace is so far beyond me that I ask for the Almighty's creativity. I try to keep walking, to trust for the long haul, and to stay ready for embracing God's gracious response.

—*June Terry*

Back to Basics

Lord, you have searched me out and known me.

— PSALM 139:1

At my orientation to Union Theological Seminary a number of years ago, James Forbes, homiletics professor and soon to be senior pastor of Riverside Church, addressed the incoming students.

Those were heady days. As new students, we were filled with anticipation about study at this fine, historic institution. We were honored to walk the halls where Neibuhr and Tillich and Bonhoeffer had taught. We were ready to dive into deep and rigorous academic work. Many of us had worked quite hard and taken big leaps to arrive at that first day. We were ready to hear what Dr. Forbes had to say to us.

He offered a simple piece of advice. He said: "Memorize Psalm 139. It will change your life." I thought to myself: *This is not why I came here. I did not come all this way to memorize Bible verses, as if this course of study was an extension of Sunday School.* I did, however, take up Dr. Forbes's suggestion, as a discipline to do in the season of Lent.

While the years since make my recollection somewhat spotty, I still have an understanding of the life-changing power of these verses, which call us to remember that as our seeking unfolds, it is always preceded, surrounded, and pursued by God's knowledge and love of us.
—*Jay Sidebotham*

Stop and Listen

Jesus promises us, "the Spirit will guide you into all the truth..." (John 16:13). How? We must be still and silent.

The English word "silence" comes from the Latin, *dēsinere*, to stop. Without silence, life is full of sound and fury, signifying nothing we'll ever figure out. We need the space of silence to separate the wheat from the chaff. We take in so much information, so many stimuli in the course of a day. What is important? What do we attend to? We need a cadence of silence to claim, compare, compost our life's experiences.

Silence for the soul is like punctuation to language. Without the silencing effect of punctuation, and without space between words, it all becomes gibberish. And so with life. Without silence, without the pauses, life is like a run-on sentence, which can be crazy-making, and will not make sense. We need silence to punctuate our soul.

We need silence to attend to God's invitation and revelation today. When we listen deeply to ourselves and to one another and to God's Spirit, we will discover life's meaning. Life is not just a random series of events, like scattered musical notes; life is actually a score being orchestrated. If you will just stay with it, you'll recognize the composition, the crescendos and decrescendos, the allegros, largos, and resolutions, and you'll notice the need for the rests, which are crucial. Life is a piece—not pieces, but an orchestrated piece. If you don't really listen, all you'll hear is cacophony.

Take time today, each day, to be still and silent. Listen. "For God alone my soul in silence waits" (Psalm 62:1).

—*Brother Curtis Almquist*, SSJE

Tethered Together

Draw us in the Spirit's tether;
For when humbly, in thy name,
Two or three are met together,
Thou art in the midst of them:
Alleluia! Alleluia! Touch we now thy garment's hem.

— PERCY DEARMER

This text, by prolific hymnist and liturgist Percy Dearmer (1867-1936), often shapes my prayer before worship. Our parish (like many, I expect) has its share of interpersonal "issues." Because we are one of only two Episcopal churches in a large area of southern Illinois, we have all sorts and conditions of people under one roof. We have high, low, and broad church Episcopalians. We have liberals and conservatives. We have military personnel and pacifists, straight and gay, the well-to-do and the hard-up, young and old, and plenty of Type A personalities. All this diversity of viewpoints and beliefs and temperaments makes for pretty yeasty dough!

As a longtime active member of this parish, I'm often aware of simmering discontents. They trouble me. But when I kneel and pray Dearmer's beautiful prayer that we might all be drawn together in the Spirit's tether, the fog of concern lifts, and I glimpse the unity God intends, the gathered community where what unites us is so very much greater than what divides us. It is indeed as if I've grasped the hem of Jesus' robe. In the presence of Jesus, how can we quarrel? How can we do anything, really, but fall to our knees—together?

I feel the Spirit's tether around us as a web, soft as silk and strong as love, knitting us up. And I'm inexpressibly thankful. —*Betsy Rogers*

A Still and Quiet Soul

I do not occupy myself with great matters,
or with things too hard for me.
But I still my soul and make it quiet.

— PSALM 131:1B-2A

The psalmist's words might be a bit challenging if you are not practiced at being still and quiet. Of course, it is not easy to be still and quiet when there are stimuli from every direction. And why would we want to be still and quiet anyway? An old English proverb, "An idle brain is the devil's workshop," might have come from scripture: "Besides that, they learn to be idle, gadding about from house to house; and they are not merely idle, but also gossips and busybodies, saying what they should not say" (1 Timothy 5:13). But there is also truth found in contemporary wisdom. For example, William Penn is attributed to saying, "True silence is the rest of the mind; it is to the spirit what sleep is to the body, nourishment and refreshment."

In the late summer months, we find our lives filled with reasons to be active. The bounty of the earth is approaching as we are reminded of God's abundant nature in the harvest. We see visible signs of God's love for us. Our only logical response must be one of gratitude and sharing.

Take a moment, seek silence where you are not occupied by so many things, and there, in the stillness, let the Spirit bring forth the harvest of God's abundant love in you. —*Debbie Royals*

A Place for Redemption and Community

This past Sunday, I stumbled across a parish in the heart of a major metropolis I was visiting. I think that if Jesus ever attended church in flesh today, he would surely worship with this parish. What they lacked in finesse, they made up in spirit. I truly felt God's presence: an interracial gospel choir that sometimes sang off-key, but with eyes closed and an open heart; the Lord's Prayer written in both English and Spanish, but prayed aloud in Spanish.

During the Prayers of the People, we prayed for all who have died in the conflicts in Iraq and Afghanistan—for both civilians and for enemy combatants. We prayed for those members of our armed services who had recently lost their lives (and the list was both written and read aloud, beginning with John F. Bruner III, 32; Paul D. Carron, 33: Scott J. Fleming, 24…and ending with Erick Yates, 26) "that their deaths may hasten the day when we shall give up war forever."

During the service, a man who was obviously mentally ill walked down the center of the aisle and handed the sub-deacon a piece of paper which she took graciously as they continued with the service, not missing a beat. At Communion, I went up to receive the bread and wine with my purse, mindful of protecting my things; likewise the homeless came up with their roller luggage and carts. And there was a toe-tapping, honky-tonk gospel song at the end of the service.

Yes, I know that Jesus would be worshipping in this place. It is a place of redemption and community. —*Westina Matthews*

Love the Questions

Be patient toward all that is unsolved in your heart and try to love the questions themselves, like locked rooms and like books that are now written in a very foreign tongue. Do not now seek the answers, which cannot be given you because you would not be able to live them.

— RAINER MARIA RILKE, *LETTERS TO A YOUNG POET*

Faith has little, if anything, to do with certainty or clear answers. People frequently asked Jesus questions, and he either told a convoluted and never-as-obvious-as-it-seems parable or simply asked another question.

Yet we still try to answer the questions of faith. Thousands, perhaps millions, of books, letters, and treatises have been written to answer our questions. Some answers are helpful; others are simply vain human attempts at certainty that do more harm than good.

God has always been fine with our asking questions. Matriarchs and patriarchs did it from the very beginning. The disciples asked many questions. Jesus asked a few. Saints and sinners across the ages have pondered holy matters. We will discuss, ponder, even argue over the questions.

What if, however, instead of putting our greatest energy into seeking answers which, as Rilke says, we may not be able to live into, we simply lived into the answer of love. That is, after all, the answer Jesus keeps giving.

Love God. Love your neighbor. Love yourself. Live each day with love. Then, at some point, we may find that the questions become less important than the life that waits each day for us, inviting us to share not certainty, not whatever "correct" answers we may think we have, but simply the grace of love with our fellow humans. —*Laurie Brock*

The Phone

I have answered many phone calls in my career. For a year I was a receptionist at a church, and I held various administrative positions that required answering the phone. For a while, the uncertainty I felt every time I answered the phone, not knowing who would be on the other end, caused me a bit of anxiety. There were always those callers seeking comfort and human contact—parishioners, strangers, the mentally ill, salesmen. I was the intermediary between them and God, or at least between them and the church.

I got the hang of it, but it was tempting to dismiss the callers as quickly as possible. I had bulletins to print and fold, tasks to perform for the staff, and sometimes I brushed the callers off. We're all busy, and it's easy to miss the cries from others in the midst of the noise.

When I took the time to listen, however, compassion would often well up in me for the people who called.

I remember callers who seemed ill—the man who claimed he was being persecuted by the Post Office—and those who just needed to talk to someone, like the woman who wanted to tell me about the trouble she and her husband were having. It was my job to listen, and this was its own kind of ministry, the ministry of empathy. I didn't have much else I could offer from my receptionist's desk.

Need comes in many forms, as does love. Many of us are isolated and disconnected from each other. We may not know where Christ—hungry, sick, lonely—might come to us, and what we may have to offer.
—*Jeremiah Sierra*

The Story of How We Begin to Remember

This is the story of how we begin to remember.
This is the powerful pulsing of love in the vein.
— PAUL SIMON, "UNDER AFRICAN SKIES"

We are storied people. From the earliest times of humanity we gathered around campfires to hear stories. Today we gather around flickering screens to watch stories unfold before us. Radio is about stories, television is about stories, YouTube is about stories, and social media is about stories. We love hearing and watching stories, we love telling stories, and we live in stories.

There is something deeply powerful about stories. They are more than mere entertainment. They both inform and form us individually and collectively. As Christians we are particularly adept at stories. Our scriptures are stories and are, as a whole, one grand story. Our liturgies are stories that harken us back to our scriptural roots and propel us forward and outward into the stories of those beyond ourselves. Our traditions remind us of the stories of who and whose we are and our call to mission in the world.

In spite of all of that storied existence, we too often forget our own stories. We fail to remember, "the powerful pulsing of love in the vein." We begin to assume that our stories, our lives, don't matter or don't count. We tend to forget that our story needs to be told or another's story needs to be heard. We need to "begin to remember" the story of God and how we all are part of that unfolding narrative. Our scriptures, liturgies, traditions, and communities are all part of that remembering of our story. —*Aaron Klinefelter*

Cows and Katydids

Last week I went to the county fair to see the Grand Champion cow. I love cows. I love the lazy flick of their tails that belie their strength, their deep piercing eyes, and the fact that as beautiful as they are, they will never make great household pets. I can safely adore them from a distance.

The county fair is a celebration of earthly abundance. Cows, sheep, and pigs vie for the honor of most perfect cow shape, or sheep shape, or pig shape. In other tents, proud folk compete for prizes for the reddest tomato, the biggest zucchini, and the biggest pumpkin.

I go to the fair to see what amazing things people can do on their plots of land. I do not have cows; I have cats. My zucchini plant rotted after the first zucchini; my one houseplant died from neglect.

For the earthly abundance around my house, I give all credit to God: The katydids and crickets are flourishing. I can hear them when evening comes. Chirps, rattles, and beeps explode from the midst of every tree. There must be gazillions of these creatures hiding in the trees.

As summer wears on, displays of God's creative abundance beckon for our attention. The bugs sound like an audio track of jungle sounds. Hillsides drape themselves in neon green ballgowns. Thunderstorms dump massive raindrops that look like little dancing men on the street.

In the fullness of summer, I can see God's glory everywhere, but especially in the trees with the katydids—and at the county fair with the cows, and where humans bring all that glory together into one big tent. —*Joanna Leiserson*

Change and Changelessness

Many people are uncomfortable with change. It often forces us to alter our routines and confront our habits, prejudices, or ways of thinking.

Our world is changing, both for better and for worse. Singer/songwriter Bob Dylan said it well in a song: "Come gather 'round people, wherever you roam, and admit that the waters around you have grown…Then you better start swimmin', or you'll sink like a stone, for the times they are a-changin'." Prophetic indeed, as we witness change brought about by economic and environmental crises and the demands of living in a globalized and diverse world.

These times require active and proactive engagement through steadfast love, compassion, understanding, peace, service, education, and reconciliation. The good news for us, as we seek God in the midst of the changes and challenges in the world, is that we worship and are loved by a God who is unchanging, who is steadfast in love and grace. While the tidal wave of change swells around us, we hold fast to the secure and unmovable foundation in Jesus Christ our Lord. No matter what happens in our collective and individual lives, no matter what changes, we hold fast to our faith and our identity as God's beloved children—the disciples and heralds of the good news.

It is my hope and prayer that the church will rise, meet, and respond to the changes and challenges of these times by remaining transfixed in the Spirit and love of God at all times and in all places—in other words, unchanged when it comes to faith. It is my hope and prayer that we will remain anchored in the Word of God and will strive daily to affect positive change in the community and wider world. In doing so, I believe the church will truly be meaningful and transformative in ways that heal, reconcile, liberate, and serve. Are you ready for that? —*Owen C. Thompson*

A Time to Leave, A Time to Learn

My son Andrew and I left late one afternoon in August to drive three hundred miles to take him to college for the first time. I'm sure we got a late start because I was looking for excuses to put off the inevitable. I considered spending the night along the way to make it all seem more distant. We drove on, arriving mercifully far too tired to think about the next day.

We got to the dorm the next morning and unloaded his belongings into what seemed too small a space. Then, though I had sworn I would not, I unpacked his things. I neatly folded every pair of pants and every T-shirt, and placed them in his drawers. I made his bed. I bought supplies.

There were orientation events. One mother told about her daughter, who had been a freshman the year before. She cried a lot. I found that particularly unhelpful. At least it delayed the good-bye.

Finally the time came. Andrew walked me to the car. I worked hard not to embarrass him. I didn't start crying until he was out of sight. And then I cried, sobbed really, for three hundred miles home.

I visited my college student son not too long after. He emerged from his room with that smile I have always loved. He hugged me. When I went in, I noticed that he had printed a picture of his family, even his little brother, for his bulletin board.

Jesus said, "Those who want to save their life will lose it, and those who lose their life for my sake will find it." In order for new life to emerge, something of the old life has to die. Tears are okay.

—*Stacy Sauls*

Lift Up Your Hearts

With a small group of interfaith activists protesting oil drilling in the Arctic, I kneel at the doors of the Department of Energy in Washington, D. C. The pavement under my knees is hard. At home, I pray on a meditation cushion, but there's no cushion today, just the weight of my body on stone. I lift up my hands. I'm dressed for Holy Communion, in alb and stole. I might as well hold out my arms as I do for Communion.

Instead of pews of parishioners, I see ranks of police. I'm afraid. I've never been arrested before. My body tenses as I place myself against the cops, the Feds, the law. I close my eyes. One by one, we pray aloud. Then I notice that behind the fear, something else is welling up: I am jubilant. I feel as defiant as a maple seedling that pushes up through asphalt. It is God I love, and God's green earth. I want to bear witness to that love even in the face of hatred or indifference, even if the cost is great.

So what if our numbers are small? So what if, in the eyes of the police and the world, we have no power? I sense the power that is ours to wield, the power of self-offering. We may have nothing else, but we have the power to say: "This is where I stand. This is what I love. Here is something for which I willingly put my body on the line." I never knew that stepping beyond the borders of what is comfortable could make me so happy—that shifting from self-preservation to self-offering could awaken so much joy. —*Margaret Bullitt-Jonas*

Living in the Comfort of the Holy Spirit

A year ago, my family suffered a terrible loss—my parents' house burned down. I was at work and felt my phone vibrating. I looked and saw the terrible news—our family home was in flames. As soon as I was able, I fell to my knees as I often do when faced with an emergency, raised my arms to God, and prayed between sobs for my family.

As I drove to my parents' house, praying, I calmed myself down by reminding myself that I had to comfort my niece Alissa and mom, Mami, who had been in the house when the fire broke out. I gathered myself and saw Mami, Alissa, my son Ellis, and the three dogs facing the burning house. We held each other tight as they recounted the events. I was able to keep my composure while I looked at the smoke threatening to take away all traces of any memory etched in the walls.

Although we shed some tears, all of us smiled and were thankful because we knew God was in control and every living being was safe. We knew, as the people in Acts 9:31, that we must live in the comfort of the Holy Spirit. People asked us why we were so calm. Some even doubted the damage was severe, since we could laugh and smile.

Yes, there was severe damage. Yes, we are still recovering. Yes, it was uncomfortable, sad, scary, and unbelievable. And yes, we are still resting in the knowledge that there is One who holds, listens, and protects. —*Sandra Montes*

In the Service of Others

The best way to find yourself
is to lose yourself in the service of others.

— MAHATMA GANDHI

Our Christian faith and Baptismal Covenant call us to respect the dignity of every human being. Labor Day is a day on which we honor the fruit of our labors and the worth of workers everywhere. Many have fallen on hard times in recent years and still others find themselves struggling to make ends meet. It seems as though the ideal of working toward something that in the end not only secures our own well-being, but also secures the well-being of others, is getting lost.

Jesus calls us to love our neighbor as ourselves. It is a call to serve others and care for the needs of others; it is a call to move beyond our own needs in consideration of the rest.

Labor Day affords us an opportunity to consider the working class, the engine that drives our nation, and the question of economic justice. Do we stand in the tradition of the biblical prophets, who relentlessly call us to the practice of justice? Do we stand in the tradition of Jesus, who served as an inspiration to the venerable Mahatma Gandhi in the service of others?

Labor Day is more than just a holiday marking the end of the summer season. As the summer season draws to a close, why not consider losing yourself in the service of others by standing on the side of economic justice? In the process you may discover the gift of experiencing unimagined beauty and grace fueled by the deepest love. —*Wilfredo Benitez*

Sticks and Stones

My heart was hot within me;
While I pondered, the fire burst into flame;
I spoke out with my tongue.

— PSALM 39:4

"Sticks and stones may break my bones, but words will never hurt me." I remember my parents offering this advice that I could brandish as a defense. And I think I've encouraged my own kids to use it on occasion.

But as an adult, I know that it's just wrong. I've skinned my knees, stubbed my toes, and twisted an ankle, but those hurts don't wake me at night. The pain of a mean-spirited jab, a precision-guided insult, or a muttered slight lingers far longer than any physical injury. Band-Aids and kisses can't repair the damage.

And yet even knowing that words can inflict such lasting hurt, I sometimes lash out, like the psalm writer, with anger or indignation boiling inside. At times, I can swallow back. But in other situations, my tongue rushes ahead of my heart and mind—and I deliver words that are hot and scathing. And sadly the targets of the verbal barrage are all too often the people I love most: my husband and children, my mom and dad. Sometimes it's coworkers and friends too.

I've been reading and studying about the Rule of Saint Benedict. Perhaps I'm not alone in the world and across the centuries of having trouble controlling my tongue. Consider that the first rule written by Saint Benedict in the 500s is to listen.

Later in Psalm 39, the writer beseeches the Lord, "Deliver me from all my transgressions." In my prayers today, I'll add, "Help me to hold my tongue, to open my ears. To listen." —*Richelle Thompson*

A Good Fight

Jacob was left alone;
and a man wrestled with him until daybreak.

— GENESIS 32:24

Jacob has tangled with others his entire life. Now he has fled his father-in-law's household with all his possessions. This puts him on a path straight into the hands of his brother Esau. Jacob believes that Esau is angry enough to kill him for usurping his birthright.

Terrified, Jacob prays to God for deliverance. Then he hedges his bets by offering Esau a generous peace offering. As night falls, Jacob takes refuge across the river. He is alone when he is attacked by a man who wrestles with him until daybreak.

This is no ordinary fight. This nighttime contest has divine consequences. Jacob is engaged in a "good fight." It ends in blessing and a character adjustment signified by Jacob's new name—Israel. This mysterious bout may just be an encounter with God! Encounters with God always end in transformation.

Jacob is at a crossroad. Running has not saved him from a night of struggle. Like him, many of us shy away from conflict, especially when we desperately need to change the direction of our lives. We have been taught that it is not good to fight. But not all struggle is bad.

In fact, struggle is almost always a prerequisite for growth, change, or reconciliation. We know this when it comes to aging, athletics, and academics. What about our relationships or spiritual lives? In the first letter of Timothy we read, "Fight the good fight of the faith; take hold of eternal life to which God has called you" (6:12). Was Jacob's prayer answered in this extraordinary encounter? —*Karen Montagno*

Recognizing Holy Space

My elders talk about the *yo ania*, the place of mystery—not necessarily physical space, but sometimes a state of mind. The *sea ania* or *seyewailo* is described as a place of complete beauty and harmony. We say it is located beneath the dawn in a place filled with flowers, water, and natural abundance of all kinds. The *sea ania* is a spiritual place; a place to encounter God, *Itom Achi*.

Place is a very important concept in the Pascua Yaqui tradition. It is the place of origin and begins to define our identity. From this perspective, land and creation are very specific places. However, there is a broader connection. We become aware of creation and Creator in diverse ways, but they all point to the same relationship. God made all of creation and no matter where we are, we can encounter God there.

Why do we want to know where to find God? We associate sacred space as a place where God dwells. Sometimes that means we think we need to be in a church, synagogue, temple, or mosque in order to find God. When we recognize that God is in all places and in all times, we open up opportunities to be with God no matter where we are.

With this in mind, stop for a moment and locate yourself in God's creation. God is there with you in that holy space.

—*Debbie Royals*

Saints on Earth and in Heaven

As for the holy ones in the land,
they are the noble in whom is all my delight.

PSALM 16:3 (NRSV)

In reading Psalm 16, I rejoice in the individuals of my faith community. I identify characteristics for thanksgiving, such as someone's sincere faith mixed with humor or another's intelligence well-blended with compassion. And there's the soprano who sings hymns in her sleep with such gusto that she awakens her husband. Delightful earthly saints!

In some churches, specific saints in heaven have a calendar date on which they are remembered. I keep my own list of delightful saints who live in God's direct presence. They're on my list because of the way they lived the Christ-life on earth. I found one on a stone on Scotland's Isle of Iona, "Here lies all that could die of Bruce Kenrick, Pastor, 1920-2007." I wish I'd known him. He was preparing with expectant hope to relinquish his physical "house" because heaven was in sight. Assured of life with God as a result of Christ's resurrection, he could even add a touch of humor and ask to have it carved in stone.

In 2011, my name and birthdate were carved below my husband's dates on a headstone for our church cemetery. That, of course, makes a person think. One result is that I find it impossible to say, as some do, that my birthday is "better than the alternative," referring to death. Absence from my body will mean being present with God! How could any birthday be better than that?

We read in I John 3 that we'll be like God, for we will see him as he is—the wondrous alternative which involves transformation and, ultimately, resurrection. Breathtaking!

—*June Terry*

The Stillness of the Basement

This past week I went down into the basement. I was immediately struck by an overwhelming sense of stillness and silence. This was particularly striking because, frankly, our house doesn't see much stillness or silence these days. We have a house full of kids and pets and a perpetually vacillating stack of dirty dishes and laundry in various stages of array or disarray. You can imagine that there's rarely a moment of solitude in our home.

For the most part I don't mind this. I love the abundant creative energy, the pure physicality, and the evolving growth of our children. I love that my wife is consistently in the midst of some art project or room redesign. I love our overflowing garden and various collections of picked plants with which our kids are experimenting.

And so, I was struck by the stillness and silence when I went down into our basement. I could hear bits of footfall and laughter and maybe a cry or two upstairs. I seem to remember chairs being readied for dinner. But somehow, in the midst of those strangely distant noises, I felt a sacredness descend upon me as I undertook whatever errand I was on at the time. And for a brief moment, I was present with myself and our house and our God. I was present in that way that the Spirit spoke softly to Elijah after the wind, and in the way the smoke ascends from a candle when an acolyte snuffs it out.

It was fleeting yet significant, ephemeral yet full of meaning.
—*Aaron Klinefelter*

A Shared Suffering, a Common Love

I am writing this shortly after the bombing at the Boston Marathon in April, 2013. In its wake, I have been thinking about how to respond to tragedy. I have no personal connection to this tragedy other than my relative proximity, being a citizen of the United States living in New York City. I cannot pretend to know how others feel, never having experienced loss of limb or an unexpected loss of someone dear to me. I can offer my thoughts and prayers and what little resources I have, give blood, and donate a few dollars.

It is tempting to isolate ourselves at such times, but that is not what we are called to do. Rather than closing us off in our fear, suffering can enlarge our empathy.

On the same day as the bombing, at least twenty people were killed and two hundred injured in bombings in Iraq. These tragedies are separate, and one does not diminish the other. Still, they can remind us that we are not quite so separate from the rest of the world as we sometimes feel in this country; that our tragedies, our pain, and our fears are connected.

Jesus, we are sometimes told, came to earth so that God could share in the experience of being human, so he could suffer and love with us. We cannot know exactly what others feel, but we can recognize that, just as we all have and will experience suffering, we also share love. We can recognize that this is one seamless world, and we are all one human community, equally loved, in need of help, equally afraid and broken.

—*Jeremiah Sierra*

A Cookie in Each Hand

I spend a lot of days home alone with the kids, and some days we completely melt down. It's tough. When the screaming gets to be too much, what do I do? I reach for a cookie. Or three.

I know I'm not alone in turning to the comforting power of a cookie when emotions are running high. It's certainly not the worst way in the world to deal with stress, but aren't there better ways?

It turns out that God created us hungry. God created us with a yearning, a "God-shaped hole" that only he can fill. God created us with a hunger for his presence and a thirst for his peace that stays with us our whole lives, that drives us to keep seeking until it is filled.

Unfortunately, we often mistake our God-hunger for cookie-hunger or beer-thirst. Instead of turning to God when the pressures of the day finally get to us, we turn to other ways to fill ourselves. We eat too much. We drink too much. We spend too much.

And seeking to fill ourselves, we end up hungrier. However, as we recognize the hunger for God that he has built into us, we can begin to turn toward him to be filled.

Today when the kids are melting down, I plan to sit down with them to pray instead of reaching for a cookie. I expect God will find ways to surprise me with goodness. I expect the kids and I will be blessed. And what better lesson can a parent teach a child than to turn to God when the going gets tough? —*Kristine Blaess*

Walking in the Fog

The storm the night before and a sudden drop in temperature caused the mountain to be coated in swabs of fog. My morning hike was going to be more like blind-man's-bluff than the inspirational communion with nature I intended. Still, I was determined and set off.

I came across a stream that I could hear more than see, but the trail eventually led me to the water's edge. I could not see the other side, just a rock about two feet ahead of me. I put my foot out and took a step. From that rock, I could see another one slightly to my left. Taking a step to that rock, I then saw two others ahead. Step by step, I followed the rocks until I eventually reached the other side of the stream.

I have always been one who loves a dramatic view. Whether climbing the trees near my childhood home or living in a house on top of a mountain, I love being able to look out and see far beyond. But sometimes the fog settles in, and there is no view. Then it is tempting to stay home, but I learned on that hike long ago that one can still travel when the journey is shrouded in fog.

You cannot forge through at the same pace as when your way is clear—you need to slow down and walk mindfully. Instead of looking ahead to some distant point on the horizon, you need to lower your gaze to a nearby rock. In recovery, they speak of "doing the next right thing." To me, that means taking the next step, even if it is only a small one, knowing that you are still moving in the right direction. Five million right steps can get even the slowest walker up Mount Everest.

Whether on a mountain trail, journeying through the illness or death of a loved one, a lost job, a troubled marriage, or loss of purpose, we are always given a next step. It may be only two feet ahead of us, but if we put enough steps together, we find ourselves on the other side. —*Chip Bristol*

For God's Glory

This illness does not lead to death;
rather it is for God's glory.

— JOHN 11:4

I was born with a 5 percent chance of survival. My dad always says that it was the only time in his life when he wished he were wealthy. The doctors told him that since he could not pay for an operation, he could take me home to die. My dad had been studying James—about divine healing—so he called a neighbor and, along with my mom and brother, prayed over me, anointed me with oil, and left me in God's will as they went to another room to pray.

But God was ready to show off that day. Ready to show God's glory. God was not finished with me yet. They prayed for a while and then went to see me, expecting, hoping, crying out for a miracle, yet understanding God's will might be different. I was sleeping soundly. God's glory revealed.

What can you substitute for illness in John 11? In my case, a respiratory illness was for God's glory. For my dad, an assault was for God's glory; he once was beaten and left for dead while working a second job, which lead him to The Episcopal Church.

In others it might be this cancer is for God's glory. Or, this set-back is for God's glory. Or, this flood is for God's glory. Let's take God at God's word and say, as I often do: God, please show off today! Let this problem be for your glory! —*Sandra Montes*

That Day

I remember that day. If you are from New York, there is a way of saying "that day" that can mean no other. And whether you were in the City or somewhere else, the words "that day," said with voice dropped and a slight nod to the sky, can mean only one thing.

That day I was working at a nursery school in Ann Arbor, Michigan. The bright room was filled with cheery artwork, toys neatly placed on shelves. A few of our students had arrived. The radio was tuned to a family-friendly morning show. We had heard about the first incident, but I was convinced it was a pilot's error. The morning team was happily chatting between songs when the host screamed, "Oh God, Oh God, there's a second plane."

Standing in that room, surrounded by things built for small hands, I felt something beyond grief. I looked at the little block area, complete with its tiny trucks and weeble-wobble people. I thought of the imaginary worlds the children build every day. I thought of the sweet way they chatter while playing. And then there was this cruel intrusion of the world we adults have built, a world where towers come crashing down with the swiftness of our hatreds and violence.

But there I was, with those small faces waiting for their morning snack, and I began the work of my day, clipping bibs and unfolding napkins. I set my mind to the small tasks and somewhere in the sweetness of the ordinary, I remembered. This matters. These tiny people who are helpless and innocent matter. I did not. I was too shocked, too busy, too overwhelmed.

I found myself praying *Jesus, Jesus, Jesus*. And I knew. This is how you get through this. You don't. Your hand makes the motions, your heart follows, and God does the rest.

—*Yejide Peters*

A Story of Forgiveness

I will call her "Julia." Like Julian of Norwich born long ago, she has relied on God's love in difficult experiences. A few of Julia's friends know about the childhood abuse suffered at her mother's hands, and we have witnessed a phenomenon of grace throughout Julia's adulthood.

Julia processed forgiveness years after danger had passed, but it didn't involve full reconciliation because her mother couldn't acknowledge the offenses. For some, a relationship would not be advisable, but for Julia, her own forgiveness changed their linked lives. Forgiveness occurred as God's grace interacted between experience and faith; forgiveness, in which Julia refused to stay stuck, no matter how justifiable the reasons to stagnate; forgiveness, in which she relinquished opportunities to "get back." Hers was a decisional forgiveness, a mental and spiritual choice before emotion supported it. One of the hardest parts: the choice to begin peeling back layer after layer to expose her excruciating pain to God's healing light.

In their last visit, her mom tenderly kissed Julia's hand for the first time. I wrote Julia later, saying, "Why haven't we been more clear in affirming the way you've responded? The actions of treating your mom lovingly came from God, but you invited the possibility. The word 'magnificent' comes to mind."

This forgiveness, though it never included a discussion toward mutual understanding, developed as a grace from God, an inward, spiritual grace with outward, visible signs. It took a long while, but in his cry from the cross, Christ had given Julia words to apply, "Father, forgive them...they do not know what they are doing" (Luke 23:34).

And Julia responded, "God, make me willing to become willing to forgive." —*June Terry*

God Dwells in Secret Places

After several visits to Paris, I declared that Notre Dame Cathedral—with its soaring arches, ancient stone saints, and palpable holiness—was my spiritual center, so I would need to make regular return visits.

A pleasant thought, but a lie. My spiritual center is a lot closer to home—the silverware drawer in my kitchen.

Forty years ago, I worked out a way that two sets of silverware could share this space yet stay separated, so I could efficiently set the table with matching pieces: one set of teaspoons neatly stacked with the handles pointing toward the front, the other set pointing toward the back; the same for the dinner forks and the salad forks that live behind them; the knives a bit more jumbled because they can't be stacked, yet still easily discerned by their orientation; the tablespoons in a plastic basket in the front of the drawer.

My husband, not naturally orderly, learned the system after a few comments about people with college degrees being smart enough to match objects. My sisters-in-law marveled at the drawer when they were helping in the kitchen during family parties—but predicted it would not last when the children got old enough to set the table. I am proud to say the children not only accepted and adhered to the arrangement, but have gone on to create much the same in their homes.

So for all of my adult life, no matter how much clutter or chaos or physical or emotional turmoil raged in the rest of the house and my life, this has been my secret sanctuary. Some people meditate, do Tai Chi, practice centering prayer. I find peace and calm by opening up a kitchen drawer and delighting in the reliable orderliness of spoons and forks. Then I can pray. Indeed, God is everywhere, even in my silverware drawer, and a quick glance in there is enough to still my soul. —*Janet Rehling Buening*

God Is...

The pig is taught by sermons and epistles
to think the God of Swine has snout and bristles.

— AMBROSE BIERCE, *THE DEVIL'S DICTIONARY*

It comforts me to know that a hundred years ago there was someone else wondering if framing God in strictly human terms was the only way to paint a picture of the Alpha and the Omega, the Almighty, the Creator of all that is and ever will be.

There *is* a God; I don't struggle with that. I do, however, struggle with all of our attempts to comprehend and explain the incomprehensible and the unexplainable.

Thousands of years ago, the ancient Greek poet and philosopher Xenophanes wrote, "If oxen and horses and lions had hands and were able to draw with their hands and do the same things as men, horses would draw the shapes of gods to look like horses and oxen would draw them to look like oxen, and each would make the gods' bodies have the same shape as they themselves had."

As far back as we know, almost every world religion has claimed to be *the way*. Don't get me wrong. I get it; the best I can do is understand something through what I can see, touch, feel, smell, taste, think. I shouldn't expect more from anyone else.

However, anthropomorphism—seeing nonhuman things in human form—can be dangerous. As author Anne Lamott quips, you can safely assume you've created God in your own image when it turns out that God hates all the same people you do. —*Bo Cox*

The True Cross

A friend was walking in the recesses of the Church of the Holy Sepulchre in Jerusalem after leading a group in praying the Stations of the Cross. He was dressed in a black cassock. A very excited, older man approached him, carefully took out a small package, and unwrapped it to reveal a sliver of wood. "Look," the man said, "I have just purchased a piece of the true cross."

My friend, a longtime resident of Jerusalem, started to scoff. Before he could speak, the old man continued. "Now I can go home to die." My friend offered a blessing instead.

Holy Cross Day commemorates not crucifixion but Saint Helena's discovery of the cross of Christ while on pilgrimage in the Holy Land. It is a hard story to swallow. But perhaps we should be careful not to scoff too soon.

The Church of the Holy Sepulchre also has a slab of marble on which the body of Christ is said to have been anointed for burial. Now, we know for a fact that that this particular piece of marble dates only from the nineteenth century and replaced an earlier one (but still not from the time of Christ) that had previously been there. Still, old women from Greece flock there to anoint their burial shrouds in holy oil, and then go home to die.

If a small sliver of wood and a relatively modern marble slab can give us the courage to face death, well then, maybe that's about as true as anyone could hope for. —*Stacy Sauls*

How Malice Dies

Years ago I had what I now call "my O. J. Simpson dream." I'd been following Simpson's murder trial with intense absorption. Convinced that he was guilty, I wanted him to be convicted and imprisoned. Not only that: I also felt malicious excitement as I watched the trial; vengeful pleasure as I watched him squirm. I was better than he was—superior, righteous, innocent.

Then one night I dreamed that I casually told someone that I wanted a couple of people killed. The person carried out my request, and in the dream I felt no remorse, guilt, or shame, just a surge of self-protective worry. Would I get away with the murders? Would I get caught? Would my bishop find out? In the dream I didn't care about the people who had died. I wanted only to save my own skin.

When I awoke, I felt a pang of shock and sorrow. I saw that I needed to pray for O. J. Simpson. I'd been visited by a dream that punctured my pride and showed me that everything I thought I saw in him—the casual violence, the capacity to kill, the failure to feel remorse, the desire at all costs to save his neck and reputation—was also in me. On a human level, we might be different, but on a soul level, we were basically alike: both of us sinners who fail to live up to the love that made us.

I still believed that Simpson was guilty and still wanted him convicted, but the thrill was gone. I could no longer watch his trial with self-righteous glee, for in contemplating his guilt, I also saw my own.
—*Margaret Bullitt-Jonas*

An Unlimited Broadcast

I love to think of nature as an unlimited broadcasting station,
through which God speaks to us every hour, if we will only tune in.
— GEORGE WASHINGTON CARVER

Perhaps because I was born in autumn, or maybe because fall always signals the beginning of a new academic year—and I have spent more than a third of my life in formal studying or teaching that commences in September—fall is my favorite season. It begins officially in less than a week, bringing crisp, cooler days and new beginnings.

I saw a hummingbird outside my window this morning, its beak nestled deep within one of our petunias. During the summer months, and with the hot, steamy days here in the South even in September, vibrant trumpet-shaped blue flowers appear on this tender evergreen perennial—attracting butterflies and apparently hummingbirds. I wondered if this hummingbird had been captured and banded at the Sagawau Environmental Center in Lemont, Illinois, the month before, but was so excited to see it that I forgot to look.

It's amazing how nature has its seasonal cycles. If we are observant and take the time, we can share in the great mysteries and delights of the universe. One can attend the hummingbird festival in Lemont, Illinois, in August. Or, for two weeks in June, one can venture over to Elkmont, Tennessee, to a small trailhead in Great Smoky Mountains National Park when the country's largest population of synchronous fireflies puts on what locals call "the light show."

Or you can just look out your window and see a hummingbird and wonder at God's creations.

—*Westina Matthews*

Gifts Even While We Sleep

It is but lost labour that we haste to rise up early,
and so late take rest, and eat the bread of anxiety.
For those beloved of God are given gifts even while they sleep.
— NIGHT PRAYER, *A NEW ZEALAND PRAYER BOOK*

Do you ever imagine what things you could do, or the sort of person you could be, if only you could get by with less sleep? I do. If I slept less, I think, I could leap from bed and run eight miles every morning, cook only healthful and budget-friendly meals, work on that novel-in-progress, edit documents like a fiend, finally crack that Josephus tome. In these daydreams, I'm also bursting with energy and extroverted and dressed like a J. Crew model.

Well, it's not gonna happen. I could start sleeping three hours a night with all these intentions toward some twisted ideas of perfection, but it wouldn't turn me into a model citizen. It would turn me into a zombie.

That's why I really like the above lines from the *New Zealand Prayer Book*. I so easily fall into the rhythm of staying up late, setting an alarm as early as I can bear, and running around sleepy and anxious. But those beloved of God are given gifts even while they sleep.

Sleep is important—and productive. It has a purpose and a place; it's part of being a creative, grounded, healthy, fully alive person. It is part of encountering God. It is also an important biblical concept: God knows that we are a people who need rest, and taking that rest is part of the Christian life. —*Alissa Goudswaard*

On the Same Team

Fall means one thing for many of us. College football.

When you are born in the shadow of Bryant-Denny Stadium, home field of the Alabama Crimson Tide, your college football allegiance is pretty much decided upon birth. Don't ask me why. That's how life works in the South.

I've yelled, "Roll Tide!" at the top of my lungs in stadiums around this country, standing next to truck drivers, doctors, fellow clergy, and mechanics. I've spotted a person in an Alabama shirt in a pub in London, England, raised a pint with a "Roll Tide," and was greeted in response with the same. At bars I've watched close games against Georgia or Florida with people sitting at the next table that I'd just met at kickoff, who instantly became colleagues in the trenches as we agonized and celebrated with each play.

I marvel at the community that sports creates. In that moment, we are a team. I cheer with people, not worrying about their political allegiance, their baptismal theology, or where they live. I cheer with them because in that moment, we are united for a common cause—Alabama.

What would happen, I wonder, if Christians were so allied with each other for the common cause of loving the world as Christ loves us? If we cared less about the adjectives that describe us and more about our unity in the faith, if we joined in grief when sadness was the response, and if we rejoiced when life burst forth?

Granted, college football is a game, and Christianity is a way of life. But every now and then, I dream of a world where I see someone in a pub, raise my pint, and say, "Hello, fellow child of God."

And s/he raises a glass to say the same. —*Laurie Brock*

Play

I like to go to the beach any time of year, but the fall is probably my favorite time. The crowds are gone, the sun is not quite so hot, and it feels a little like playing hooky to be at the beach after summer vacation is over.

On one of my off-season beach trips, I came upon an interesting sight. As I was walking, I saw a man way up ahead picking up things, doing something in a particular area. Then he finished what he was doing and walked on down the beach. My curiosity was piqued.

When I arrived at the spot, I saw that he had created a sort of art display: a collection of driftwood and found objects that looked a little like a boat filled with some rope, a bit of netting, and two very colorful but nonmatching rubber gloves stuck on sticks, swim goggles, and two plastic children's beach shovels. It was delightful. Of course, I had passed many of these items on my walk. But the man saw a way to play with these things and to create something fun out of them.

As an adult, I find it hard to play. I'm afraid I'll look silly. I'm afraid I won't be taken seriously. I'm afraid I've forgotten how to play.

One of my favorite Bible verses is Psalm 104:27: "There is that Leviathan, which God has made to frolic in the sea." For the fun of it, God made whales, or sea monsters, or whatever the psalmist meant by Leviathan, to play!

We, too, are made to create and be playful. So perhaps we should play today. —*Penny Nash*

In the Images of God

Separated from me only by glass, the ancient *Book of Kells* was fetching my soul. Through the experience, I was attracted to explore the meanings of the illustrations. Each gospel includes exotic and mystical paintings of the images of the four evangelists taken from Ezekiel and Revelation. The eighth-century Celtic monks knew artistry could better capture the mystery of God than volumes of words. Thankfully, the monks of Saint John's Abbey are carrying on the same tradition in their beautiful new illustrated Bible.

The Celtic symbol representing Matthew's Gospel is a human figure sporting wings—Jesus, human and divine. The text begins with the genealogy of Jesus. His family lineage was "interesting," like ours. The divine came into the world, like us, born of woman, to walk the messy road of life. The gospel writer's artistry crafted this story of hope, bringing the divine intimately into our human story through Jesus' earthly journey of trials.

The Gospel bearing Matthew's name is a narrative of everyday people. This apostle, whose feast we celebrate today, was a publican, an average person, struggling to survive in a rugged world. As evangelist, and artist, he created a portrait of the weak, wounded, and vulnerable who followed the Teacher. If Jesus, the winged human, could include Matthew, Martha, Peter, and Mary Magdalene in the inner circle, then we too are sketched into the picture, sitting at the table with Jesus— divine art, indeed. —*Gil Stafford*

Face Up to Fears

What you fear is an indication of what you seek.
— THOMAS MERTON

We spend a lot of time trying to suppress our fears, to keep them at bay, to make believe they aren't there, perhaps even running from them. But what if we were to look at our fears head on, to use them to discover something true about ourselves?

This is not to say that we go out of our way in search of fears, as if we needed to do such a thing. They show up on their own. It is really about acknowledging them so we can work through them. Maybe it's what Saint Augustine had in mind when he spoke about the restlessness of our hearts, how we are indeed restless until we find our rest in God.

That rest is what we seek. Our fears keep us from it. But we are not powerless in the face of those fears. Begin today by taking an assessment of the fears you're facing. Write them down, if that's helpful. Don't write too many, at least today. Then take some time to see if those fears indicate some sort of seeking.

What hopes are blocked by those fears, what dreams deferred? Say a prayer for each one, committing them all to God's power, a power greater than yours. Ask God to bring you to that resting place. And remember that the power you invoke in prayer is the power of love—and as scripture tells us, love casts out fear. —*Jay Sidebotham*

Home

"How can you stand living in Miami—aren't you just scared to death?" exclaimed my parents' neighbor.

It was the mid-1980s, the time of *Miami Vice* and the *TIME* magazine cover that proclaimed, "Paradise Lost."

"No," I responded firmly, explaining that as in any large city there were parts of town we knew to avoid, and that yes, we did lock our doors. But I realized I was offended: How dare she malign my *home*?

Then I thought, "But *this* is home, too." My daughter and I were visiting my parents, and we were standing in the living room of the house where I grew up, in the town where I was born.

One of the compelling themes in scripture is the search for home, from Adam and Eve banished from the garden, to Abraham called by God to leave his birthplace, to the Israelites' forty years in the wilderness on their way to the land promised to them, to the Christ with "no place to lay his head," who promised us an eternal home in the house of his Father—and ours—where there are "many rooms."

That moment in my parents' living room, when I realized that "home" for me meant at least two places, was an invitation to begin looking for "home" in other locations, too. Home includes not only the places where I've lived, but also places I regularly visit and places I may have visited on only one occasion that resonate in memory. I have found "home" in days with friends and moments with strangers, in work, in play, in sorrow, and in joy.

Those "many rooms" Jesus promised are right here in this life, too. Look around. God says, "You're home." —*Mary W. Cox*

271

Mother Wasp

The searing pain struck suddenly. I dropped the garden hose that I was about to put away and squeezed my throbbing hand. Then I saw my assailant—a black wasp, flying up from the ivy toward me.

"Go away!" I screeched. "I'm sorry! I didn't mean to do anything bad to you!"

My neighbor noticed a tiny nest nestled in the ivy near my hose rack, and he quickly knocked it down. Mother Wasp flew away.

Later I picked up the tiny nest. In the holes were two yet-unborn creatures and a baby wasp. The mother had lashed out at me when my hand threatened her nest of babies. The maternal instinct chased me away, but the babies died anyway. I felt sorry for her and for the little babies she was trying to protect.

When we feel threatened, we lash out, too. What do I do to protect and defend? What do I defend? My children? My pride? My reputation? My right to privacy?

A woman barks at me when I accidentally bump her grocery cart in the aisle. I don't know that she is drowning in debt, that the food in the cart I so callously bumped is all she can afford to feed her children until the end of the month. I know she is hurting, because she just hurt me.

"I'm sorry," I say, meaning it.

Her face softens for just a second. No longer the mean-looking woman who yelled at me, she hears me repeat, "I'm sorry." I don't expect anything in return and I get nothing, but perhaps I have at least buffered her day. Sometimes that's all we can do—just be kind.

—*Joanna Leiserson*

God's September Glory

"Glorify the Lord, every shower of rain and fall of dew,
all winds and fire and heat.
Winter and summer, glorify the Lord,
praise him and highly exalt him for ever.

— CANTICLE 12: A SONG OF CREATION,
THE BOOK OF COMMON PRAYER, P. 88

Canticle 12 celebrates the glory, power, abundance, and mystery of God in creation. The canticle is a glorious hymn that rings with joy in the march of created life, its fullness and its fierceness.

Autumn is upon us. Birds move in formation across the sky. Their haunting cries herald change. Slowly the days become shorter. There is crispness in the air. The trees dazzle us with leaves of yellow, orange, and red. The sun no longer scorches, but slides from the sky in a ruddy blaze.

I notice that when weathering the latest heat wave, I wish for fall or spring. After spending time out in a blustery winter day navigating icy walkways, I am grateful for summer. I look for the change in seasons. I find I am less tolerant of seasons changing in my life.

The challenge for us is that life does change and has its seasons. In human life, there are times of harvest, death, rebirth, and growth. There are seasons of celebration, seasons of struggle, and seasons of rest.

There is also hope in the seasons of life. In them, we can experience the fullness and richness of life. Things come. Things go. We change. The hope is that our lives are an invitation to grow— an invitation to discover the ways God's glory, power, abundance, and mystery are with us throughout it all.

—*Karen Montagno*

Relationships

Whether you are reading something someone has written, meeting someone new, studying sacred texts, or interviewing for jobs, you know how important relationships are to us. We want to know who someone is and where they came from. Sometimes we even want to know things that will give them credibility in our eyes. But rarely do we see the lives of people, birds, animals, fish, or otherwise as relatives just because we are all the creation of the same Creator.

Relationship often determines how we interact with another being. In fact, I think that when we don't think we have a relationship, we are often less willing to connect, making our interactions more superficial or minimal.

I am challenged by this concept each and every day. The more exposed to the world I am, the more challenging my day. As an introvert, this can take a lot of energy. However, working toward acknowledging the God of creation abiding in everything is changing my view of relationships. I am naturally related because God made me and all of creation—they are all my relatives. —*Debbie Royals*

Give and Keep Giving

People grumble and groan whenever the subject of stewardship is brought up. They associate it with having to open up their wallets to put more money in the plate or increase their annual pledge. Money is an essential aspect of stewardship, but it is not the central part. Christian stewardship is about compassion, commitment, faith, and faithfulness. It is about who we are, and who we say we are, as God's people.

Stewardship is a way of life; a continuous way of being as one seeks and strives daily to give back to God, who has abundantly and so generously given to us. Yet we don't often think of ourselves as stewards. There are thousands of people who are in financial debt because they have not been good stewards of their finances. We have been terrible stewards of the earth. We waste oil and water, cut down trees without replanting, and pollute the very air we breathe. The list of poor stewardship goes on and on.

The ministry of Christian stewardship to which God calls all of us allows us to see how blessed it is to give rather than to receive, to care for rather than to abuse and neglect. When people are generous, their love for God, church, and each other is palpable—and they reflect God's transformative and saving love and grace into a world that so desperately needs it.

So the next time you hear the word "stewardship," it is my hope that you will not cringe, but step up and do your part for the glory of God, for the future of the church, and for the sake of the planet; so that our lives may be blessed, our congregations flourish, and our environment improve; so that at the last, we may hear the words of God, "Well done good and faithful steward! Inherit the kingdom prepared for you!" —*Owen C. Thompson*

Rest

I once worked as a senior underwriter. The job was simple; just make about a hundred decisions per day, all of which had to be exactly correct. My boss came around at 10:00 a.m. and 3:00 p.m. to make sure we were taking breaks; the company knew good decisions are made when underwriters are rested.

As a parent, I am best when rested. But how often, as parents, do we feel that way? Parenting happens amidst anxieties and on too little sleep. I saw a parent get angry at her child the other day. She looked worn out. I don't think she's a bad person or parent; she was simply tired and making bad decisions.

I wonder if God was weary when he created the avocado pit or the carrion flower that smells like death. Genesis says God made heaven and earth, and on the seventh day he rested. Jesus sent out the twelve, and when they returned, "there were so many people coming and going that Jesus and the twelve did not even have a chance to eat. Then Jesus said, 'Let's go to a place where we can be alone and get some rest.'"

At church, two retired priests approached me; one said he'd like to preach on Labor Day Sunday and the other said, "Then I'll celebrate," and in unison, "And you can take the weekend off." I did! And it was good!

The Letter to the Hebrews says a sabbath rest remains for God's people, and the person who has entered God's rest has rested from his own works, just as God did from his. May we find time today to rest from our labors. —*Dave Marshall*

Marked with Love

The island of Portland, off the coast of England, is famous for its "Portland stone"—used for centuries to build such famous structures as the United Nations building in New York City and St. Paul's Cathedral in London. Sir Christopher Wren, the architect of St. Paul's, would spend days walking through the stone quarries on the island, carefully choosing the various shaped stones for different parts of his cathedral. He had in mind exactly what he was looking for, and, wherever he came across a stone with the right shape, he would mark it with a particular mark. Each stone was different, but each had a unique part to play in the fabric of the great cathedral.

At a baptism I attended recently, the candidate was signed on her forehead with the sign of the cross, and the priest spoke these beautiful words, "You are sealed by the Holy Spirit in baptism, and marked as Christ's own forever."

Like those stones on Portland, each one of us has been marked, through baptism. God, the master builder, has chosen us, formed us, and marked us for a purpose. We each have a unique shape, and each of us is called to be what Saint Peter names "living stones…to be built into a spiritual house" (1 Peter 2:5).

We might not always like our particular shape—we may wish we were more like someone else—but God has made us as we are and God loves us. So what shape are you? What particular gifts do you have to offer? What unique place do you have in God's spiritual house? You and I are marked men and women—marked with love.

—*Brother Geoffrey Tristram*, SSJE

Learning Humility

John's disciples came to him and said, "Rabbi, the one who was with you
across the Jordan, to whom you testified, here he is baptizing,
and all are going to him." John answered, "You yourselves are my witnesses,
that I said, 'I am not the Messiah, but I have been sent ahead of him.'
He who has the bride is the bridegroom. The friend of the bridegroom,
who stands and hears him, rejoices greatly at the bridegroom's voice.
For this reason my joy has been fulfilled.
He must increase, but I must decrease."

— JOHN 3:22-30

How strange John's words sound in Western ears! Our self-referential, self-absorbed, self-obsessed culture teaches us to put ourselves first, to compete tooth and nail, to strive relentlessly toward the top.

Not John. Here's a man who is clearly passionate about his message. And he's had a real measure of success. Disciples have gathered round him, crowds follow him, even Jesus himself comes to him for baptism.

And then John's crowds turn toward Jesus. "All are going to him," John's disciples observe resentfully. Can't you just hear them muttering among themselves and plotting strategies to win back their following?

God's ways are not our ways—thank heavens!—and God's saints do not resemble Western culture's icons of success. Far from struggling to regain his position, John freely gives it over. "He must increase," he says simply. "I must decrease." And he relinquishes his following willingly—with joy!

There is so much in this small narrative for our hearts and minds to learn. May God give us the grace to grow beyond self, to learn to say, with John, "Jesus must increase, and I must decrease." —*Betsy Rogers*

Sustain and Comfort Us

Hearts starve as well as bodies: Give us bread, but give us roses!
— JAMES OPPENHEIM, "BREAD AND ROSES"

I was standing in line at the neighborhood drugstore, preparing for the super storm that was heading our way. The woman ahead of me was purchasing two six-packs of beer. She laughingly told anyone within ear shot, "I'm from Louisiana; we know how to get through hurricanes and storms!" The young couple behind me had two DVDs in their hands. I had three candy bars, bread, a bag of potato chips, and flowers.

Comfort. That's what we were all looking for as we awaited the storm that promised to be a doozy. We needed sustenance, but we wanted comfort. I had been so busy checking off my list of "to do's to get ready for the hurricane" that I had nothing in the house that would comfort me.

Walking the streets in my neighborhood, I saw others also in various stages of preparing for the hurricane/tropical storm. Young mothers with their toddlers, hoping to get them exhausted by letting them play outside before they are cooped up inside for who knows how long; expectant mothers with big bellies, sitting on stoops with water jugs and overnight bags, waiting for their rides to get them to safer territory; joggers getting in their final runs; animal lovers walking their dogs; and last-minute grocery shoppers loaded down with water and paper towels.

Stay safe. That's what everyone was saying to one another, friends, family, and strangers—in emails and texts, on the telephone, on the street, in the stores, on the news. Stay safe. And we all prayed that we would. —*Westina Matthews*

Being Christ

I was talking recently to a guy I'd describe as a nonbeliever. We met at a local, rather hip, coffee shop. I might have been the only person there who did not have a tattoo or some sort of piercing. Eric, in his late twenties, was wearing a black shirt that covered up a tattoo that started on his left wrist and ran up to his neck.

Normally folks chat about work and family before getting around to talking about God. Not Eric. We sat down, and he immediately jumped in. A town in Oklahoma had just been leveled by a tornado. "Why did God let this happen?" he asked. Before I could answer, he asked about AIDS, then earthquakes, and then tears welled up in his eyes as he asked why his dad had died of a heart attack when Eric was only twelve, just three years after walking out on him, his mom, and his sister. The sounds of the coffee shop faded away as I talked about a loving God working in a broken world. I told Eric about Jesus who is loving and forgiving and who would not take away a father—even if his angry son prayed that he would die.

Eric later asked why I do the "church thing." I said the church equips everyday people to be Christ for others.

He replied, "Hmm, like 'being Christ' to people who are angry at God and meet in coffee shops."

Sometimes seeking God is being like Christ for someone. Incidentally, Eric is now serving at a small downtown church. He talks to people who "have issues with God." *—Dave Marshall*

The Sun Hides Behind the Clouds

When the Ego speaks on behalf of God it is a terrible thing, and the Sun hides behind the clouds.

How do we keep faith at a time when there are so many contradictory voices in the world claiming to be speaking on behalf of God? We hear these voices from different parts of the world and in our own nation; voices claiming to know the absolute truth of God, and yet these voices often lead to division, strife, and sometimes violence. What is it about the human Ego that can make such a bold claim as to profess it speaks on behalf of God?

The Ego, by nature, is self-absorbed and seeks to assert itself regardless of consequences. Too often God is ignored in the process. How often has this tendency seeped into our own houses of worship, reaping havoc and planting seeds of division? The almighty Ego often competes with God, unwilling to be silent before the majesty of the Most Holy.

As children of God, made in the image and likeness of God, it seems we are both blessed and cursed. Blessed by the ever-presence of the Holy Spirit that dwells within each and every single one of us, and cursed by the weakness of the Ego in wanting to have its own way. Some might even call this the nature of sin. Why drown the indwelling voice of God in this manner?

People of faith are called to be still before the presence of the Lord (Psalm 46:11). God invites us to put our Egos to rest so that the Sun may stop hiding behind the clouds of our lives. —*Wilfredo Benitez*

The Saint of Generous Nature

All praise be yours, my Lord, through Sister Earth,
our mother, who feeds us in her sovereignty
and produces abundant fruits and colored flowers and herbs.

— SAINT FRANCIS OF ASSISI, "CANTICLE OF BROTHER SUN"

As I walk the sidewalks of my urban neighborhood, I notice the yards as I pass by. Some are well-kept; some are overgrown. Well-kept or not, in many of them stands a sentinel. Statues of Saint Francis keep watch.

Saint Francis is the founder of the Franciscan order and the patron saint of animals, ecology, and the poor. He is often depicted with animals and the infant Jesus, for whom he had a special devotion. It makes sense that he would find a home here in a diverse, vibrant neighborhood.

As a gardener, I have spent many spring mornings with aching fingers working damp ground. The garden is bare. I wait for the promise of growth to push through the earth. I dream of Saint Francis surrounded by growing plants and birds.

This year, I indulged myself with a glorious flower garden. More butterflies sailed overhead and more goldfinches fussed among the sunflowers than in years before. Admirers stopped and encouraged my work.

My little city garden, squeezed between house and pavement, was bountiful and filled my time, imagination, and heart. I felt the fullness of God's blessing. The garden enriched my mealtimes, and I was generous to my neighbors. I have a new appreciation for Saint Francis. I have been inspired by the generosity of God in nature.

—*Karen Montagno*

Alleluias Aplenty

Tucker's idea of "success" involved barking at the mailman to chase him away. It worked! Tucker's person always put him into his kennel for discipline, but he would bark anyway and then run to relax in his kennel. Success was worth the penalty.

I may follow Tucker's example and start saving my quarters this fall to pay a penalty in the spring—an optional "fine" applied lightheartedly at church. In some churches, the practice of not voicing aloud the word "Alleluia" is a discipline during Lent, a practice rooted in history over a thousand years ago. Our church displays a small bank labeled "Alleluias, 25 cents each." If I start saving now in October, I could pay for the privilege of saying "Alleluias" aplenty next spring. And the money goes for a good cause.

Actually, I could claim an exemption, because our choir rehearses alleluia-filled anthems for weeks before Easter. Randall Thompson's anthem has around sixty alleluias per singer! The music begins quietly, as if with a sense of loss, but recovery seems to follow, and the music builds to jubilant praise. The alleluias are then marked *movendo*, meaning "Get a move on." And *triple forte* reminds the singers, "Give it all you've got." Thompson wrote this music during World War II, allowing for the reality of deepest distress, but he moved the music expectantly toward relief and exuberance.

Such progress in the anthem makes sense. We may merely whisper "Alleluia" during a struggle, anticipating that issues will be resolved. At such times, we're not pretending to praise, but rather choosing to trust, praising in faith that we will return to a *triple forte* of strength and joy. And God's understanding embraces us all. Alleluia!

—*June Terry*

Exercise Love

I do not love the gym, despite the fact that I spend four or five hours there every week. It's hard work and time consuming, and the gym often smells funny. Still, I go every week, partially because my girlfriend helps me do so. She gives me a list of exercises to do, and when I ask her, "Should I go the gym today?" hoping she will say, "Why don't you take a day off?" she almost always says, "Yes." Which is what I need her to say.

Sometimes it's not discipline we need but someone to watch over us. Knowing you are loved helps you love yourself. You know that when you suffer, someone else suffers, and when you are well, it gives someone else joy.

Being loved changes us. Love is not a static thing. We like to hear that we are loved just as we are, and that's true, but it's also true that love calls us to be better.

This is the message of God incarnate, Christ in the world: that we are loved. Who we are and what we do matters because someone—many people, God and the community of Christians—cares about us.

Of course, sometimes I skip the gym and don't take such good care of myself, especially when my girlfriend is out of town. I'm reluctant to tell her about these times, but her response is not to become angry. She is gentle with me, even when I know she wants something better for me. Love calls us to be our best selves, even when it's not easy.

Love forgives us when we fail. —*Jeremiah Sierra*

But Only Speak the Word

I have never met anybody who has such strong faith as my mom. She is the best role model I could have. She has taught me to pray. She has taught me to believe. She takes God at God's word. She knows God is bigger than any of her worries, troubles, or doubt.

Whenever anybody in our family has a need, we go to Mami. She prays for us daily. She wears different colored bracelets each day to focus on one person. For example, I'm the yellow bracelet. Every time she wears her yellow bracelet, I know I am the focus of her prayer for that day.

There is a song by Phillips, Craig, and Dean called "Midnight Oil" that speaks of Mami—"Mama liked to burn the midnight oil down on her knees in prayer....Mama always talked to Jesus..." You can find Mami on her knees praying for us many times throughout the day. She prays over us, blesses us, intercedes for us. She knows Jesus can. She knows Jesus just has to speak the word, and miracles happen.

In Luke 7:7 we find a man who has the same kind of faith Mami has. He says, "But only speak the word, and let my servant be healed." What I have seen in my life is that even when I doubt, even when my faith is tiny, my God continues to be huge and miracles happen when I pray.

I have often told people—get on your knees, raise your hands to the sky, ask, and wait. Whatever your situation, Jesus just has to say the word, and things can change. Healing. Miracles. Life. —*Sandra Montes*

Inextricably Closed Off

As a child, I hated autumn. I use that strong word quite deliberately, because for some reason that is no longer accessible to me, the waning sunlight and changing colors evoked a deep sense of despair in my soul.

I can remember from an early age dreading the change of season. Somewhere in the recesses of my mind, I can still vividly recall a particular car ride with my family through the rolling hills of Kentucky. The sun was setting in that way that only happens in the fall. The colors were full and rich and autumnal. The daylight was slowly sinking into the hills as we drove along with traffic. And in the midst of all that, I remember feeling a heaviness and sadness that was unnamable and undistinguished, yet oddly specific and acute.

I've always attributed this dread of the fall to grief over a summer lost, that the academic year with all its structure and schedule and expectation had eclipsed the freedom and frivolity of summer's yellow sun. But I wonder if perhaps it was also a grieving over the close of a growing season. I think living in our small town in Kentucky kept just enough agrarian memory alive that any possibility for seeing newness in the fall was inextricably closed off.

As a child, I didn't have the foresight to know that winter was necessary and that spring would come again. Autumn felt like death, and it came in an unyielding driving descent, just as the night sky pushed the last stretches of sunlight down below those Kentucky hills.
—*Aaron Klinefelter*

Going Willingly

The days are cooler, as are the nights. The sun is rising a bit later each day and setting as it gives way to the moon and night stars. Tree branches that were once filled with leaves and fruit are now dropping them as they prepare to rest. And the leaves and fruit that have glorified the tree now go willingly to the next stage—they slowly turn from greens to reds, yellows, oranges and eventually fall to the ground.

This is the life of the leaf: I was born as a bud on a tree branch. With so many relatives gathered around the branches, I helped make a tree appear as if it were a green sphere; we filled the tree. We acted as a sail for the winds and helped to speak the language of Creator, whispering secrets to all who listened. I protected the tree from fierce weather—heat from the sun, winds, and rain. But the time has come for me to carry my message to another time.

I will not go without notice. I will first display my diverse gifts through the colors of the rainbow. When the time is exactly right, I will let go of my attachment to the tree and float ever so slowly to meet my new home in the earth. We will work together to form a new creation, and maybe even a new tree. —*Debbie Royals*

The Finish Line

"I will see you at the finish line."

The words stirred me in a place so deep I practically gasped. The young girl was giving the final meditation before the assembled group ran a marathon; she was speaking of the conclusion of our upcoming race, but, for me, her final sentence spoke of a different race and location.

Maybe it was my nerves about running such a distance, my more reflective stage in life, or the fact that our group was made up of religious souls, but the power of her words haunts me still.

What if there is such a place? What if there is a finish line? What if one day we reach it and feel the utter joy of completion? Is there a moment when we look down the way and see our journey's end, and, like at a marathon, see people holding signs and cheering? Are there familiar faces in the crowd?...A grandparent?...Father or mother?... Beloved friend or mentor?...Child?...Are they there, waiting for us, welcoming us home?

If such a place exists, if ever I experience such a moment, "heaven" would be the only word for it. Such a place or moment would be enough to put my daily struggles in perspective, lift the significance of my present race, and give my heart its deepest hope.

God has never spoken to me in a distinct, clear voice. Instead, I seem to hear things in whispers and see them out of the corner of my eye. Whether through a particularly beautiful place, a loving moment with a child, or a comment made by a young girl standing in front of a bunch of nervous runners, these whispers are fingers pointing to something I can only fathom in small bits and pieces— but they're enough to get me to lace up my shoes once again, with renewed enthusiasm, profound gratitude, and, most of all, hope. —*Chip Bristol*

288

Safe Harbor

Anne Lamott, in her beautiful book *Bird by Bird*, says writing is like singing on a boat in a storm—it doesn't stop the storm but it cheers the heart. I love that image, but not boats themselves. I am not a good swimmer, so being out on large bodies of water frightens me.

There are a lot of boats in the Bible—Noah, Jonah, Jesus and the apostles all got on boats, usually with a good end.

And then there is Tom Stoppard's play *Rosencrantz and Guildenstern Are Dead*, in which the title characters are happy to get on a boat to England; it gives them purpose and direction. Until they learn Hamlet has switched the letter they carry, and they will be executed upon landing. Then their plaintive cry is, "Where we went wrong was in getting on the boat." My family has adopted that line as a catchphrase, wry shorthand for "bad choice" or "you just don't want to go there."

But one year, in a why-not moment after major illness and surgery, I agreed to get on a boat—a huge cruise ship—with my daughter for two weeks, something I had never planned to do. We sailed across the Mediterranean Sea and up the Black Sea, visiting nine countries—some I certainly never meant to go to—on three continents. It was the most amazing journey of my life. So maybe I was wrong about boats.

There is one boat I surely want to get on. My friend Audrey, dying from breast cancer, in her final days often said she was getting in the boat with Jesus. I can't imagine what it feels like to know your life will end in a few weeks and your three young children will grow up without you, but I know Audrey found immense peace in that image.

When my end is near, and I am standing on the edge of that river, I want to get into the boat with Jesus. And I hope others are there with me, and we are all singing.

—*Janet Rehling Buening*

When You Become No One

Let's say you take your kayak to a pond one October morning. You're in no hurry to get somewhere else. You're simply here, awake and still, welcoming each moment as it comes, floating wherever the breeze may take you. From your boat in the middle of the pond, you watch the dark water, the white birch trees leaning overhead, the golden-green grasses on the shore.

The rising sun warms your face, you see a pair of bluebirds sitting motionless in a tree, and you listen to the lapping water. A yellow leaf floats by. You need nothing, want nothing, exclude nothing, and welcome everything, drifting as freely as a feather that is carried on the breath of God. Just then the birch trees release their leaves. A cascade of tiny yellow leaves is tumbling through the air around you, landing on the field, the pond, your legs, even your face. What can you do but laugh for joy?

Wandering in nature invites us to practice effortless attention. In that contemplative state of mind, we relax our unconscious effort to define the rigid edges of ourselves (*I am this, not that*), and we invite the Spirit to disclose our true identity. What if our self does not stop at the boundaries of our skin? What if we were created for communion with the web of life that surrounds us? In moments like these, we are no one—we have no fixed self to protect or promote. In such moments we are in the tree, the grass, the leaf, the pond. We belong to a larger whole that is infused and sustained by the living Mystery we call God.
— *Margaret Bullitt-Jonas*

Growing Pains

You've got to do your own growing,
no matter how tall your grandfather was.

— IRISH SAYING

In the fall of 1986, a sheriff's car pulled up to a gate in the Lexington Assessment and Reception Center's double razor-wired, twelve-foot fence. The deputy rolled his window down, reached outside, and grabbed a phone out of a steel box. "Yes, I've got three from Coal County," he said into the phone. Across from him was a young man, barely twenty-two, trying not to look scared and failing.

"You ready for this?" He looked at me with compassion in his eyes.

Every cell in my body wanted to wrap my arms around his legs and beg him to not make me get out of the car when we pulled through the gate. Instead, I took a deep breath and tried to steel my nerves as I nodded yes.

Less than an hour later, I was strip-searched, given an ill-fitting jumpsuit and had my head sheared. Standing alone and still trying not to look scared, I thought maybe if I explained to someone that I really wasn't a bad person—that I was a normal enough guy who'd just made a terrible mistake, certainly not a criminal—then they'd understand and maybe I wouldn't feel so alone.

"Sir, my name is," I began. I was going to tell him who I was, where I was from, who my grandpa was, who my father and mother were. Surely he'd see then that I was not a bad person.

"Back up against the wall, 150656. That's who you are here."

Little did I know my life was on its way toward a great healing. —*Bo Cox*

The Kid with Brown Hair

I always wanted to be one of the popular kids. I watched the popular girls, so I knew exactly what it would take: Guess Jeans, a denim jacket, and two Izod shirts to layer on top of each other. A Swatch watch, straight blond hair, and parents who would let me stay out late wouldn't hurt, either. But none of that ever happened. In the end, I was happy enough to be the kid who got along with everyone.

As I got older, I realized that changing how I looked in order to be popular probably wasn't going to fit who I actually was (I played the pipe organ and loved algebra, after all). And a funny thing happened. As I got more comfortable in my own skin, other people got more comfortable with me, too. As I became secure enough to show people my heart, they wanted to be part of my life. I'm still a work in progress—still learning who I am and how to live it out.

There is an attractive beauty that clings to people who are authentically themselves. We're attracted by their quiet confidence. We're attracted by their joyful clarity about life. We're attracted by their kindness and generosity. Because they're secure in themselves, they can pour themselves out for other people. We want to be like them.

And how do we live into that attractive beauty? As Jesus shows us more and more who we are to him, we live into the security of our identity as children of God. And as we cling to that identity, we look more and more like Jesus. Which is beautiful. —*Kristine Blaess*

Confession

When I was a child, I tried very hard never to be wrong. At least, I thought I was trying not to be wrong. But really, mostly, I was trying not to admit that I was wrong. Being wrong made me feel badly about myself, and, I admit, I was afraid of getting in trouble. Better to just conceal real or imagined wrongdoing, I thought, to be on the safe side.

As a result, I wasted a lot of emotional energy on this way of being in the world. It is hard work to keep one's foibles concealed. Further, in trying to avoid some kind of pain, I deprived myself of the experience of confession and forgiveness. I limited my own growth by trying to play it safe. And of course, I didn't really ever feel safe. I was always afraid I was going to be found out.

What a mess.

There is great freedom in confession, for only after confession can we experience forgiveness. Only after admitting our wrong can we let go of it and move on. We can't grow from our mistakes if we can't admit our mistakes. Covering them up uses valuable resources we could be using for something else, like learning how to forgive ourselves, to forgive others, to know what it is like to be reconciled to God and to neighbor.

From our own experience of forgiveness comes the freedom to risk living life fully and becoming the person that God made each of us to be. That's so much better than a life of concealment and self-protection. —*Penny Nash*

The Key to Gratitude

I remember a writing assignment I was given in the fifth grade. The teacher had asked us to write a paragraph, naming some things for which we were grateful. I can still recall the scene to this day, because I had the most terrible case of writer's block! I sat and stared at the blank page on my desk for several minutes, unable to think of a single thing for which I was grateful.

I'm ashamed to recall it now, because my life was full of gifts. I had a wonderful home, loving parents, close friends, a terrific school, a healthy body and mind. I was *surrounded* by gifts—and yet I didn't *recognize* them as gifts. As a result, I didn't feel much gratitude for them. I assumed that everyone had these things, that they were the normal lot of kids my age. I took them for granted.

Unless we become aware of the gifts that surround us and fill our lives, we will not experience gratitude. Awareness and gratitude go hand in hand. While it's true that sometimes gratitude arises unexpectedly, it is also a quality that can be cultivated, simply by paying attention to the gifts that come to us from the hand of God, moment by moment, day by day.

For this reason, we pray, "give us such an awareness of your mercies, that with truly thankful hearts we may show forth your praise, not only with our lips, but in our lives..." (*The Book of Common Prayer*, p. 101). Today, see if you can walk through the day with awareness of the many gifts it holds—and give thanks. —*Brother David Vryhof,* SSJE

Crossing a Line

When I was six years old, I memorized and recited the Presbyterian *Catechism for Young Children*. I still remember parts of it, including:

    Q. What is sin?

    A. Sin is any want of conformity unto, or transgression of,
       the law of God.

I asked my father what "transgression" meant.

"Crossing a line," he said.

I've thought about that answer many times, as it's become clear to me that "conformity unto" the law of God seems to lead to crossing lines. Jesus surely did—healing on the sabbath; dining with known sinners; treating women, children, Samaritans, and even lepers as beloved daughters and sons of God.

Those we honor as saints and exemplars of the faith crossed lines, too: people like Paul, who gave up his privileges as a Roman citizen and a representative of the Jewish religious authorities to become a member of the community he had persecuted; Francis, born to wealth, yet choosing radical poverty and unity with all of creation; Joan, the shepherdess called to lead armies. In our own time we've known Martin, who laid down his life in the cause of freedom, justice, and peace; and Teresa, who saw and ministered to Jesus in the sick and dying of Calcutta's slums—crossing lines.

My prize for learning the catechism was a New Testament with my name embossed in gold on the cover. My Sunday School teacher invited me to read from it, and pointed to John 13:34: "A new commandment I give unto you, that ye love one another; as I have loved you, that ye also love one another." Conforming to that law leads us across many of the world's lines, some petty, some life-altering. Love is the line we hold. —*Mary W. Cox*

Dancing in the Margins

Each Tuesday the minister met his trusted friend to discuss the week's sermon. After he described what he planned to say on Sunday, about living lives of gratitude, his friend asked if he was going to mention being grateful for the challenges and difficulties of life. After an awkward pause, the minister replied: "Well, it's not in my outline."

They both laughed, knowing how often the important things are not in our outlines. Whether in the pulpit, at a kitchen table, or on a walk, some of the most important things we need to say are not in our outlines. No matter how carefully we plan what we want to say, we leave out what we need to say. With outlines all neat and tidy, sometimes the most important things are scribbled in the margins.

The same is true of the lives we live. No matter how hard we plan our lives, how much we anticipate, some of the most important things happen in between our scheduled lives. Whether a call from a doctor, a "you have a second?" from a boss, or a "we need to talk" from a spouse, our scripted plans are often interrupted, forcing us to abandon our outlines.

In all my insecurities and fears, I long for outlines. What will this week be like? Who are my children becoming? What will I make of my life? Answers would be so comforting, but life would lose much of its magic. Like the wise member of AA who said that if he had written down all his dreams when he first got sober he would have sold himself woefully short, my plans could be far short of what God intends.

As much as I want to create and stick to an outline, such a life would become stagnant and dull. Better to live in the in-between spaces and dance in the margins. —*Chip Bristol*

The Space Between

Recently, our nine-year-old daughter came home from school and proclaimed that she was learning to play "Mary Had a Little Lamb" on piano in music class. She plunked out each note with a precision reserved for launching a nuclear weapon or signing your first mortgage. Our five- and three-year-old children had their own musical compositions to show us. Suffice it to say, their renditions had a cacophony of notes with unique harmonies and uncertain meter. They were free-form to the extreme. But for our oldest daughter—and in our lives—it is the spaces between the notes that come to take on as much, if not more, meaning.

We need to carve out space in our busy, hectic lives. Our identity is not bound to our ability to make, acquire, produce, consume, or develop. Sometimes we think that making or consuming, whether that means products, connections, or experiences, will fill the gaps in our souls. But when we let those gaps become places where we meet God, amazing things happen.

It's the space between the notes that matters.

Recently I've been talking with a friend about the uncertain, in-between place that she's been in. She's living with a good deal of ambiguity and unknowingness. It's a place that we all find ourselves in from time to time. We enter into this in-between space and time holding one set of assumptions and ideas, and we exit a different way. To truly enter the cauldron of transformation, metanoia, repentance, and rebirth is to enter the space between where we meet God and are changed.

Because, it's the space between the notes that matters.

—*Aaron Klinefelter*

Picking up the Pieces

Where I sit on Sundays in my parish choir, I don't face the altar; I face the sopranos and basses, and behind them, a wall of windows. My church building is old and has some really beautiful stained glass. The jeweled rainbow of glass pieces—cobalt, violet, gold, scarlet—fit together to create light-catching pictures: Saint Cecilia with her organ, the Spirit-as-dove descending, flowers and hands and intricate patterns.

First, though, the glass has to be broken.

Stained glass, in its un-windowed form, comes in panes like any other glass. It has to be cut—broken—to be leaded into a patterned window like those that dapple my church with rainbow-colored sunlight. In other words, all those magnificent windows are really just shattered glass, masterfully arranged.

Panes of colored glass may seem nice enough as they are, but when they're broken into pieces and soldered together, they're transformed into works of art. This is a violent process—cutting and soldering. The artist, too, experiences the violence. Glass doesn't cut neatly; it splinters into shards that cut and pierce and burrow into unprotected hands. Lead, the traditional metal for soldering, is poisonous. The creation of stained glass is messy, painful work, but the results are stunning.

To be with people in pain is difficult. It's difficult because sometimes things are not okay. Sometimes God seems far away. Sometimes really bad things happen to really great people, and there is no silver lining, escape hatch, or happy ending. Sometimes everything shatters, and we have to believe that God will be there to pick up the pieces, and to put them together into something even more beautiful.
—*Alissa Goudswaard*

Clouds and Fog

My love of flying began when my parents took me to Tampa at age six. What I remember most is my excitement and curiosity. I wanted to see what was on the other side of the clouds. I expected angels.

As the DC-6 lifted off into the sky, my nose was pressed against the window. We passed from the blue into the whiteness of what had appeared to me from the ground as fluffy but solid.

The cloud was completely disorienting. I could see neither below nor above, just fog and haze. I had no idea where I was or where I was going. We emerged on the other side. There was no one there. I was perplexed.

For one thing, I learned that heaven was not exactly how I had imagined. For another, I learned that clouds were not what I thought they were, either. The clouds and the fog are the same.

There is a basic part of being human that we are only aware of in the fog. It is the fact we do not know. It is somewhat painful, vulnerable, and frightening. It also is exciting.

No effort on our part can clear the haze. In fact, like the headlights on a car or the flashing lights on an airplane wing, our best efforts to cut through the fog only reflect blindingly back at us. In the end, we have no choice but to wait and see.

Clouds and fog, over time, encourage us to dwell in the unknowing and let God reveal Godself as God will. They give us the opportunity to be aware of our unknowing, and that makes us particularly available to God, whether we want to be or not. —*Stacy Sauls*

The Gospel and the GPS

"And you know the way to the place where I am going."
Thomas said to him, "Lord, we do not know where you are going.
How can we know the way?"
Jesus said to him, "I am the way..."

JOHN 14:4-5

Thomas needs a GPS.

My own sense of direction is, to put it mildly, nonexistent. Once I got lost going home from work—and that was after having lived and worked at the same places for over a year. My excuse was that I tried a new route, but I cannot deny that I am geographically challenged.

A GPS is a wonderful invention for the geographically challenged. You punch in your destination and the lighted screen shows you how to get there.

It's a funny feeling when I don't know where I am going, but I know how to get there. But that's the strange thing about using a GPS. It knows the way, but it does not know the place where I am going. In that way, the GPS is blind; the place is simply "your destination."

I hear Jesus telling me both the destination and the way: God is our destination, Jesus the way to get there. Like a GPS, he even allows stops on the way. But he leads us unwaveringly to God, our final destination and our true Home.

Jesus is the GPS for all of us spiritually challenged. When I occasionally get lost going Home, I look at Jesus through the lighted screen of the gospels and let him remind me how to get there. He never fails to bring me to that place.

—*Joanna Leiserson*

A Welcoming Faith

Today is the Feast of Saint James of Jerusalem, first leader of the church in Jerusalem. As he pastored that community, he convened a church meeting to talk about an important issue. Could Gentiles be part of the community? Paul and Barnabas presented the case that the church should be more welcoming than folks had previously imagined. They had seen the power in such inclusivity.

As leader of that church, James came to embrace the good news from Paul that Gentiles were to be welcomed. He broadened the welcome of the community to folks who had been excluded, and saw this step as fulfillment of prophecy in the Hebrew scriptures, specifically the verse which promised that Jerusalem would be rebuilt as a place where all people may seek the Lord (Acts 15:12-22a).

In observance of this day, give thanks for an expansive and inclusive faith, one begun by adventurous, faithful disciples, change agents in that first century, many of whom ended up giving everything for the sake of this new community. Take a few minutes to read about Saint James of Jerusalem. Consider ways you can open the doors for those who are seeking God's life in their lives. Consider ways the Christian community can extend welcome. —*Jay Sidebotham*

Make Haste to Love

A friend of mine died suddenly in 2012. Madelyn was in her early thirties, and one day she fell and hit her head and was gone.

We had been roommates for a year in New York City. I lived in a small room in her three-bedroom apartment off 30th Avenue in Queens. We hadn't spoken in a long time when she died, though I had often thought of calling her up and returning the keys to her apartment. Keys I still have somewhere.

I was lonely when I moved in with her. There was a huge television in the living room, and she'd often be there watching television when I came home, inviting me to join her. She'd invite me out for a drink every now and then. It was a relief to have others around after living by myself for a year. She was kind and generous with her time and space.

The memorial announcement I received included this quote from philospher and poet Henri Frédéric Amiel: "Life is short, and we do not have much time to gladden the hearts of those who travel with us, so be quick to love and make haste to be kind."

At the service, people who knew Madelyn much better than I gave remembrances, and it was lovely and heartbreaking. What I felt then and still feel is sadness, shock, and also, beneath that, gratitude for her friendship. Death can leave us mute and rend our hearts.

Death can teach us, too. I learned that Madelyn's warmth and joy had been a gift to many, including me. I was reminded to be quick to love and make haste to be kind, as Madelyn did. —*Jeremiah Sierra*

Ask. Search. Knock.

When I read Luke 11, I am encouraged. I am invited to ask, search, and knock. I have taken God at God's word, and I ask for anything. Yes, *anything.* My parents would do anything for me. And in the Bible I am told God is my parent. I can ask my parents for anything—from lunch to a car, from a Diet Coke to an international trip. *Anything.* So why wouldn't I ask God for anything I need, want, and desire? The Word says it will be given to me.

I lose things all the time. I am often searching. Mami always tells me to pray like this: "God, you know exactly where this thing I'm looking for is. Please reveal it to me." No, it's not a magic prayer. But it does work. If I will ask God to reveal where my left shoe, car keys, or tax information is, why wouldn't I also ask God to reveal jobs, ideas, and opportunities? I will keep searching because with God's help, I will find.

There are so many doors I long to open. Right now, I am knocking on the singing opportunities door, scholarships/monies for graduate school door, and career success door. I know God will make a way for the doors to be opened wide for me. Will you take God at God's word? What are you asking for? What are you seeking? On what doors are you knocking? Continue. Do not cease. Have faith. As you ask, search, and knock, have faith you will receive, find, and that doors will be opened.

Do not go through life wondering if the scripture is true. Ask. Search. Knock. —*Sandra Montes*

Back to Basics

Anyone watching the "madness" that marks our political season may feel dizzy from all the wrangling between our political parties. How divisive and unconstructive it has been for our nation as a whole. Families are divided. Neighborhoods are divided. Friends are divided.

In the midst of this, I hear the poignant words of the late singer/songwriter Marvin Gaye, who sang in "What's Going On?" about the turbulent times facing our nation in the aftermath of the Vietnam War and the civil rights movement. It troubled Gaye that a nation he and countless others had fought for and were returning home to would be a place of division and unrest, and so he asked: What's going on?

History does repeat itself. According to recent polling, our nation is more divided now than at any other time. What's going on? Many people seem to have lost sight of our commonality as citizens and our need to come together for the benefit of the entire nation.

Sadly this dynamic also affects the church and the Christian faith today. With numerous denominations, dogmas, doctrines, and inherent ideologies, a person could easily get lost in the maze of institutionalized religion. I long more and more for the Christ-Center, to get back to the basics: the heart and root of our faith and life in our loving God.

The church has a vital role to play in all this. Christ needs to be revealed and his love shared with this broken and wounded world. We need to be the Body of Christ, doing the work of reconciliation, healing, liberation, feeding, clothing, building, loving, and peace-making. It is my prayer that we will hold fast to Christ, and seek in all things to love and serve only him. It is my hope that when Christ comes again to bring forth the kingdom of God, he will recognize his followers—you and me—as those who reflect and radiate his light and love. —*Owen C. Thompson*

Spaces in Your Togetherness

Let there be spaces in your togetherness,
And let the winds of the heavens dance between you.

— KAHLIL GIBRAN

I took the plant that I had in my apartment to the office this week. In this garden studio apartment that I am renting for the year while on a fellowship, little (if any) sun comes into the one window. There is some natural light coming into the apartment, but no sun.

As you may recall from your elementary school science classes, without sunlight plants cannot make chlorophyll, which makes the plant green. I was watching the leaves of the plant slowly becoming lighter and lighter, and I knew that it would eventually die if I did not do something about it soon.

It made me a little sad to take the plant over to my office. It was a gift presented during my first week in my new abode from a very special person. I will visit the plant often at the office and remind it how much it is loved.

Isn't that what we must do sometimes with our relationships—intentionally move them away from us where they can receive more light? Parents do that with children, managers with employees, volunteers with organizations, friends sometimes with other friends. Oh, we may visit from time to time, but we know it is best for them to be somewhere else—away from us—fearing that if they stayed with us much longer, there might be a certain and eventual death. So we let go with love, creating spaces in our togetherness, visiting from time to time, offering a much-needed remedy and renewed hope. —*Westina Matthews*

Rearview Mirrors and Honest Reflection

And in my mind, this settles the issue.
I would never drink cologne,
and am therefore not an alcoholic.

— AUGUSTEN BURROUGHS, *DRY*

During my first four years of prison, I continued to use chemicals as my solution for living in the mess I'd made of my life. Quantities were sometimes scarce, so people found alternative ways to ingest intoxicants. At first, I had my limits; no way was I going to do some of the things I saw going on. To me, this even proved that I didn't have a problem. Despite the irrefutable fact that my existence was a complete train wreck, I believed it was okay, especially when I was intoxicated.

One old man used to trade people to get their cologne. Once he had enough gathered, he'd pour it in a big plastic tumbler and gulp it down. The day came when I asked him exactly how many bottles I would need to get drunk.

Looking back at years fifteen to twenty-seven of my life, I see a road littered with the shards of broken promises and dreams wadded up and tossed out the window. My tire tracks don't stay on the road; they veer from one ditch to the other, knocking down signs along the way. Turning the signs over, I see hundreds of things I'd never intended to do, with my tire tracks right down the middle of them.

The scary part of this is that, during that time, I believed I was on the right road and having a pleasant trip. Sometimes spiritual awakenings are disguised as simply the ability to see oneself and one's actions clearly. —*Bo Cox*

Love to the Loveless Shown

For God so loved the world that he gave his only Son.
— JOHN 3:16

Perhaps the best-known and most quoted verse in scripture, this statement of God's limitless love brings to my mind a hymn: "My song is love unknown, my Savior's love to me, love to the loveless shown that they might lovely be" (*The Hymnal 1982*, #458).

Loveless: not "unlovely" or "unlovable," but lacking in love.

How do we lack love? We are "loveless" when we exhibit unloving behaviors and habits of mind, when judgment, self-righteousness, ready anger, sarcasm, arrogance, and meanness take up residence in us and leave no room for love.

Jesus sees past all that, all those sorry habits that make up our false selves. He sees that God made us to be lovely, and that love itself is the only way to uncover the loveliness deep within, the very image of God at our core. He shows divine love in all its immeasurable infinitude to us, the loveless, that we might lovely be—and that we "may not perish, but have eternal life."

When we, lacking in love, are shown love, we become lovely. Haven't we all had such experiences, when in a tense or angry moment someone speaks a gentle word or performs a loving deed, and the whole tenor of things changes? That's what Jesus did in his life, in his death, and in his resurrection. He spoke gentle words, performed loving deeds, and *everything* changed. And that's what we are called to do as his followers: simply show love. —*Betsy Rogers*

Things That Go Bump in the Night

Are you afraid of the dark?

I am, sometimes. If I've watched a scary movie or read a collection of old Southern tales and legends (because those *always* have a ghost), the pile of laundry on my floor suddenly looks a bit ominous. And the trees blowing in the wind outside my window seem more like shadowy banshees than branches.

Because the dark is scary. We don't see as well in the dark. The dark has often been a cloak for those who are up to no good. And, according to the tales and legends, ghosts, witches, goblins, and creepies come out in the dark.

The season of Halloween, with its blend of the secular and sacred, invites us to be scared in a fun way. Dress up, decorate, scare yourself silly, all to live into the truth that yes, the dark is scary for many, many reasons.

Jesus came to remind us of the truth that the darkness will not overcome the light. The Light of Christ shines when the ghosts of life's trauma come back to haunt us, when the goblins of life capture us with their grief and pain, and when the ghoulies of life make us crawl under the covers in fear. Life brings scary darkness, and the Light of Jesus shines in love.

Not to make the darkness go away. No, darkness still remains, but like the Paschal Candle shining at funerals, Jesus is present in the dark places of our lives.

The Light does not make the darkness disappear. Life is still dark and scary at times. Yet the Light of God shines. And that is Good News. —*Laurie Brock*

Of Saints and Souls and the Rising of the Son

The Grange Stone Circle in County Limerick, Ireland, is older than Stonehenge. The impressive circle is the largest in Ireland, with 113 stones. The giant black entryway provides a "V" for the setting sun of the Feast of Samhain, All Hallows' Eve. The feast, celebrated in the stone circle, marked the beginning of the darker half of the year. Cattle were brought down from the hills and preparations were made for winter. Bonfires of purification were lit. The night was considered a thin space, an opening for those who had died during the year, journeying to the other side.

The ancient festival was a precursor to Halloween and influenced the creation of All Souls and All Saints' Day—our celebration of the dead who have touched our lives. At our parish on All Saints' Sunday, people bring pictures and memorabilia of their loved ones and place them on the altar. With the communion of all the saints, we celebrate the Eucharist and invite the Holy Spirit to sanctify all present, the living and the dead.

I find myself imagining the saints of the faith, the Virgin Mary, the prophets, the apostles, the martyrs, and the loved ones of our parishioners dancing in a circle around the table. We celebrate the One Holy God, Creator, Son, and Spirit. We celebrate the Rising of the Son in our lives. We honor the setting of the sun in the lives of our loved ones. Together, we experience the grace of communion, sharing the Holy Meal, the presence of the Son, and our eternal life together.

—*Gil Stafford*

Beyond the Open Door

Describing Staffa stumps me. Writing about this eighty-acre island, words come fast, tripping and tumbling into a heap. Staffa boasts basalt columns, upended and six-sided in natural artistry. I climbed slippery steps, knowing the precarious climb might quickly end, head over heels. ("American meets Atlantic off Staffa.") On top, rock piles represent the prayers of climbers past, now including my own thanksgivings.

Telling this story helps me sympathize with the evangelist John, who wrote his vision on an island. His wild report sends words sprawling, breaking communication rules we thought we knew, but we have an advantage in reading his New Testament book, The Revelation to John. We know how to accept what we understand, letting the rest slide by. We know how to give in and be transported beyond the everyday.

Try Revelation 4 and 5. Heaven's door stands open. Participants are too joyful to stop singing. Songs overlap. Why aren't the singers bored? Because at last, they "get" what we only imagine: how worthy of praise God is, how appropriate gratitude, how total their health. Glimpsing adoration, we learn that eternity flies when you're having fun.

If you've watched a favorite person leave earth to sing in God's direct presence, just imagine: when he or she arrived in heaven, it was like turning a page of earthly music, suddenly singing with precise pitch and rhythm in full voice without missing a beat, expressing joy. But you say you cannot carry a tune? Just wait.

When your pastor says in a communion service, "We praise God, singing with all the company of heaven," draw your deepest breath, and sing. Let it rip! You're in grand company. —*June Terry*

God in Your Own Image

*You can safely assume you've created God in your own image
when it turns out that God hates all the same people you do.*
— ANNE LAMOTT, *BIRD BY BIRD*

When I was a girl, I subscribed to the typical image of God-as-white-bearded-old-man. That was what I saw in pictures, after all—surely those devotional prints wouldn't lead me wrong! As I grew in age and in my faith, I came to realize this was a construction I'd built of how I thought God would be. While I can't erase those white-bearded pictures from my head, I can pretty easily dismiss them.

Now, though, the images I create of God are subtler and harder to dismiss. I try to seek God's will, and so I hope and believe that at least some of what I think and do mirrors a little piece of who God is. I have to be careful, though, because I'm not perfect (shocking, I know), and sometimes what I think is God isn't at all.

Sometimes I need a reminder that God loves where I fail to love and sees where I fail to see. God loves those who I think are profaning the gospel message, those who commit acts of unspeakable evil, even those who just irritate me every time they open their mouths—you get the idea.

We are created in the image of God; thank goodness God is infinitely vaster than the gods we create in our own image.
—*Alissa Goudswaard*

A Close Race

Do you not know that in a race the runners all compete,
but only one receives the prize? Run in such a way that you may win it.
— 1 CORINTHIANS 9:24

I once managed the campaign of a businessman who was running for U.S. Congress. My candidate was well-recognized in the area and had the support of the local party establishment. The only other person who filed to run for the party nomination had no political experience, did not actively campaign, and did not even raise or spend any money. Media sources were predicting that we would win an easy landslide victory.

As the results rolled in on the night of the primary election, everyone on my campaign was suddenly nervous. It was neck-and-neck. "How could this happen," I wondered, "when we were a shoo-in all along?"

When the dust settled, we were defeated by only sixty-two votes out of more than twenty-thousand that were cast. Since we were not expecting much of a contest, we had delayed our official announcement, refused to buy many advertisements until after the primary, and held only one public event. It had never occurred to me that I might have been taking victory for granted.

The complacency that led to our surprise defeat can also plague the Christian life. It seems fine to hit "snooze" instead of getting up early to pray, or to put off reading scripture for another day. And it's all too easy to procrastinate on caring for those in need. Sometimes it helps me to remember that, like campaigning, Christianity is not a part-time enterprise, and salvation is not a victory to be taken for granted. We must love God zealously, as if everything depends on it.

Because it does. —*Charles Graves IV*

Frivolous Play

When my daughter insists on raking leaves together for a pile to jump in, I find myself ever so slightly annoyed. Why redistribute the hard-won efforts of a tree's summer work, now cast off with abandon, into a pile just to jump in? The frivolousness of it all seems a waste of energy. Why not put that eight-year-old eagerness into reading or cleaning or doing math? Why expend such focus and determination merely to fall uncontrollably into debris?

And why should it annoy me such? Is there any harm truly done? Might the tree look down from above and relish with delight in its leaves being recycled? Might the leaves exclaim for joy as children giggle and toss about? Might I forgo my chores and the pressing needs calling from my to-do list to roll helplessly down the hill? And perhaps I will, because this may well be the best use of eight-year-old energies there ever was—of delight and abandon, of recycling and determination.

So today, we—you and I—are invited into the holy work of play. The immeasurable expanse that is childhood beckons us come. Jesus knew something of this. He speaks to his disciples, both then and now, "Truly I tell you, unless you change and become like children, you will never enter the kingdom of heaven" (Matthew 18:3).

—*Aaron Klinefelter*

Solid Ground

*Grant us, Lord, not to be anxious about earthly things
but to love things heavenly.*

— *THE BOOK OF COMMON PRAYER*, P. 234

Who hasn't felt anxious from time to time about things that are going on around us in the world? We feel anxious about external situations that are very real. Not only are they real, but they can be overwhelming. We think we must keep everything in place. Yet the tighter we clutch, the more we feel life slipping through our fingers like sand.

Jesus urges his disciples not to worry about their lives, but the reign of God (Luke 12:22-31). Today science reminds us of the debilitating impact of stress and worry. The collect passage above anticipates that things will come our way that will give us cause for concern.

The prayer is for God to empower, surround, and free us so that we can turn our attention, our love, our action to things that will lift us up and support us. I find support when I think about people of love, faith, or courage who have gone before me. We might call them saints, heroes, or sheroes.

I can remember in church, the "old saints" singing a particular hymn during times of trial, "On Christ the Solid Rock" (*Lift Every Voice and Sing II*, #99). The chorus says, "On Christ, the solid Rock, I stand. All other ground is sinking sand." The hymn suggests if we set ourselves on solid-ground Jesus, there we can find a sure place to negotiate our lives.

Our hope lies in the generosity of God providing saints and moments of solid ground in the midst of things passing away. —*Karen Montagno*

How History Holds Us

On a hillside in Colorado sits a small wooden church called St. Philip in the Field. It was built by my family generations ago, and many of them are now buried in the graveyard that surrounds the church. Last year, about forty members of my extended family squeezed into the church to pray and remember my grandmother. It was a somber day but also a good day, with so many members of my family, living and dead, gathered there to lay my grandmother to rest.

There are plenty of unhealed wounds in my family, as there are in most, but for a few hours that little church, with its history and tradition and liturgy, and our relationship with my grandmother, were enough to hold us together.

The past supports and guides us. This is certainly true in The Episcopal Church. It's not our agreement on doctrine that keeps us together, thank God, but a long history, a thoughtful liturgy, a shared faith, and the relationships we form in that context.

On that day, we prayed and remembered and ate, because these are things we can do together in our grief. This is how we come together, with the help of a history and faith that holds us and points us toward our hope. The wooden church, scripture, prayer books, bread and wine: these are the instruments of faith that help us find our way through life and death to love. —*Jeremiah Sierra*

Do 4 U

Misconceptions of what Jesus does in our world have been going around lately. You've probably heard this: "If God is loving and all powerful, why are there people starving in Africa?" I presume this implies that if there is starvation, there is no God. So what is God in charge of? Making life and the things we eat, certainly—but we're in charge of distribution.

Jesus does what we cannot do for ourselves. He gives us a path to salvation, turns mourning into joy, is the light in darkness, and gives us grace upon grace. One day he gathered a large group of followers and sent them out to heal and proclaim the Good News of God. He gave them, and now us, the power to heal and proclaim.

What will Jesus do for you? Jesus encourages you to diet for your heart, but he won't do it for you. He will sit with you in AA meetings, but won't slap the bottle out of your hand. Jesus will gladly jog with you in the morning, but won't force you out of bed to do it. These are things you have to do for yourself.

But when you are in situations with no way out, he'll show you a way. When you are weighted down with sin and self-loathing, his grace will set you free. And, on the last day, when you cannot save yourself, he will reach out with his arms and carry you home, just like he does starving people in Africa—and even for an overweight, stressed out, chain-smoking father of a fifteen-year-old. These are the things Jesus does for you. —*Dave Marshall*

Organ Donor

It won't work.

The stage whisper echoed in the sanctuary, and I forced my face to keep a smile. After all, the entire audience was standing, waiting for me to walk down the aisle.

The musician pushed pedals and flipped switches. The organ only sighed in response, with puffs of air, not notes, coming from the pipes.

It won't work, the organist muttered again. In a flurry, she gathered the sheet music and the worship bulletin and made her way to the grand piano on the other side of the altar. Never were sweeter sounds heard than the first notes of Wagner's "Bridal March."

I leaned into my dad: *Well, every wedding has something go wrong. That was our thing. Now I can relax.*

And I did. I was nervous, sure. But the gaffe of the music actually set me at ease. I was able to savor our vows, to politely blush when the long kiss elicited giggles. Even seventeen years later to the day, I can remember the feel of Jeff's hand in mine, the look in his eyes, the rising wave of deep and abiding love.

It might be a stretch to say that God messed with the organ. It was probably a fluke; the organ was only a few years old, and they often need decades to sort out their false stops and unpredictable ways. But I think God had a hand in it.

God knit me in my mother's womb. God knows me, so God knew I was sweaty palms and racing heart. God knew I needed something to settle the nerves so I could be fully present at one of the most important days of my life.

And wouldn't you know: the organ fired right up as soon as the service ended.

Maybe it worked correctly after all. —*Richelle Thompson*

Abundant Life

Months and months of miracles have produced fruit from the earth. We have enjoyed the abundancy that supports life and nurtures us. Our relatives have learned to savor these gifts and prepare them in ways that will continue to nurture us while the earth is resting. It is our way of nurturing the earth as well. We do not take from her anything that we do not need at this time. It is her time to regenerate.

Walking in step with the season is important for us as well. When we take an inventory of our life over the past months, we begin to realize how much we have to celebrate. Our life has provided us with abundance. Have we needed to use all that has been gifted to us? Are there things that we received that we might want to savor a bit longer, so we understand the full depth of the gift?

Taking our cue from God's creation invites us into both this time to celebrate all that we have and a time of sorting through all that we still need to glean knowledge from. It is a form of canning, preserving, and saving for a time until we need nourishment and sustenance. There is always plenty of everything that we need. When we realize that we don't need to take more than we need, we feel comfortable preserving some for later. —*Debbie Royals*

My First Love Story

The minute I heard my first love story,
I started looking for you,
not knowing how blind that was.
Lovers don't finally meet somewhere.
They're in each other all along.

— RUMI, *THE ILLUMINATED RUMI*

Too often we think of God as a wise old fatherly figure with a long white beard, sitting on a cloud in heaven. In the process we separate ourselves from God, deceiving ourselves into thinking that God is above and we are below. Jesus reminds us that we are the light of the world and the salt of the earth (Matthew 5:13-14). In our eucharistic celebrations we seek to be one body in Christ. This all points in the direction that in reality there is no separation between God and us.

Rather than thinking of God as somewhere outside of us, why not think of God as a Love within? The Spirit of God is within us, calling us into perfect union. God invites us to dissolve into God's presence as lovers dissolve into each other. The great Christian mystic Meister Eckhart once wrote: "The eye through which I see God is the same eye through which God sees me; my eye and God's eye are one eye, one seeing, one knowing, one love."

Separation from God is only an illusion. Our journey toward God is truly a love story. It is the narrative of lovers seeking each other and finally coming to the realization that they were in each other all along.

Why not dip your toe into the universe of God's infinite Love, which is a vast ocean inside your very heart? God is waiting and calling to you! —*Wilfredo Benitez*

Wounded World

Oh, the First World War, boys, it closed out its fate.
The reason for fighting I never got straight,
But I learned to accept it, accept it with pride,
For you don't count the dead when God's on your side.

— BOB DYLAN, "WITH GOD ON OUR SIDE"

I cry when I see wounded veterans being honored, whether by a hat removed, a hug, or a standing ovation in the airport. The Vietnam Memorial Wall left me speechless, with a lump in my throat and a sadness in my heart. I am grateful to have been born in the United States, my part of the world.

Children, when shown pictures of earth from outer space, often remark they don't see the lines that separate one country from another.

Later, we "teach" them what those borders represent and, sadly, often tell them that it has a lot to do with right and wrong; generally, that the people who live within our borders are right and others are wrong, usually in matters of politics, religion, and economics.

Meanwhile, the adults in other parts of the world are doing the same with their children—children across the globe who also didn't recognize boundaries and, thus, differences until they were taught to.

And, so, on a day where we remember and honor those who gave their lives and who continue to risk life and limb in conflicts that have everything to do with boundaries and lines, let us also seek to learn from the children of the world and see the world and its population as one.

No boundaries. Different, yes, but more same than different. —*Bo Cox*

Working Our Muscles

The first time I take my friends on a horseback ride, they are surprised at how sore they are afterwards.

"I thought riding was just sitting!" one friend complained, as she took another Advil.

Riding a horse is just sitting—along with balancing using those all-important core muscles, holding on through thigh muscles, keeping feet and knees at appropriate angles, and keeping shoulders relaxed but engaged, just to name a few.

Being a Christian can often seem just like sitting and doing nothing else. Come to church, sing a few songs, hear a sermon, then leave. And God loves you. You can do just that, and God loves you. God loves us just as we are—and loves us enough to invite us to change, as well.

One way we change is to be active in our ministry. Serving Christ is not just about sitting, but also about doing. Living a life in Christian love is filled with opportunities to develop new muscles—to listen with our hearts without judgment and condemnation, to love our neighbor, to forgive those who have hurt us, and to be a servant of peace and mercy in our communities. Following Christ means we open our hearts and minds to have the muscles of our own prejudices and biases stretched into stronger muscles of love and inclusion.

Being a Christian is responding to God's love for us by *doing*. And trust me, exercising new muscles is initially uncomfortable, maybe even a bit painful.

But stick with it. Keep working on love, grace, mercy, and forgiveness—those things that give Christians strength, balance, and endurance in a life of faith. —*Laurie Brock*

Shaking the Foundations

I'm watching an institution collapse. The foundations of the church are being shaken, and everything that can be shaken loose, is. I've never seen so many things fall apart all at once. If it weren't so awful, it would be funny.

Leaders are sacrificing themselves trying to contain the damage. But frankly, trying to hold back the collapse is like trying to catch a tsunami with a milk jug. No amount of brilliant visioning, strategic skill, charisma, or hard work is going to hold back the inevitable. This outcome was set decades ago. This institution as we know it is going to die.

However, this is not the end.

Once the dust has settled, we'll see how the pieces that are left can build something new. In the shearing and tearing of the old institution, the pieces will have new shapes. Like a jigsaw puzzle that has been recut, the pieces will fit together in new ways. Some pieces will be destroyed or set aside. Others will be newly important.

I am confident that in a generation or so, when the pieces are finally fit together again, the institution will have been renewed. Feudal structures will have given way to something that looks much more like the Body of Christ. Power and privilege will be flattened and shared. The impulse to prop up dying congregations will be replaced by the impulse to bring kingdom life to people who are dying.

"Those who lived in the land of deep darkness, on them light has shined" (Isaiah 9:2). New life is coming. Do not be afraid! Our Lord will not disappoint. —*Kristine Blaess*

Keep the Pilot Light Lit

When our father died, my brother and I, searching for a place of safety, a retreat from uncertainty, and space to give voice to our deep sadness, bought an old stone chapel. It had been converted into a unique home. I remember the wood-burning stove and the bathroom in the bell tower, complete with a stained glass window. It was a special place that will always hold my heart in its hand.

It was also a drafty place. In the winter, the wind blew right through the stones and came in continuously under the doors. We struggled to keep the pilot light of our furnace lit. When the breeze blew it out, we had about an hour before the cold house alerted us to the problem.

It took me thirty-three years to learn what the chapel, the pilot light, and the breeze were trying to teach me.

I have been born with a pilot light, a small blue flame burning quietly within, waiting to ignite my being and bring warmth to the world around me. It is a primal light that resides out of sight and often goes unnoticed. When needed, it is there to bring my true self to life.

But often, the relentless winds find their way through stones and under doors and cause my light to go out. When the cold awakens me to what's happened, I need to relight the flame. The torches are many: sitting quietly, going to church, talking with a trusted friend, going for a walk, looking out at the ocean, listening to music, going to a twelve-step recovery meeting, or reading an inspirational work. All of these, and more, are effective tools for relighting the pilot light within, but I also need to be mindful of the cracks and gaps through which the breezes flow. I want to make my house air-tight, but there will always be breezes that find their way inside.

Today, I am grateful to have a flame at all, and will do what I can to keep it lit. —*Chip Bristol*

Caution—Deconstruction Zone!

In his most recent book, *Mere Churchianity: Finding Your Way Back to Jesus-Shaped Spirituality,* the late Michael Spencer (known as "The Internet Monk") argues that churches need to be covered in caution tape to warn that serious deconstruction is going on within. Spencer argues most convincingly that the Christian faith, as it manifests itself within the institutional church across the denominational spectrum, has failed God's people, both those in the pews and those seeking to know Christ outside of the church. The church, he says, has failed to represent Christ faithfully in the world.

As Advent approaches, how might each of us undergo some deconstruction and reconstruction on the way we "do church" and live our lives as followers of Christ? We need to ask ourselves some tough questions: Am I glorifying God with my life? Have I loved my neighbor as myself? What role do or can I play as a member of the Body of Christ? Do I pray enough (without ceasing)? Do I participate in regular worship? Am I reading the Bible? What can I do to make Christ known? Am I afraid to commit myself fully to Christ and the proclamation of the gospel? Do I understand the Word of God and God's will for me? Am I prepared to meet my Lord when he comes in glory?

These are tough questions, but we must do our best to answer them in words and deeds. We must tear down some of the old ways of doing and being so that we build up our faith. Like a construction zone, there will be some hazards, rearrangements, setbacks, frustration, resistance. Yet, with God's help, the cross of Christ ever before us, and the tools of faith, hope, and love, we will build up and truly become the Body of Christ in the world, doing the work that God has given us to do. —*Owen C. Thompson*

Yes or No?

One of my strengths as a teacher is classroom management. I know, I know, that's teacher talk for discipline.

Several times a year I am asked, "What is your secret?"

I always say, "Consistency."

Do not say something unless you mean it. In essence, let your *yes* be yes and your *no*, no. Usually, when teachers have a very unruly class it is because they do not follow through.

How do you fare in this? Does your *yes* mean yes or does it mean: if I have time, if there is nothing better, if I remember? Does your *no* mean no, or does it mean: maybe, I guess, or yes? I am so glad God's *yes* is always yes, and I believe God's *no* is "there is something better for you"!

God says "Yes, your future is filled with hope. Yes, I will supply all your needs. Yes, I will give you strength, power, self-control, victory, peace, and eternal life." —*Sandra Montes*

Grab the Rope

I'm a descendant of John Howland, who arrived on the Mayflower. He's not a household name, like Myles Standish or John Alden, but he sometimes shows up in accounts of the Plymouth pilgrims, because he not only sailed on the Mayflower, but he fell off!

The story goes that after several days of rough weather, the young man thought the storm had abated, so he went up on deck for some fresh air. Unfortunately, the wind and the sea had not calmed as much as he'd imagined. Slammed by a large wave, the ship heeled over precipitously, tossing Howland overboard, but he was able to grab a rope dangling off the deck and was hauled up to safety by the crew.

I imagine the terror of my ancestor, thrashing and gasping in the frigid autumn waves, yet with the presence of mind to reach up and grab the rope, and to hold on, so that he could be rescued. Maybe he felt a bit like Peter, who had walked for a moment across the waves, but was definitely sinking, and needed to reach up and grab Jesus' hand.

I can identify with the feeling of being suddenly swept into stormy waves, of stepping out in confidence and then finding that my own faith is not enough to keep my head above water. Sometimes I've been perilously close to going under before I admitted I needed someone to hold out a rope or a hand. But whenever I've reached for that help, it's always been there.

If John Howland, that self-reliant pilgrim, had not been quick to reach for help, I—and his thousands of other descendants—wouldn't be here.

When you're sinking, grab the rope. —*Mary W. Cox*

I Want to be Ready

"Are you ready?" I asked her, as she collapsed in my arms. Her husband had just been wheeled down from surgery where doctors had inserted a portacath beneath the skin on his chest. We were standing in the hallway outside of his room while four attendants carefully put his frail, thin body back into the hospital bed.

I thought about this question of readiness over the days that I made a daily trek to the hospital to sit with her, sit with him, or take her out for a meal. Are any of us ever really ready?

"I Want To Be Ready" is the title of one of the old spirituals. As Christians, each of us strives and desires to be ready. Yes, like that song that was sung by slaves long ago, we want to be ready to walk into the "new" Jerusalem wearing our long white robes.

Advent begins in just a few days. God's love is placed in our hearts each Christmas, yet there is a season just before—this season of Advent—that asks us to awkwardly wait. Expectations have a lot to do with how we experience holy days, and the fruits of our waiting—hope, joy, love—are spiritual habits of the heart indeed worth cultivating.

And so today, I wait with my two dear friends as we prepare for whatever is waiting for us just beyond the horizon. On the calendar, Thanksgiving, Advent, and then Christmas are marked. Still, I will focus only on this day. I only hope that I am ready. —*Westina Matthews*

And All the Mornings After

Those who wait for the LORD shall renew their strength,
they shall mount up with wings like eagles,
they shall run and not be weary, they shall walk and not faint.

ISAIAH 40:31

When my husband, Jim, was admitted to Intensive Care, the first employee I met was Aquila. When she said that her name meant "eagle," I responded, "Aquila, you've comforted me. In my mind, eagles connect with sprouting wings when weary. I needed that!" She asked for the verse and seemed to savor it.

We glimpsed one another over ten days, as I was slowly becoming aware that Jim wouldn't recover. Having waited on the Lord for years through less grueling tests, I clung to the reality of trusting God as an absolute must. Clearly, I would need enormous grace to let Jim go if healing were to occur, not on earth, but in God's immediate presence. Too numbed for well-worded prayer, I relied on the prayers of others.

No eagle, I received strength "to walk and not faint" when Jim died. Afterwards, Aquila came to express sympathy as I sat overwhelmed in the lounge with friends. Gently, she asked for the verse again, and so the promise which began my hospital ordeal concluded it. And the next morning, the promise echoed upon waking.

And so it has been for all the mornings after. For all the *mournings* after. Two years later, by God's grace, I'm in flight—not soaring, but off the ground. I've been given spiritual strength to walk and to run, overcoming weariness. God has not disappointed me in the slightest, but has graciously granted cleansing tears, strength, peace, courage, and even laughter. For such gifts, I love my Comforter all the more. —*June Terry*

Seek and Serve

Will you seek and serve Christ in all persons,
loving your neighbor as yourself?

— THE BAPTISMAL COVENANT,
THE BOOK OF COMMON PRAYER, P. 305

This promise from the Episcopal baptismal service is one of the several promises describing what it means to be a Christian person, to live the Christian life. It fits with the theme of seeking in this devotional book, and tells us that if we are seeking God, in Christ, we don't have to look any further than the person across the breakfast table, or riding the bus with us, or sneaking in front of us in traffic, or speaking too loudly into a cell phone. In the mystery of our faith, we read that we can seek Christ in all persons.

A friend who serves an open, urban parish nailed it when asked how she manages the mix of humanity who come through the doors. She said: "I try to see Christ in all persons. Christ often comes well-disguised." She refused to tell me whether the well-disguised Christ was the irascible homeless person in dire need of a shower or the entitled business executive throwing her influence around.

If you have any interest in what it means to seek God in Christ today, for better or for worse, you can start right where you are, with your neighbor. Especially those who are irksome or annoying. Seek and serve Christ in all persons. Believe Christ can be found there.

—*Jay Sidebotham*

Everyday Incarnations

Sometimes God shows up in unexpected places. When I was nine, my parents and I were involved in a bad car accident on a snowy road. I escaped with only scratches, but both my parents sustained injuries. While we waited for the police and ambulance to arrive, a car full of strangers stopped and welcomed me into their warm car. When we arrived at the hospital, my parents were whisked off to operating and examination rooms. I was checked over, then shuffled to an empty bed in a whimsically decorated children's room, where I was joined by an on-call chaplain.

I don't remember much about the chaplain—his age or appearance, if he wore a collar, whether we talked about God or about how I was feeling. What I remember is talking about my purple junior bridesmaid's dress for my brother's upcoming wedding. I was astounded to learn that the chaplain was colorblind, unable to distinguish purple shades from blue, and my love of rainbows left me feeling sad for this man, who seemed to be missing so much. What I didn't see then was that, colorblind or not, he saw more than most. On a dark and tumultuous night, this flesh-and-blood chaplain was Christ to me.

I wasn't looking for God when my world was turned upside-down by slick roads. God found me, nonetheless, in the strangers who came my way that night, and I've continued to find God in the people I meet along life's journey: everyday glimpses of incarnation, even when I'm not looking for it. —*Alissa Goudswaard*

Redeeming the Day

We are entering the season of celebrations. Thanksgiving is just days away. To give thanks is to be reflective. What brings gladness to our heart—a newborn child, a fresh start, a change of scenery, family strength, maybe the celebration of a long partnership?

We look back. But for some events, we struggle to give thanks. This day, in 1963, would be one of those days, the loss of the young president, John F. Kennedy. Grief and thanks rarely hold hands. As a ten-year-old boy, I remember my fifth-grade teacher, Mr. Peace (ironically, yes, that was his name) telling us the grave news. The days following were filled with tears of confusion and fright.

Yet, either by odd coincidence, or, I would like to think, synchronicity, on this day forty-five years ago, I asked my future wife out on our first date. Two years later, on this day, we married. Friends reminded us how strange it was for our wedding to be on such a tragic day—a bad omen, they said.

Whenever any day seems doomed, I have to wonder, what will redeem its memory? The prophet Isaiah wrote, "For I am about to create new heavens and a new earth...no more shall the sound of weep-ing be heard...the wolf and the lamb shall feed together" (Isaiah 65:17, 19, 25). While the horror of some days may never find redemption in our life's pilgrimage, we do have the promise that God is creating a new Jerusalem where, "the former things shall not be remembered" (Isaiah 65:17).

Indeed, our tears of confusion and fright will be turned into a celebration of thanksgiving. Thankfully, the peace of Jesus has come to deliver Good News. —*Gil Stafford*

Freedom in Limitations

An ancient monastic principle about inner freedom is both challenging and inviting: "Freedom is known in the context of limitation." This is quite countercultural. We are identified as "consumers" in a market economy constantly alluring us with *dis*satisfaction, where what is next or what is new is presumed better than what is now. The notion that what is now is enough is quite radical; however there is buried treasure to be found in the grace of contentment.

Contentment, from the Latin *contentus*: to be "satisfied" or "contained." Contentment is not passivity. Contentment is actively engaging with what is *now*, living into the depth of life we've been given *today*. Contentment is not being seduced into thinking we must stretch our soul ever broader, ever thinner, to take in ever-new experiences, to always read new books, taste new pleasures, hear new things, master new skills in order to be complete. Rather it's to grow our soul downward, deeper, into the ground of our being. The psalmist prays, "Out of the depths, O Lord, have I cried to you; Lord, hear my prayer" (Psalm 130:1). Contentment means that we stretch down into the depths of ourselves and accept that we and this moment are enough. Contentment is about *being* rather than about doing, or acquiring, mastering, disciplining, craving, searching.

To find contentment, start with what is *now*: with your breath, and with what you can see and hear and feel *now*. Savor your life. Don't add the confusion of more choices. Be content. And be thankful.

—*Brother Curtis Almquist,* SSJE

Thankfulness

The week of Thanksgiving begins today in many American homes. Those of us who have let the planning slide are now beginning to feel the pressure. There are recipes to collect, traditions to be remembered, spoons and forks to be counted, travel plans to be finalized, or guest rooms to be prepared. The Monday of Thanksgiving week is always a day of anxiety for me.

In the middle of all of this planning and preparing and doing, it can be hard to remember the "thankful" part of Thanksgiving. Because being thankful requires some reflection. And this time of year, many of us are short on time for reflection. Perhaps we could wait a week or so until Advent, a traditional time of reflection.

Except, we all know what Advent is like these days. Shop! Buy! Decorate! Cards! Gifts! Parties!

Much better, I think, to try to cultivate a regular practice of taking a few minutes each day during which to reflect and be thankful for the many blessings we have received from our Creator who loves us and wants us to have abundant life. If we stop and breathe during "normal" times, then we've developed our spiritual muscles to continue to stop and breathe during hectic times. And by breathing, I mean stopping and letting myself savor something or recognize something important or wonderful or lovely or special. I mean stopping the "go, go, go" world of producing and accomplishing and resting in the arms of God for a few minutes each day. For me, those are ways to practice being thankful.

The busy time is here. Don't forget to breathe. —*Penny Nash*

Love Every Leaf

"Love every leaf." So says Father Zossima, the Russian Orthodox abbot in Dostoevsky's *The Brothers Karamazov*. From his deathbed, the abbot evokes the ecstatic perception of reality that inspired his life, and the ethics that flow from that perception. By learning to love every part of God's creation, every leaf and grain of sand, every creature, every moment, we come to perceive the "divine mystery in things" and to love with an all-embracing love.

But, I splutter in protest, is it possible to love every aspect of my life and every person in my life? Is it possible to love the world as it actually is, not as it once was or as I hope it will one day be? Is it really possible to love my enemies? Can I learn to love what is "other" than myself, what is unknown, disturbing, or disappointing; to love what is mortal and will one day die? Left to my own devices, I "love" only what pleases me, only what is useful and supports my own agenda. My love is often partial, tuned merely to personal preference. It seems sensible and natural to love like that—in a limited, self-interested way.

Yet I am haunted by the possibility of a greater love—the love I see in people who sacrifice for the common good, who reach out to the poor, who welcome the stranger, who speak words of selfless kindness rather than of judgment or contempt. Jesus Christ loved like that, and, as we share in his crucified and risen life, he lures us to do the same. Today, like every day, is a good day to be love's apprentice.

—*Margaret Bullitt-Jonas*

Thanksgiving Eve

I descended the steps to the subway in a dark mood, even if it was the day before Thanksgiving. The weather was cold and gloomy. I dreaded the commuting hassles of New York City. It did not help that I missed my train.

When another train came, a boy and grandmother sat across from me. She was telling him a story in Chinese while holding his hand and stroking his hair from time to time. The boy's brow would crinkle in puzzlement. Then his eyes would grow wide with surprise. He would laugh, and his eyes would nearly close. It made me smile. Thanksgiving.

A young mother and her baby got on. They watched each other adoringly. The baby glanced at other faces occasionally, once at mine. It made me smile. Thanksgiving.

There is a man who plays the accordion at the station where I change trains. He makes me smile. Thanksgiving.

Then there is the man who hands out newspapers and greets me with a wide smile, "Good morning, Pastor." This morning he wished me a happy Thanksgiving. Then he followed me halfway to the street, insisting that I give his Thanksgiving greetings to my family. "Have a blessed day," he concluded. "And a safe one." I smiled. Thanksgiving.

I began to remember how my morning had begun, my mood notwithstanding. I walked out of the apartment, which I never do without my wife reminding me that she loves me. The dog wagged her tail. More smiles. Thanksgiving.

By this point I was seeing things differently simply by seeing what was really around me. Cold and gloomy became fresh and crisp. The energy that is New York City replaced any sense of being hassled. Thanksgiving at last. —*Stacy Sauls*

Growing in Gratitude

My in-laws always said the simplest of graces before meals: "Lord, make us thankful for these and all our blessings." My husband brought this grace into our own household. I used to tease him about it, because it is so short, seemingly over before it starts.

Over the years I've come to appreciate this humble prayer. Of course, it is a thanksgiving for the food before us. Even more, it's an occasion to stop and think about all God's many blessings. And when we do, when we cooperate as God accomplishes in us the thankfulness we pray for, it helps us become ever more conscious of God's extravagant generosity and *presence* in our lives. Thus we draw near to the throne of grace.

When our children were small, we'd go around the dinner table and each would give thanks for particular things. One night our son Nick, eying the peas on his plate, thought to thank God "even for the things I don't like." (For a little boy, it was fairly profound theology.)

Counting our blessings is an ancient and invaluable discipline. Family and friends, our church, God's healing power at work, opportunities to serve, beautiful days, autumn's sensory pleasures, learning, safe travel, inspiring music, great books, the night sky, laughter, fragrances and flavors, our pedestrian-friendly neighborhood and the health to walk, our ebullient dogs, and yes, even peas and the things we don't like—truly, when one begins to enumerate God's blessings, one quickly discovers the list never ends.

Thus we grow in gratitude, for how can we consider all these gracious gifts and not be thankful? And thus, in gratitude, we draw nearer to God.—*Betsy Rogers*

Strange Herald

I can't face the crowds at the sales that start before the turkey is barely cold. I need a time of reflection to transition from the gratitude and family gatherings of Thanksgiving to the waiting time of Advent. So I will spend this day at home getting out some Christmas decorations. It's too soon for Baby Jesus. I will start with the snowman.

Folk art or family icon, this snowman was made by my mother in the late '50s, from newspaper she crumpled into balls, covered with tinfoil, and stuck on a coat hanger; metal strips from coffee cans (in the days when coffee cans were opened with a key) pulled into coils for arms; and mismatched glass balls for eyes and buttons. He's trimmed with a hat hastily cut from red satin and stapled together, the pipe from our Mr. Potato Head set, and once-vivid ribbon from a liquor bottle. Created to entertain my sister and me on a dreary winter day, the snowman was displayed each Christmas for a decade or so, then tucked away in the attic and forgotten until Dad moved, forty years later.

The snowman is ugly, in a cute sort of way, and has been known to frighten small children to tears. It is absurd, but not as absurd as the Son of God being born in a stable and laid in a manger. It is beautiful, as it speaks of a time when life really was less materialistic and tacky homemade decorations were a part of Christmas, when mothers had time to sit and make crafts with their children, when we were less likely to casually throw things away and a lot better at valuing what really matters, when things didn't have to be perfect to be cherished.

Now the battered little guy has a place of honor on a pedestal in my foyer. A strange angel heralding tidings of comfort and joy, he calls up memories of Christmases past and the people who made them special, and reminds me every day to fill Advent with peace and love, joy and prayer. —*Janet Rehling Buening*

Dancing in Place

In Russia, a highway is blocked due to construction delays. Cars are stopped for over an hour. When the passengers realize that the wait will be a long one, they begin getting out of their cars. One man begins to dance the traditional Cossack dance. Others join in, and people begin playing music and singing. When the road finally clears, the people pile back into their cars and set off on their way.

I have yet to see this scene in a traffic jam in the United States. We are an impatient, time-pressed, multitasking, goal-oriented people. We do not tolerate waiting with such an open mind that we could even imagine dancing in the streets. Is it any wonder that we may dread the coming of that season of waiting we call Advent?

For many, Advent is mostly a time to prepare for Christmas—time to shop, bake desserts, wrap gifts, host parties, untangle Christmas tree lights. We struggle to squeeze a multitude of activities into a few weeks. Such is the psychological traffic jam of Christmas planning that we often treat Advent less as a gift of stilled time on the road, and more as a kind of exit ramp as we rush headlong and at breakneck speed toward Christmas Day. In a season of waiting, we are charging full speed ahead.

But Advent is God's gift of precious time, when we can slow down and watch for the coming of Christ in our lives. Advent is God's construction delay, stopping our internal traffic and inviting us to enjoy this time on the road. May we then dance ourselves into Christmas!
—*Joanna Leiserson*

Ichthus

My early morning runs along the water—in river cities, country lakesides, or ocean front roads—bring sight of many different fishers. Human beings with poles fixed to long docks or leaning over bridges—silent, solitary, intently focused, or sometimes napping. Cormorants diving, seagulls chasing others away from "their" territory. Nary a crew of fisherfolk, hauling nets ashore.

One can find fishing buddies casting flies in mountain streams—far enough apart to avoid the tangles. Observers from afar will never see the small bands of strong and stubborn fishers who go to sea on boats bearing crab pots, herring nets, and longlines or squid jigs—you have to join the crew and take the journey with them.

Jesus called fishers who worked together, Andrew first among them (John 1:40-42). Andrew soon called his brother. Others joined the motley crew. Post-resurrection, feeling lost and abandoned, they didn't scatter to the four winds but went fishing—together (John 21).

We remember Andrew first of all at the year's Advent. He brought another.

Who and where will I discover companions as I wait? What catch awaits us? —*Katharine Jefferts Schori*

The Still of Winter

The earth has gone quiet. She reminds me of that period of time when I lie still in my bed, not yet asleep and still aware. I am quiet. My breath slows, and I am still. In that space my senses are making their transition from active to a dream space. The cold and crisp air feels good as I cuddle up under soft and cuddly blankets. I imagine the earth is doing the same. Being still in the winter helps us preserve our energy to keep us warm. As the earth stills, she seems to be keeping warm with blankets of snow sheltering her against the cold. I wonder what she is thinking. Is she dreaming and sorting through more active times?

Our ancestors always used this time to gather around fires and talk. We heard our origin stories again and spoke about times past. It was also a time to talk through difficult topics that might be separating us from others or from God. There were no lectures or admonitions. We did not expend energy in that way. Instead, we were still—listening and learning. We were embraced by the blankets of love and relationships against the cold, hard truths.

In the still of winter, all things were made right, and we rested in the confidence that this rest would give us the break we needed for our next step forward. —*Debbie Royals*

Fear-less

I've noticed, and maybe you have too, a fair bit of hand wringing going on about how consumer-driven Christmas has become. And yet, every year our consumptive impulse to out-do, over-spend, or out-gift just seems to become more and more the fabric of this season.

What if we're just missing the point? What if we could enter into the "great joy" that the angels proclaim without going into debt? I have been deeply taken by this passage in Luke where the angels appear to the shepherds and say, "Do not be afraid; for see—I am bringing you good news of great joy for all the people" (Luke 2:10).

Do you hear that? Really hear that? *Don't be afraid.* Fear cuts us off from others, God, and ourselves. Fear isolates, divides, and confines. Fear drives us away from each other and away from joy. When we are afraid we stand naked, vulnerable, and alone. So our fear-laden response is to fill our homes, our stomachs, and our hearts and minds with more and more stuff. We consume, collect, and categorize, all in an effort to waylay the fear we feel creeping in when we are still and silent and in solitude.

That's why practicing Advent is so important. It gets us prepped for Christmas so we can truly hear the angel's announcement. We do not need to fear.

When we enter into this great joy of God-with-us that the angels proclaim, we can stand fear-less. We can be confident in the surprising good news of a king born in a stable. God is with us. Emmanuel.

—*Aaron Klinefelter*

New Beginnings

Advent. A beginning. A new beginning. This is the time of the year when we prepare for Christ's birth.

When Jesus was born, the shepherds knew something was afoot. The wise men knew God was doing something special. The angels were singing God's praises, too.

But most of the people who saw Jesus thought he was just another baby. One of many. The littlest. The least. Most people didn't have any idea that in Jesus, God was doing something new.

And I suspect that most people didn't think Jesus was anything special until he grew up and began his ministry. Crowds flocked to see his miracles and hear his teaching. Even then, most people didn't understand that God was doing something new. They crucified him, after all.

When Jesus was born, God did something new. And it's strange that it was thirty years—a whole generation—before people noticed. It was as if the people were startled awake one morning, noticing something that happened decades ago.

God is doing something new in our lives, too. God has been up to it for quite some time—our whole lives, in fact. God is giving us a new beginning. God is giving us a chance to start over, a clean slate. God has made us his children. Have we noticed? Does the new beginning that God gives us in Jesus mean anything to us? Is it our greatest treasure? Or are we asleep?

It's Advent. Jesus is calling us to wake up and discover this new thing he's been doing in our lives. Do you see the new thing he's started in you? —*Kristine Blaess*

A Time of Journey

Advent is a time of waiting and anticipation, and unless we have evolved and matured, waiting is never fun. Most of us would prefer immediate gratification to waiting. When all our focus is placed on gratification, we can easily lose sight of the process that leads us to that moment. Life is more about the journey than anything else. The very meaning of life is about the voyage—how we get there—and not necessarily the arrival.

During this season of the church year, we wait. It is a time of pondering and reflection, of sitting still in the presence of the Lord as we consider the mystery at hand: the Incarnation of God in our midst, and the implications for all of humanity. Advent is a mystery worthy of deep reflection; it is a knowing that God is not done with humanity and a reminder that we do not walk in isolation. God is present.

In the coming weeks, we will draw nearer to the beauty and majesty of the birth of our Lord. The sense of anticipation will increase and opportunities for grace will abound. The coming newborn King is a magnet pulling us in the direction of the Divine whether we are conscious of it or not, and we can almost breathe it in the air.

Why not swim in the liturgical colors of blues and purples as we move closer to the birth of our Lord? Why not move beyond all logical thinking to a place of mystery and awe?

We are on a journey toward God. Be still, go slow, and savor each step along the way.

It really is about the journey! —*Wilfredo Benitez*

Calling "Come"

Advent marks one of my favorite times of year. I love the changing seasons—the chill in the air; winter creeping in. Strings of lights and artificial candles in windows push back at the early dark. The meteor showers of the Geminids are followed by the winter solstice. In church we light candles and sing minor melodies. Everything seems to glisten.

This is a time of expectation and joyful anticipation. A time to get ready, preparing hearts and hearths for the advent of Christ. We get ready so we can call "Come" to the Messiah. We sing the prayer, "O come, O come, Emmanuel."

The thing is, we don't really know what's coming.

There is no event or arrival that we can really know ahead of time, and when we call "Come" to Jesus, we face the very real possibility that the Jesus who comes will shatter all of the hopes and expectations and boundary lines we have so carefully constructed—after all, that's what happened two millennia ago in Israel.

When we call "Come," we are not calling someone or something we know—or are capable of knowing—fully in advance. We call "Come" with all the risks and ambiguities the word carries. This is a time of joyful anticipation, but there's nothing safe or comfortable about it. To call "Come" to Christ is, perhaps, the most dangerous and the most important thing we as Christians can do. —*Alissa Goudswaard*

Pruning for Life

When I lived in England, I had a beautiful garden with some spectacular rose bushes. I got the best advice ever from a wise old gardener, who said to me, "You should get your worst enemy to prune your roses, because he'll be ruthless. And the following year the roses will be more beautiful than ever!"

Sometimes we need to be pretty ruthless about pruning our lives, too. We can become so busy, we can take on so many commitments and activities that, like a rambling rose, our lives become dissipated, and we feel scattered and stressed.

Pruning roses and pruning our lives both take vision and courage. We need a clear vision of the direction in which we want to grow, as well as the courage to lop off all those branches, all those activities in our lives which, although they may be good in themselves, exhaust and diminish us, preventing us from growing strongly and vigorously in the direction in which God would have us grow. In John's Gospel, Jesus compares his Father to a vine-grower and says, "Every branch that bears fruit he prunes to make it bear more fruit" (John 15:2).

Advent is a good time to examine our lives with absolute honesty, to ask: What sort of person does God want me to grow into, and what parts of my life are preventing me from doing so? We may need real courage to prune whole parts of our lives that drain us of life but do not bear fruit. We may need to spend time in prayer with God asking for a renewed vision and commitment, that our lives may glorify God by bearing fruit, fruit that will last. —*Brother Geoffrey Tristram*, SSJE

A Day That Will Live in Infamy

Franklin Delano Roosevelt coined this phrase in 1941, but every generation has some date indelibly marked by a tragic, shocking, unpredictable event. Across the generations, depending on our age, we recall where we were, what we wore, and what the weather was like as we heard the news of the attack on Pearl Harbor (which happened on this day), or the assassination of the President in Dallas, or the gaping hole in lower Manhattan created on a crystal clear September morning. Our common life is marked by days we remember for infamous reasons.

In addition to these seismic events which affect us all, we each contend with unexpected experiences, what one friend called personal tsunamis. So our lives unfold in the mystery of why these things happen. They prompt us to go deeper in the spiritual life, to seek God in the midst of those tragedies. Our prayer book calls us to pray in the midst of things beyond our understanding. It does not offer or ask for explanation. But it affirms that in the darkest moments, we can seek God's presence, knowing the message of the cross is that God in Christ is present to the suffering of the world.

At this early point in the season of Advent, when we wait with expectancy for the arrival of Christ into our darkened world, hold on to that bit of light, that spirit of hope that is coming—the promise that God is with us. —*Jay Sidebotham*

César

I was twelve when I met him. He had full lips and sad eyes. He was sixteen. Everyone knew I liked him. I am certain he did, too. I called once just to hear his voice and remained silent when he said "Hello?" about eight times. Then he said, "Sandra?" I hung up and hid behind my bed.

I never spoke to him. I would smile a lot and gaze. Nothing ever came out of my mouth—except maybe a shy hello—even though our families were friends and we saw each other often.

April 9, 1983. "Sandrita," Mami began sweetly, "please sit down. I need to tell you something. Your César had an accident. *Murió*. He died."

I could not stop the tears. My regret: never telling him how I felt. Not that I liked him. But that I thought he was amazing. That I thought he dressed well. That he was very funny and intelligent.

That day changed the way I talk to people. I try to say what I feel to those close to me and even to strangers: "Your eyes are beautiful!" "Your smile is sweet!" "I love you!" "You're hilarious!" In 1 Thessalonians 5 we are told that as children of the light we must encourage and build each other up. I always wonder if giving César an encouraging word might have changed something. I found out later he had committed suicide.

Let's be children of light and encourage and build each other up while there is time. If I could, I would pick up the phone and instead of staying quiet, say, "César, you are loved, missed, and oh so handsome!"
—*Sandra Montes*

Good News?

Prophets generally don't tell us what we want to hear.

In the familiar Advent lessons, John the Baptist calls his hearers a "brood of vipers," warning that unless they repent, they might be fuel for "the unquenchable fire"—and then we're told that this was the way he "proclaimed the good news." Reading or hearing this, I feel myself doing an inward adolescent eye-roll. Good news? Really?

A few weeks after my daughter entered high school, I had a call at work from the school counselor she had visited to discuss a schedule change. "Your daughter seems very nervous," the woman said. "Is there a problem at home?"

I explained that I had just come back to work after gallbladder surgery, and that my recuperation (this was before the days of laparoscopic procedures) had been stressful for our family, with my husband and our daughter taking on unfamiliar tasks for a time.

"Well," said the counselor, "You're an adult—you'll get over it. But your daughter seems very anxious, and I think you'd better get some counseling for her!"

I suppose I thanked her before I hung up and burst into tears.

This woman had probably dealt with many situations of domestic abuse, and may have thought she'd encountered another one. She was wrong about that, but her harsh words shocked me and my husband into doing for our daughter's sake what we had not been willing to do for each other—family counseling.

She may have saved our marriage; she certainly set us on a path that led my husband and our daughter, then at odds, to the blessedly close relationship they still enjoy.

Prophetic words make us squirm; but if we pay attention, yes, we'll hear the Good News. —*Mary W. Cox*

To Mary, His Mother

Dear Mary,

I'm writing to apologize. For years I've held you in one stage of life, as a teenager who has given birth to God's Son. Now, I honor your whole life. Weren't you almost fifty when you were in the upper room, praying with other believers after the resurrection?

Thank you for your example in your conversation with the angel Gabriel. Your response to God, "Let it be with me according to your word," alerts me to keep shifting my own attitude to "Your will be done." Thank you for demonstrating faith into maturity.

I'm grateful for your habitual pondering, reflecting on events and relationships in heart and mind. After Simeon told you during Jesus' infancy that a sword would pierce your soul, I think you listened in privacy as God reassured you of the comfort and courage you would be given. Thirty-plus years passed before you stood by Jesus' cross where you experienced, at last and in depth, that sword's piercing. And you must have relied heavily on God for three long days, waiting for an unimaginable resurrection.

Though I will remember you as a young mother at Christmastime, I will also remember you as a gray-haired woman of seasoned endurance. You personified energetic postures that help me today: waiting for God to speak and act, hoping in God, trusting God.

My experience cannot hold a candle to yours, but dear Mary, you have my thanks. You've shown me that waiting can become a sacred activity, that James was correct when he wrote, "Let endurance have its perfect work."

With affection and respect,
—*June Terry*

O Come, O Come, Emmanuel

In the weeks before Christmas, our spiritual energy can easily be kidnapped by the hectic rush to buy gifts, send cards, mail presents, decorate the house—the host of holiday tasks that we cram into lives that are probably already pressured and over-scheduled. But beneath the din of cash registers and the countdown of days left to shop, a deeper, more authentic longing stirs within us. *Come, thou long-expected Jesus.*

We hunger for so much: for wholeness, fulfillment, and meaning. We thirst for so much: to love and to be loved, to know and to be known. We ache for an end to war, for an end to violence and poverty. Grab a pen and we could list all the things that we long for, but behind them all is a longing for we-know-not-what, an infinite desire that we can barely put into words. We sense a desire for a beauty that can never fade. We yearn for a love that can never die. We touch our longing for God.

For those of us who grew up believing that our desires don't matter, what a sea change it is in the psyche, what a turnaround, to begin to listen to our longings! What a marvel it is to realize that at the very center of our desires, we will find something sacred, something that is of God! In Advent we renew our dedication to the long, patient process of listening to our souls, as we inquire, "What do I long for most? What do I truly yearn for? What do I love and value more than anything else? What am I eagerly waiting for?" —*Margaret Bullitt-Jonas*

The Wisdom of Compassion

Today, the Feast of Our Lady of Guadalupe, is also my wife's birthday. She is a retired school superintendent who spent twenty years working in a predominantly Hispanic community. On her birthday she would receive statues of Our Lady. Over the years, her dresser has become a shrine to the miracles of Mary's life.

The thought of being born on such a holy day can be daunting. We have no choice of our birthday, but we can choose to lean into what Lady Wisdom has woven into our sacred blanket.

"Although [Wisdom] is but one, she can do all things...in every generation she passes into holy souls and makes them friends of God and prophets; for God loves nothing so much as the person who loves wisdom," (Wisdom of Solomon 7:27-28). Lady Wisdom carefully draws the weaver's needle across the loom of our life. Some threads are worn, the colors are faded, and the design may be flawed. Yet our imperfection is beautiful to the Creator.

The first day of the school year, my wife would be outside as classes were dismissed. One kindergartener had never been on a giant yellow bus. Frightened and screaming, he clung to my wife like an infant koala to his mom. With his limbs strangling her, the superintendent climbed aboard the bus. His eyes were squeezed shut. As the lullaby of her whispering words comforted, he slowly released the death grip and opened his eyes. Intrigued with passing images, he let go. Peering through the window, he proclaimed, "It sure is high up here!"

Ah, the miracle of a rug woven of wisdom brings comfort to the child within us all. —*Gil Stafford*

On the Freight Train to Christmas

Christmas comes with all the subtlety of a freight train—and with like baggage. There is the unmistakable magic of the baby in a manger, stars and angels, shepherds and kings, miracle and mystery. Then there are the shopping malls, cookies and sweets, fancy trees, gaudy lights, and frenzied parties.

Christmas is an impossible juxtaposition of burdensome expectations and fervent hope. Sometimes it feels like a tug-of-war between two conflicting world views, two parallel universes.

I think God would be amused at the world's clumsy attempts to recreate outwardly the holy joy that we hold within us. I even think God blesses our union of the profound and the tacky, the simple birth and extravagant gifts, our contemplative wonder and our raucous parties.

And why not? God is a God of paradox. God came to dwell with us in all the messiness and disarray of daily life. Jesus' birth was a mingling of the earthy and the divine, the lowly and the noble, situated in history and rooted in eternity. Is it any wonder that our Christmas celebrations are also steeped in paradox?

We seek to honor the gift of Christ to us. Our celebrations are a heartfelt, if clumsy, sacramental offering of the world given back to God. They are a gift of abundance to the God of abundant joy.

In this light, we can forgive ourselves for our indulgence of joy in the name of Christ, whose birth we so piously and so riotously celebrate this month. For soon, the world will finally grow hushed as we sing "Silent Night," lost in wonder, love, and awe. —*Joanna Leiserson*

Jesus Is the Reason

I spent most of today decorating the apartment, bringing up boxes marked "Christmas" from storage, unwrapping tissue paper while ooh-ing and ah-ing over forgotten treasures. But the sure sign that it is Christmas is bringing out the nativity scene.

About five years ago, as a gift to myself, I ordered a very special folk craft nativity scene. Eagerly, I unpacked the pieces and assembled them for display. Much to my surprise, I had a camel, but no wise men! When I went on the website, I realized that I needed to order the wise men separately.

I shared my dilemma with a colleague at work, who remarked, "Have you noticed the nativity scene down in our lobby? There's no Baby Jesus?!"

I explained to him that in some traditions, the Baby Jesus does not appear until Christmas Eve.

"I don't care what you say," he replied. "I'm from the South; and in the South, we have a Baby Jesus!"

Which got me to thinking: did I have a Baby Jesus? I rushed home to carefully examine my newly acquired nativity scene. Sure enough, there was Baby Jesus in the arms of Mary. But I had no manger. I was reluctant to go back on the website to see if you had to order the manger separately. I've got three wise men, Mary, Joseph, and Baby Jesus—what more do I need?

But isn't it all a nice reminder about the true meaning of Christmas? Jesus *is* the reason for the season. And now we wait with great expectancy—with or without the manger—for the coming of our Lord. —*Westina Matthews*

Look for the Lord

People, look east and sing today: Love, the Lord, is on the way.
— ELEANOR FARJEON, "PEOPLE, LOOK EAST"

We are surrounded by lights this season. It is, after all, a time when lawns and homes are displays of twinkling brightness. Yet for many, it is also a season of darkness, filled with joy and with reminders of those losses in our lives—loved ones who have died, relationships ended, and expectations unfulfilled.

We live a life that is not fair or even fun at times. Tragedy, sorrow, disappointment, and grief are part of the human experience. And God is with us, loving us when life is glorious and loving us and comforting us when we are grieving.

As Christians, we do not live life in Christ so bad things won't happen, but to support and sustain us when bad things do happen. We do not pretend that life is filled always and only with joy, but that life is a complex blend of light and darkness, and that somehow, some way, God needs the darkness so we can see the comforting light. Comfort may be God's work alone—some act of love, mercy, and understanding in the sole purview of the Almighty—and our job is simply to trust in the Holy Comforter.

May we know deep within our valleys of sadness and despair that our comfort is with God, even when we're not sure how that comfort will happen or even if it can happen. May we lift up our heads and hearts, heavy with whatever sorrow, grief, or desperation we may have, and look to the place of new birth, of new life and resurrection, and of new hope.

People look east and sing today: Love, the Lord, is on the way! —*Laurie Brock*

Giving and Receiving

One of the most meaningful aspects of my work as a priest is distributing bread at communion. I walk along the altar rail every week and see people standing or kneeling with their hands stretched out to me, open, ready to receive the gift of the Body of Christ, the bread of heaven.

I particularly enjoy sharing communion with children. While some feel that children should not receive communion until they "understand" what they are doing (which understanding is sometimes thought to be awakened at confirmation), I find that generally, even the youngest communicant fully understands this rite. Perhaps we've been overthinking this. The children know they are being given a gift, and they reach out to receive it eagerly, eyes bright. They know this is a holy time, even if the bread they receive is a plain wafer. They are glad to be included in receiving the gift of God for the people of God (as we say just before we distribute communion) along with everyone else.

The children understand they are receiving a gift, they hold out their hands in anticipation, and they receive it with joy.

This time of year we can get mighty anxious about gifts. We want to pick out just the perfect thing for each person on our Christmas gift list, if we are the giver, and many of us receivers spend a little too much time deciding on what we want to receive. Perhaps we don't need to overthink this, either. For in an atmosphere of genuine love (and dare I say, holiness), the experience of giving and receiving itself is a joyful and wonderful mystery. —*Penny Nash*

O Christmas Tree

Our family went Christmas tree hunting at a place called Sulphur Creek which, true to its name, stunk of eggs. After lots of hiking through the snow and looking at trees, son Jack picked out a big tree. We cut it and tied it to the car with our trusty bungee cords.

We've been doing this task for years; we're not novices. Nevertheless, as we drove down the highway, we soon heard a thud behind us. I craned my neck to see out the back window. There, in the middle of the road with cars swerving around it, lay our tree. I watched a pickup truck aim for it and drive right over it (It was pretty much okay—when we got home, the flat side fit nicely against the wall).

Michael retrieved the tree and the broken bungee cords while I walked back along the road. Surprised, I noticed a wad of rope lying on the shoulder. A wad of rope, in fact, exactly the length we would need to tie the tree onto our car. If we had lost our tree even twenty feet earlier, we wouldn't have found that rope.

It could be just a coincidence. But eyes of faith see God at work. I wonder, did God orchestrate this, from the rope's previous owner losing the rope, to our bungee cords failing, just so we would wake up and notice? Or did God know our bungee cords were going to fail and gave them a little help at just the right time? The details of God's work so often remain shrouded in mystery. But we are blessed when we open our eyes and find God, right there with us. —*Kristine Blaess*

Some Brighter Life

Often, around Christmas time, I read a poem by Mark Doty called "Messiah (Christmas Portions)." It captures an experience I've had again and again. In the poem Doty describes going to a performance of Handel's *Messiah* at his church, not expecting much but finding it transformative. His words, "Everything, the choir insists, might flame; inside these wrappings burns another, brighter life," describe a feeling I've had many times, that of being connected to something greater and more beautiful than I had imagined possible at an unexpected moment.

As someone who experiences a lot of doubt, I find these experiences welcome and surprising. I felt that way the first time I listened to the music of Thomas Tallis, when I read certain poetry or life-changing books, or on occasion when I step outside under a bright blue sky. The feeling is something like joy and longing.

"Aren't we enlarged by the scale of what we're able to desire?" Doty asks in his poem. Perhaps my longing is evidence of God in my doubt, bringing me closer to God.

I feel this most when singing and praying with my community on Sundays. During those moments, my heart, so often small and irritable, feels larger. It seems to grow to encompass all those people singing together.

These feelings are usually fleeting, of course. Peter wanted to build a place to stay on the mountain when he saw Jesus transformed, but it was not to be. Likewise, we cannot live in these moments. But they are necessary to help us see beyond ourselves and our doubt, to manifest the brighter life that burns within us. —*Jeremiah Sierra*

Expecting?

I have a friend who is pregnant. It's her first child so everything is new. For anyone who has experienced the miracle of conception, the world changes, and sometimes the changes are strange and unexpected.

After a major shopping spree for baby items, the happy, expectant couple bought six crispy tacos. While the husband unloaded the car, the smell of tacos haunted him. He could hardly wait to get to the kitchen and chow down on some much deserved taco meat, lettuce, and sour cream held in a deep fried crispy shell. Much to his surprise, on the kitchen counter he found five empty taco wrappers; he also found his sleepy wife on the couch. He said, "Hey, what happened?" His wife rolled over and said, "The baby made me do it."

Another day, he came home from work and was welcomed by the smell of interior latex paint. He saw his wife lying on the couch with paint splatters on her clothes. Through the hallway, he saw a freshly painted light blue nursery. He said, again, "Honey, what happened?" She murmured through her nap, again, "The baby made me do it."

As we await the celebration of Christ's birth, we might wonder what Mary did in anticipation of her unborn son. And, as we are expecting Christ to be born into our hearts, what should we do in the name of the baby?

Why do we pray for the sick and feed the hungry? Why do we give gifts to loved ones and display kindness to strangers? Why do we worship Christ and invite others to do so? I don't know about you, but the Baby makes me do it. —*Dave Marshall*

Set the Prisoners Free

I avidly watch *Nurse Jackie*, a television drama whose main character, the eponymous Jackie, is an emergency room nurse, mother, wife, and drug addict. What breaks my heart as a viewer, and makes the show so real, is how powerless Jackie is to prevent her own destructiveness. A loving mother and brilliant nurse, she is driven to steal, lie, cheat, and even neglect her beloved children. Recovery eludes her. She lives in a prison of pain and obsession.

As someone who has known many people who live in recovery from the terrible disease of alcoholism, I have witnessed dozens of walking miracles. At its heart, recovery is about the healing power of God and the willingness to acknowledge God's grace and gift each day. It is about the willingness to say to oneself, "Thank you, God, for the gift of sobriety. Dear God, how do I live today with integrity? How might I help others?" The profound reality of such "ordinary" miracles is visible to those who have passed through the valley of the shadow of death. Such people live their lives in the bright light of the miracle they have witnessed or experienced.

And perhaps that is half the reason we come to church: so that we might be witnesses and recipients of such liberations. And I tell you, friends, they are everywhere, and in the most unexpected places. Stick around long enough and you'll see one. Stick around long enough and you may even experience one. And when you see it, go into the world proclaiming what God has done.

Don't be shy! Tell a friend or two. Tell prisoners and wonderers of every kind the Good News of great joy. For the One who is coming into the world has set them free. —*Yejide Peters*

The Gift that Matters

The recently arrived Christmas card was displayed on the mantle, and the unopened gifts lay under the tree, when the phone call came and changed Christmas forever. "There's been a tragic accident," the voice on the other end sputtered. "Everyone in the airplane was killed."

Time stopped in an instant, memories of what was being said blurred, confusion and panic overwhelmed. The family in the photograph was gone. The gifts would never be opened. Even now, the news and implications are unfolding, but, looking on, I can only feel the importance of holding my family extra close this Christmas and appreciating every single second of time I have.

Help me remember when someone calls at an inconvenient time...

Help me remember when the line is long at the cash register...

Help me remember when the bills arrive...

Help me remember when my children are fighting over who opens their gifts first...

Help me remember when I am stressed over creating the perfect meal...

Help me remember when someone doesn't really care for what I gave him or her...

Help me remember when I am lonely and feeling sorry for myself ...that I can open this Christmas, this very minute, like the gift it is or take it for granted; that I can focus on what truly matters or get distracted by what doesn't; that I can be present or distant, passionate or indifferent.

The choice is mine. The moment is not.

It's a gift.

The only Christmas gift that matters. —*Chip Bristol*

The Infinite Gift

A ship came in for my husband and me, and we found ourselves in the happy position of being able to make a substantial gift to a parish building project.

Some weeks later, serving as an acolyte at the altar, my mind wandered to this building project and the support we were able to offer. To be painfully honest, I was feeling mighty pleased with myself, quite smug, really, that we could play a good role in the capital campaign.

A voice penetrated my reverie. It was our rector, reciting the Eucharistic prayer: "This is my Body, which is given for you."

The words pierced my heart. Here I was, self-satisfied and self-absorbed, musing happily about what was, of course, a very finite gift. And then here is Jesus, self-giving and self-sacrificing, giving his very life, his flesh, without measure, for all the world, through all time: an infinite gift.

My first reaction was mortification, a profound sense of being humbled, brought up short. My second was thanksgiving, as the stark contrast between our gift and his made the magnitude of what he has done for us, for me, unmistakably clear. My heart filled to bursting with gratitude. My third reaction was a question that I still struggle to answer: how might I begin to move beyond my small, self-centered thinking into the stretching, all-encompassing generosity of God?

"Were the whole realm of nature mine, that were an offering far too small; love so amazing, so divine, demands my soul, my life, my all" (*The Hymnal 1982*, #474). —*Betsy Rogers*

Following Christ

I like your Christ, I do not like your Christians.
Your Christians are so unlike your Christ.

— MAHATMA GANDHI

Jeff and I were riding mountain bikes in the mud. We were coming up a hill, wheels spinning, feet pedaling as fast as they could to keep us upright. The terrain dropped off sharply on both sides of the trail; to fall would be to tumble down sharp precipices.

Every time I'd feel either wheel slide in the mud and the accompanying lack of control, I'd panic and want to put my foot down, afraid that if I didn't, I would lose control and wreck. However, less than ten feet in front of me, I could see Jeff's wheels successfully navigate the course and continue on safely. Seeing this gave me the courage to not give up when I felt my bike slipping and, instead, pedal harder and follow his wheels.

In two days, Christmas will mark the celebration of the birth of Jesus. Many people believe many different things *about* Christ. As a person who strives to follow Christ's example in living, I want to remember to simply believe *in* him and not get caught up in what I (or others) believe *about* him.

Maybe someday when, and if, I can safely say I've successfully believed *in* Jesus and followed the example of his life, I'll tackle the subject of what to believe *about* him.

Until then, I'll do well to watch his tires as I slip in the mud.

—*Bo Cox*

Here Will I Dwell

Christmas Eve is a tender time. We welcome the birth of a much longed-for baby. God comes to us as a child, vulnerable and needing support. A child cannot exist alone. A child survives only in relationship to someone else, only if there is someone close by who will guard and keep watch, who will cradle, wash, and feed. With infinite trust, God in Christ takes the form of a baby and is yielded into our hands.

What will we do with this gift? For we, too, participate in the birthing of God. "This shall be my resting-place for ever," God says to our souls. "Here will I dwell, for I delight in [you]" (Psalm 132:15).

Will we consent to God's birth within us? Will we give shelter to the hidden One who longs to be born right here? Just as the Holy Spirit came to Mary, so, too, it comes to us, inviting our response. Sometimes our hearts leap for joy, and at once we say yes. But sometimes we pull away, frightened or perplexed. Sometimes we lean forward, opening our arms to receive the love for which we've yearned for so long. But sometimes we pull back, afraid to trust that this love is real, afraid to lose control.

It's a dance that we play at the borders of the self, testing the edges, sometimes moving toward love, sometimes moving away, now opening to relatedness, now closing fearfully in. God is always patient and never forces, never compels. The Spirit comes to us just as the Spirit came to Mary, and waits for our assent. Will we say yes this time? Will we let go? —*Margaret Bullitt-Jonas*

In the Beginning

In the beginning was the Word...

—JOHN 1:1

Beginning today, the whole universe has just changed—because something inconceivable has just been conceived.

How do you put a name to God in human form? How would you describe an impossibility that has become a reality? How can you talk about a person who personifies Glory?

John ponders for years: Who is Jesus? How far back in time do I need to go until Jesus makes sense? From where I sit, it is as if the whole universe was dark, and now it is light. It is as if I was blind, and now I can see. It is as if we were in the beginning—the deep beginning—and then God spoke the Word and it became light, right before our eyes. It is as if the Word, the light that was there at the beginning, is with us here.

To John, the universe did not really begin until Jesus came into it. So John concludes his pondering with what we call the Prologue: "In the beginning was the Word, and the Word was with God, and the Word was God." That is what John knew in his bones about Jesus. *This* is who Jesus is.

God incarnate is born among us. This is a love story unlike any other, and it needed new language, new words. But the language was always there—in the beginning. And so on this day, the baby is born, and our hearts are open to receive him, and our minds are deepened to understand him, and our universe has been lit up by him. Can you see his glory now? Come, let us adore him.

—*Joanna Leiserson*

And Then There Is Stephen

The Christmas season is nothing if not filled with traditions. Family traditions, church traditions, and cultural traditions are the backbone of this holiday season. I expect most of us feel our traditions are good things, even if they are sometimes a little over the top. Most of us would not consider our holiday traditions too much of a burden, I think, and certainly not insidious.

But here we are, the day after the Nativity, confronted with the story of Saint Stephen, the first Christian martyr, who, we are told in the Book of Acts, was stoned to death for speaking out against mindless adherence to religious traditions that left no room for the work of the Holy Spirit.

Yikes.

Even if we have romanticized the baby in the manger and the angel song and the fluffy lambs dotting the countryside around Bethlehem, there is no way to romanticize the story of Stephen and his charge against the church leadership. This story brings us quickly back to earth about the consequences of God coming to live among us as one of us.

God did a new thing in coming to live among us as one of us. It is hard to make room for God's new things when we have made our traditions into idols. There are still eleven more days of Christmas. Will we leave room for the working of the Holy Spirit to bring new life to a broken world, or will we worship and cling to our traditions as if they could bring us salvation? —*Penny Nash*

Beloved Disciple

In the Gospel of John we encounter a mysterious figure described only as "the disciple whom Jesus loved." He is never named and he is not remembered in any of the other gospel accounts. But in John's Gospel, he is a key figure who is present at some of the most significant moments in Jesus' life.

We see him first at the Last Supper (John 13:23), reclining against the breast of Jesus, enjoying intimate companionship with him. He is the only male disciple to stay with Jesus at the cross, and Jesus entrusts to him the care of his mother (19:26-27). This beloved disciple and Peter are among the first to witness the empty tomb, and he is the first to believe (20:1-10). He is with the disciples in Galilee and is the first to recognize the stranger on the shore as Jesus (21:7). Jesus hints that this beloved disciple will not suffer a martyr's end, but will remain until Jesus comes again (21:20-23). This man's testimony is at the heart of the fourth gospel (21:24).

This beloved disciple can be a model for us all: a model of the kind of intimacy that we are invited to share with Christ in prayer; a model of fidelity even in the face of suffering; a model of one who "abides" in Christ and who testifies to what God has done for him. In John's Gospel, the chief characteristic of a disciple is that he or she loves Jesus. Jesus asks each of us who follow him, "Do you love me?"
—*Brother David Vryhof*, SSJE

The Boat Box

My mother never threw anything away. She had jars of safety pins, a closet full of fabric scraps, and shelves of old coffee cans. Her garage was packed to the rafters with items salvaged from the spring cleaning of others.

Knowing that all this was one day going to be my problem, I had been threatening for years what I would do. I told her I would one day rent a truck and haul all of what she called "stuff," but what I called "junk," to the dump. She would say I couldn't do that. I would say she wouldn't be there to stop me. It became a game.

After she died, I started with the garage full of junk. I noticed a box near the top of a set of shelves labeled "BOAT" in big letters. My mother knew how much I have always wanted a boat. I reached for the box thinking I might find a set of keys.

There were no keys, just a note written with a red marker in my mother's handwriting. "Dear Stacy, I knew you'd look in this box first. Please don't take all my stuff to the dump. I love you. Mom."

Often it takes something incongruous to reach those places in the recesses of our hearts and call forth love. It takes a baby king born in a stable. It takes angels singing to the shepherds in the fields. It takes a tomb with no body. It takes a box labeled "BOAT" with a mother's last word in a game she and her son played about her "stuff." It is the calling forth of love where love could not be sure to have been. In that Christ is born in us over and over again. —*Stacy Sauls*

Included in Incarnation

In the midst of Christmas joy, the church celebrates the Incarnation of God in our midst. Through the birth of our Lord Jesus Christ, the shining face of God comes to a broken world. We live in a realm desperately seeking to find its way back to God. As Christians we put all our hopes and dreams on the Christ Child and turn to him to see the face of God. Jesus becomes our hope as we plunge through the darkness of life in search of the radiance emanating from a child born on the run to refugee parents.

It seems we are all running from something at some point in our lives. Fear abounds and suffering is never far, yet this birth points us in the direction of a different and divine reality. It reminds us that even in the midst of despair, God is present!

The birth of our Lord is also a reminder that God's divine light shines in the world and the very light that shined in Jesus shines in us. We all feel a sense of awe when we reflect on the Nativity. God is calling us to have that same sense of awe when we reflect on our own birth. We too are children of God—born of God into an earthly realm. As followers of Jesus the Christ we are his very presence in the world, his very light, and his very hope.

Why not be bold in your interpretation of the Incarnation and include yourself in that equation? Do you not become one with Christ and God when you partake of the Holy Eucharist? You are the new Emmanuel! —*Wilfredo Benitez*

What Do You Seek?

How is the season of Christmas a season of seeking? I get it about the other seasons: Advent is about waiting, about expectancy. It's definitely about seeking. Lent is a season of preparation, a time in the wilderness, clearly about seeking refreshment in a dry land. But what about Christmas?

What do we seek in this season? What are we looking for? Mary seeks an answer to the question: *How can this be?* Joseph seeks an answer to this question: *What do I tell the neighbors?* The innkeeper's wife is wondering: *Who are all those people in my backyard? And can somebody please turn out that bright light over the stable, for God's sake?* Shepherds run from hillside to town according to angelic instruction, seeking the baby in the straw in the stable in the back alley. Magi from the east travel miles until they find the one worthy of their gifts. Herod's just looking to hold on to power.

And you? What are you looking for this Christmas? Where do you fit in that nativity scene? There is, after all, a place for you. The mystery, the miracle of the season is that the answer to our searching will be found in the Christ Child. The hopes and fears of all the years meet in that baby. Can you see all that in that manger?

—*Jay Sidebotham*

The Work of Christmas

*After the star is gone, and the shepherds return to their flocks
and the wise men have returned, the work of Christmas begins.*

— HOWARD THURMAN, "THE WORK OF CHRISTMAS"

The Rev. Dr. Howard Thurman, mystic and theologian, reflects on the tasks of the Christmas season and gives us direction. Just a few days ago, the season of Advent called us into a time of anticipation and preparation for the birth of Christ. Now Christmas is a reality. Not just a day of birth, but a season of birth. As anyone awaiting a child knows, birth is just the beginning. Now begins the nurturing.

In scripture, we catch glimpses of the family as the shepherds leave their flocks to seek out the holy child. The family is visited by mysterious seers from afar who bring them rare gifts. Their pilgrimage confirms the glorious messages of the angels.

At the same time, scripture reveals a growing tension. We hear that the birth does not go unnoticed and is a threat to the prevailing spiritual and political powers. Yet wise elders have spent their lives waiting for this child. They rejoice at the new light God's favor has brought into the world. Joseph dreams, and Mary ponders the meaning in all that has happened. But they cannot return to life as they knew it.

Thurman's words are an ancient call to the real work of Christmas. Thurman suggests that the birth of Christ calls us beyond mere celebrations. The birth of Christ urges us to continue the transforming ministry of Jesus in the new year ahead.

How might we feed the hungry, proclaim the Good News, stand with the poor? How might God be calling us to proclaim the Lord's favor with our lives?

—*Karen Montagno*

Contributors and Index

Curtis Almquist, SSJE, is a monk at the Society of Saint John the Evangelist, a monastic community of The Episcopal Church. He is active as a spiritual director, retreat leader, and conference speaker.

A Lifelong Conversion 30
Be Kind to One Another...94
Believe Less...145
Stop and Listen...237
Freedom in Limitations 332

Wilfredo Benitez, an Episcopal/Anglican priest, is the current rector of historic St. George's Church, Flushing, New York. He is actively involved in interfaith peace and justice work. Prior to ordination in 1991, Wilfredo was engaged in counseling and community organizing in the city of New York. He is also a passionate photographer with a contemplative, prophetic eye. His website is www.benitezrivera.com.

A Journey in Darkness..24
Are You Up For It? 44
Walking the Desert 79
The Garbage Jesus...89
A Still, Red Light 97
Hallelujah, Easter!...124
A Wet and Soggy Bed Is a Lonely Place to Sleep.............168
Nothing Is Ordinary with God 200
Hostage from Love...218
In the Service of Others 249
The Sun Hides Behind the Clouds....................................281
My First Love Story 319
A Time of Journey..343
Included in Incarnation 368

Kristine Blaess is an Episcopal priest and associate rector for Disciple-making and Missional Communities at St. George's Episcopal Church in Nashville, Tennessee. She is also a coach and consultant for 3dm, an organization that equips leaders and congregations as they seek to be transformed by and to share Christ's abundant life.

Taking a Load Off..10
Potty Trained..35
Fie, Death..57
The Land Got Its Rest 77
Peter's Faith 108

A Light on the Stand..138
Blackened Baby 163
Traveling Hearts..188
Paddling Upstream..213
Lord, Let Me Trust You...232
A Cookie in Each Hand...256
The Kid with Brown Hair..292
Shaking the Foundations...322
New Beginnings..342
O Christmas Tree..356

Chip Bristol serves as chaplain and program director of Prodigals Community, a long-term rehab community in Winston-Salem, North Carolina, for men with a history of chronic substance abuse. He has served as chaplain and headmaster at a number of schools and is a graduate of Taft School, Hamilton College, and holds a master's in divinity from the Virginia Theological Seminary.

Doors and Other Thresholds..15
Colors of Faith..38
Lowering the Centerboard 62
A New Song 88
Cloudy Days at the Beach..98
Emptiness..118
Shallow Streams and Deep Rivers.....................................129
Hobbits and Adventures...144
Enough Is Good 171
Bare Feet 187
Adjusting the Knobs...211
Riding Waves 231
Walking in the Fog...257
The Finish Line..288
Dancing in the Margins 296
Keep the Pilot Light Lit 323
The Gift That Matters 360

Laurie Brock serves as rector of St. Michael's Episcopal Church in Lexington, Kentucky. She has written and contributed to books published by Morehouse/Church Publishing and Pilgrim Press. She allows horses to teach her about soul, spirit, and humility as she cares for and rides them. She blogs at www.Dirtysexyministry.com.

Resolve to Remember 7
Nameless...36
Does This Make Me Look Fat? 47

Soul Soil 73
Waiting... 114
But I Hate Them! 130
Emmanuel, God With Us...............................154
The Wisdom of Wounds 172
Trust, Live, Pray..194
Transfiguration...223
Love the Questions...241
On the Same Team...267
Things That Go Bump in the Night 308
Working Our Muscles....................................321
Look for the Lord...354

Janet Rehling Buening came to Forward Movement as an editor in 2006, after careers as an English teacher, marketing manager, columnist, communications consultant, freelance editor, and college professor. A community activist and chronically overcommitted volunteer, she has a patient husband, three adult children who are grateful she always has a lot to do, a head full of stories, and a house full of books and life-souvenirs.

Of Light and Stars, and the Radiance of a Soul 16
Unexpected Mercy...196
Poured Out..220
God Dwells in Secret Places...........................261
Safe Harbor 289
Strange Herald 337

Margaret Bullitt-Jonas serves the Diocese of Western Massachusetts as a Missioner for Creation Care, with a foucs on addressing climate change. She leads retreats, has taught courses on prayer at Episcopal Divinity School, and served as chaplain to the House of Bishops. She is the author of *Holy Hunger* (Vintage, 2000), *Christ's Passion, Our Passions* (Cowley, 2002), and *Joy of Heaven, To Earth Come Down* (Forward Movement, 2012). An environmental activist, she has been a leader in Religious Witness for the Earth (rwearth.org) since 2001. Her website is holyhunger.org.

In the River with Jesus 17
You Are the Music While the Music Lasts.........48
Beside Still Waters 86
When a Leaf Needs to Speak 117
Get Real 131
New Every Morning Is the Love 148
God Is In the Details.......................................178
What Do I Want?...203

With You Always...222
Lift Up Your Hearts 247
How Malice Dies...264
When You Become No One 290
Love Every Leaf..334
O Come, O Come, Emmanuel...350
Here Will I Dwell 363

Bo Cox is familiar to Forward Movement readers, having written for *Forward Day by Day* and other publications numerous times since 1995. Released from prison in 2003, Bo enjoys life with his wife Debb at their home near Norman, Oklahoma—a sanctuary in the woods. When not creating at home, Bo plays well with others for a living, leading therapeutic activities at a psychiatric hospital. His most recent book, *I Will, With God's Help*, is a collection of selected works (Forward Movement, 2013).

Freedom's Shadow 14
The Mirror 40
Passing it On 64
Just Another Poor Soul.......................................83
Waste Not..104
Mom...137
The Universe Inside.. 161
Master of the Universe 185
Disguises 207
Attitude of Gratitude 228
God Is..262
Growing Pains...291
Rearview Mirrors and Honest Reflection.................306
Wounded World 320
Following Christ...362

Mary W. Cox retired in September 2012 after twenty years as a member of the staff of the Diocese of Southeast Florida, where she first served as assistant to the canon to the ordinary, and, from early 1999, as director of communications. She writes light verse and haiku, and practices photography as both communication and art. Her cartoon character, EpiscoRat, still occasionally appears on her Facebook page.

After Twelfth Night 22
Supporting Role 46
Yelling at the Lord...91
Saving Gracey...109
Backlighting 146
The Blessing of Babel 166

For the Sport of It..209
The Runaway Bunny's Mom 225
Home...271
Crossing a Line...295
Grab the Rope 326
Good News? 348

Alissa Goudswaard is a member of the delightful parish community at St. John's Episcopal Church in Lafayette, Indiana. She has a master's degree in rhetoric and composition, and enjoys journaling, reading young adult novels, building playlists, and making scrambled eggs. Alissa blogs on matters of faith and life as a twenty-something Episcopalian at www.episcotheque.wordpress.com.

A God Who Hides 19
Deeply Loved 50
Enter the Wilderness, Enter Abundance 70
Scars and Stories..120
God Shines Through...139
Impossible Things Before Breakfast.................155
Like a Little Child..170
Hindsight Miracles...192
Jesus Is Real..215
Live Without Fear 233
Gifts Even While We Sleep 266
Picking Up the Pieces..298
God in Your Own Image....................................311
Everyday Incarnations 330
Calling "Come" 344

Charles Graves IV is a seminarian in the Berkeley Divinity School at Yale University and previously worked as a political strategist. He lives in Cincinnati between school terms and enjoys woodworking, riding his bicycle, and spending time at the beach.

Listening for the Silence.....................................65
No One Will Notice 149
A Close Race 312

Katharine Jefferts Schori is the twenty-sixth Presiding Bishop of The Episcopal Church. She was previously the bishop of the Diocese of Nevada. She holds a doctorate in oceanography and is an instrument-rated pilot.

Beginnings...6
Windows into Heaven 164
Ichthus 339

Aaron Klinefelter serves as minister for young adults and families at The Church of the Redeemer in Cincinnati, Ohio. He is also a parent, husband, PTO co-president, gardener, bicycler, and networker. He loves coffee and hospitality.

Snowmageddon 26
The Blessings of Snowstorms 61
Harbingers of the Kingdom.....................................68
The Dance of the Dandelion 106
Practice Resurrection...140
Breaking Boundaries 159
Jesus Is Lord 190
Conspicuous Othering...205
Sitting Down...226
The Story of How We Begin to Remember.........243
The Stillness of the Basement 254
Inextricably Closed Off...286
The Space Between 297
Frivolous Play 313
Fear-less..341

Joanna Leiserson is an Episcopal priest in the Diocese of Southern Ohio, most recently serving as canon for Christian Formation at Christ Church Cathedral, Cincinnati. She has a special interest in quirky but deep preaching, scripture-to-life storytelling, and creating a just community. She is also author of *Weaving God's Promises*, a curriculum for children in The Episcopal Church. She has three grown children and three grown cats.

Our Home Up Ahead...21
Plundering the Egyptians.......................................45
Turning on the Divine Autopilot...........................63
Rush Hour Sabbath 80
A Planet Named George 121
Old Mountain, New Earth 143
This is God Calling...169
Are We There Yet?...184
Sleepless Bird..212
Cows and Katydids..244
Mother Wasp...272
The Gospel and the GPS 300
Dancing in Place 338
On the Freight Train to Christmas......................352
In the Beginning 364

Dave Marshall is husband to Christi and father to four: adopted daughters Galina and Veeka and biological sons Ethan and Elijah. He is also a new grandfather. An Episcopal priest in sunny Chula Vista, California, Dave is priest-in-charge at Saint John's Episcopal Church and School in the Diocese of San Diego. He writes a weekly column for his parish, at saint-johns.org. When not in the office, you can find him at the beach.

Letters of the Kingdom 49
Time to Seek 78
A Lottery We Win 123
Learning War No More 160
Waterloo 174
Temperance 189
Lifesaving 219
Rest 276
Being Christ 280
Do 4 U 316
Expecting? 358

Westina Matthews, Ph.D., is an adjunct professor at General Theological Seminary where she teaches contemplative spiritual direction, and she serves on the vestry of Trinity Wall Street. A retired corporate executive, she is now an author, inspirational speaker, retreat leader, and spiritual director whose practice reflects contemplative living through "holy listening." She has contributed to several Forward Movement anthologies, including *Finding God Day by Day* (2010) and *Wisdom Found* (2011).

Sticking with Love 25
Callused Prayers 56
How'd You Know My Name? 72
Seen and Unseen 90
Too Much or Just Enough? 111
Acts of Kindness 142
Stepping Out in Faith 158
Bestow Your Love 179
Nowhere to Lay Her Head 199
A Place for Redemption and Community 240
An Unlimited Broadcast 265
Sustain and Comfort Us 279
Spaces in Your Togetherness 305
I Want to be Ready 327
Jesus Is the Reason 353

Karen B. Montagno is an Episcopal priest and director of Congregational Resources and Training for the Diocese of Massachusetts. Her work involves equipping lay and ordained leaders in order to promote healthy worshiping communities. Her ministry also includes spiritual direction, retreat work, and writing spiritual reflections. Karen finds joy and a lively challenge in her adult children. Her inspiration also comes from vegetable and flower gardening, cooking, camping and her two cat friends.

Fishing for People...31
Beloved Community 99
Sour Grapes..162
Christmas in July 216
The Ladies Who Let Their Light Shine.........................230
A Good Fight..251
God's September Glory...273
The Saint of Generous Nature.......................................282
Solid Ground..314
The Work of Christmas...370

Sandra Montes is a daughter, sister, singer, dreamer, writer, teacher, aunt, and mother (in chronological order). Born in Perú and raised in Guatemala and Texas, she now lives in Houston where she finds inspiration for songs, stories, pictures, and meditations in the mundane, for through God all is holy. She has been healed, forgiven, transformed, blessed, and loved more than she can recount. But she tries.

Delight! 28
"I Have Called You Friends"..60
Eternal Springtime..84
If You Are Able! 100
¡Aleluya! Cristo ha resucitado ¡Aleluya!.........................116
"If It's Still in There…"..156
Shout! 183
Enciende Una Luz…..204
The Woman Bore a Sinister Son,
    and Named Him Ellis...229
Living in the Comfort of the Holy Spirit.......................248
For God's Glory..258
But Only Speak the Word 285
Ask. Search. Knock...303
Yes or No?...325
César 347

Penny Nash is the associate rector for Youth, Children, and Families at Bruton Parish Episcopal Church in downtown Colonial Williamsburg, Virginia. She parks her car next to a horse and is often asked what women priests wore in Colonial times. (Answer: pants.) She is also an amateur photographer, and you can find her photographs illustrating prayers and reflections at her blog, One Cannot Have Too Large a Party (www.penelopepiscopal.blogspot.com).

Making Room Again..12
Winter Treasures 39
Stuck..59
Awesomeness...76
Fragrance...107
Love and Mothers 136
How Does Your Garden Grow?............................152
Smile 176
Faithful and Forgiven 208
Busy...234
Play..268
Confession..293
Thankfulness..333
Giving and Receiving 355
And Then There Is Stephen.................................365

Yejide Peters is an Episcopal priest and (often disappointed) New York Mets fan. She currently serves as rector of All Saints' Episcopal Church in Briarcliff Manor, New York. She is passionate about peace-building, theology, writing, music, silly jokes, cooking, and spending time with friends and family.

Broken Heart, Open Arms......................................20
Who Would You Have Me Be? 103
A Friendship Firmly Planted................................165
That Day 259
Set the Prisoners Free 359

Betsy Rogers is a freelance writer and editor and a member of the Forward Movement Board of Directors. She and her husband are the parents of three grown children (and two comical English setters) and divide their time between Belleville, Illinois, and Sister Bay, Wisconsin. In these sesquicentennial years, they are pursuing her husband's deep interest in the Civil War, visiting every major battlefield in that great American tragedy.

I Have No Sideways..9
Whoever Heard of Sinibald? 33

The Robin's Lesson 53
Grace Makes Us True...85
Lessons from the Civil War..105
Summoned From the Tomb..125
Out of the Mouths of Babes 141
The Old Man by the Sea 157
Choosing Compassion, Choosing Life 182
An Interval of Gladness...197
Tethered Together 238
Learning Humility 278
Love to the Loveless Shown 307
Growing in Gratitude..336
The Infinite Gift 361

Debbie Royals, Pascua Yaqui, is an Episcopal priest who is serving part-time at Grace St. Paul's Episcopal Church in Tucson, Arizona. She is chair of the Standing Commission on Mission and Evangelism, serves as a faculty member for CREDO, and works with the Indigenous Theological Training Institute. Debbie has written for Forward Movement's *Forward Day by Day* and many other publications as a part of her call to share her Native American spirituality.

Resting 27
Margins 43
Dust and Tears—Glue that Binds 66
Worry 93
Holy Time 110
Welcome...132
Fire...173
Warrior Spirits..191
Clutter 221
A Still and Quiet Soul..239
Recognizing Holy Space...252
Relationships 274
Going Willingly 287
Abundant Life 318
The Still of Winter...340

Stacy Sauls is the chief operating officer of The Episcopal Church and previously served as bishop of the Diocese of Lexington. He enjoyed a career as a lawyer before ordination. His passion is mission, and he has been involved in mission projects both in Africa and Japan. He draws much of his inspiration from his family—his wife Ginger, their two adult sons, Andrew and Matthew, and Andrew's wife Jessica.

Epiphany and Transformation 11
Hoping Against Hope 34
A Scary Story.. 54
Repentance 74
Annie on Lent... 92
The Shoe Shine Man....................................... 112
The Sick and Tired....................................... 133
Sunday in Ocean Grove....................................... 150
Fishing with Mattie....................................... 175
Griffin: Another Name for Grace 201
A Time to Leave, A Time to Learn........................... 246
The True Cross....................................... 263
Clouds and Fog....................................... 299
Thanksgiving Eve....................................... 335
The Boat Box....................................... 367

Jay Sidebotham is an Episcopal priest and director of RenewalWorks, a ministry of Forward Movement that nurtures discipleship and encourages spiritual growth. Jay previously served as rector of Church of the Holy Spirit in Lake Forest, Illinois, where he led an intensive period of spiritual growth and renewal, and of four other congregations. He is well-known for his cartoons about church life and his animation work on the television cartoon *Schoolhouse Rock!*

Safe Questions....................................... 23
"I Found It" 55
A Season for Sincerity 67
In the Wilderness 87
Look in the Right Place....................................... 115
Now!....................................... 134
Extravagant Love 153
Search the Scriptures....................................... 177
Praying Shapes Believing 210
Back to Basics....................................... 236
Face Up to Fears 270
A Welcoming Faith 301
Seek and Serve....................................... 329
A Day That Will Live in Infamy....................................... 346
What Do You Seek? 369

Jeremiah Sierra is a writer living in New York City. He received an MFA in creative writing from The New School. He blogs for Vital Practices for The Episcopal Church Foundation and is a co-founder of *The Daily Cake*, a webzine for young adults. He is currently the managing editor in the communications and marketing department at Trinity Wall Street.

Come and See..18
Useful Guilt...41
Life in the Midst of Death 82
A Cyclical Faith...126
Co-creators with God..151
An Outward Silence...181
A Healthy Disillusionment 198
God of Words..217
The Things We Cannot Hold 227
The Phone..242
A Shared Suffering, a Common Love 255
Exercise Love 284
Make Haste to Love...302
How History Holds Us..315
Some Brighter Life 357

Gil Stafford is vicar of St. Augustine's Episcopal Parish and chaplain for Episcopal Campus Ministry (St. Brigid's Community), Arizona State University. Previously he spent five years in professional baseball, then taught high school in Coolidge, Arizona. He was head baseball coach at Grand Canyon University for twenty years, winning three national titles, and then served four years as university president.

A Pilgrim's Poem..8
From Heart to Heaven...29
Walking with Brigid 37
The Extraordinary Ordinary 51
Simply God 75
Stories That Last...95
A Different Kind of Opening Day 96
The Wedding at Cana 128
Stories to Learn By..135
Stepping Out 193
Transformation..224
In the Images of God 269
Of Saints and Souls and the Rising of the Son......309
Redeeming the Day..331
The Wisdom of Compassion 351

June Terry taught nurses in South Africa for ten years before returning to the United States. She earned a master's in New Testament and met her late husband when they worked as seminary administrators. She has served as a nursing home chaplain and is active in The Society of the Companions of the Holy Cross and in her Rhode Island parish. She is thankful for friends, dogs, books, music, and the ocean nearby.

On Being and Becoming 13
Saying Her Prayers 42
The Whole Picture 71
Mulled Grace 102
Warmed Hearts, Informed Faith 119
Give God a Little Credit 147
Mutual Blessing 167
Strength of Presence 186
Of Turtles and Skunks 202
Becoming a Presence of Peace 235
Saints on Earth and in Heaven 253
A Story of Forgiveness 260
Alleluias Aplenty 283
Beyond the Open Door 310
And All the Mornings After 328
To Mary, His Mother 349

Geoffrey Tristram, ssje, is the Superior of the Society of Saint John the Evangelist, a monastic community of The Episcopal Church. Brother Geoffrey has pursued a ministry of teaching, spiritual direction, and retreat leading, and for three years he served as chaplain to the House of Bishops.

Up to a High Place 52
How Shall We Mend It, My Dear? 113
My Soul in Silence Waits 180
Marked with Love 277
Pruning for Life 345

Owen C. Thompson, rector of Grace Episcopal Church, Nyack, New York, received his master's of divinity from General Theological Seminary and holds a master's in Educational Communication and Technology from New York University. He is the son of the late Rt. Reverend Herbert Thompson Jr., Bishop of Southern Ohio, whose ministry motto he has adopted as his own: "To reconcile. To heal. To liberate. To serve." He is married and has two young sons.

Faith, Prophets, and Economics 58
And They Will Know We Are Christians
      by Our—Foreheads? 69

Live the Risen Life 122
Through the Wilderness 195
Change and Changelessness 245
Give and Keep Giving 275
Back to Basics 304
Caution—Deconstruction Zone! 324

Richelle Thompson is the managing editor for Forward Movement. She and her husband, an Episcopal priest, have two rambunctious children and live in God's country in Kentucky, just south of Cincinnati. She worked for several years as a journalist and served for ten years as the director of communications for the Diocese of Southern Ohio.

Patience and Providence 32
A Good Thing to Give Up 101
Love Grows 214
Sticks and Stones 250
Organ Donor 317

David Vryhof, ssje, is a monk at the Society of Saint John the Evangelist, a monastic community of The Episcopal Church. He currently serves as Novice Guardian for the community, training the new men who enter the monastery. He is an experienced retreat leader, spiritual director, and teacher.

Yearning for God 81
Do You See This Woman? 127
Making All Things New 206
The Key to Gratitude 294
Beloved Disciple 366

About the Cover Artist

Roger Hutchison is a writer and painter who has served for more than sixteen years as Canon for Children's Ministry at Trinity Episcopal Cathedral in Columbia, South Carolina.

"Painting is the way I talk to God," says Roger. "I find joy when I move my fingers through puddles of color and across blank canvas. I am always surprised—and blessed—by the conversation that takes place."

Roger's paintings have been shown in various galleries and collectors hail from as far away as New York and Australia. His first book, *The Painting Table: A Journal of Loss and Joy,* is set for release January 1, 2014. Visit www.thepaintingtable.com